Contempora

Contemporary Australian Plays

edited and introduced by
Russell Vandenbroucke

Hotel Sorrento
Hannie Rayson

Dead White Males
David Williamson

Two
Ron Elisha

The 7 Stages of Grieving
Wesley Enoch and Deborah Mailman

The Popular Mechanicals
Keith Robinson and Tony Taylor

Methuen

Published by Methuen 2001

3 5 7 9 10 8 6 4 2

This collection first published in Great Britain in 2001 by Methuen Publishing Limited,
215 Vauxhall Bridge Road, London SW1V 1EJ

Hotel Sorrento first published by Currency Press, Sydney, Australia, in 1990, revised 1992,
2001, copyright © Hannie Rayson, 1990, 1992, 2001; *Dead White Males* first published by
Currency Press in 1995, copyright © David Williamson, 1995; *Two* first published by
Currency Press in 1985, revised 1990, 2001, copyright © Ron Elisha, 1985, 1990, 2001;
The 7 Stages of Grieving first published by Playlab Press, Brisbane, Australia, in 1995,
copyright © Wesley Enoch and Deborah Mailman, 1995; *The Popular Mechanicals* first
published by Currency Press in 1992, copyright © Keith Robinson and Tony Taylor, 1992

Introduction copyright © Russell Vandenbroucke, 2001

The authors and editor have asserted their rights under the Copyright,
Designs and Patents Act, 1988.

Methuen Publishing Limited Reg. No. 3543167

A CIP catalogue record for this book is available from the British Library.

ISBN 0 413 76760 4

Typeset by Deltatype, Birkenhead, Merseyside
Printed and bound in Great Britain by
Cox and Wyman Ltd, Reading, Berkshire

Contents

Russell Vandenbroucke is a stage director, producer and writer. His other theatre books are: *Truths the Hand Can Touch: The Theatre of Athol Fugard* and *The Theatre Quotation Book: A Treasury of Insights and Insults* (Limelight Editions, 2001). Plays and adaptations include: *Eleanor Roosevelt: In Her Own Words*, also broadcast on television; *Holiday Memories*, his stage version of Truman Capote's 'The Thanksgiving Visitor' and 'A Christmas Memory'; and *Atomic Bombers*, a behind-the-scenes drama of Richard Feynman and the making of the bomb. Broadcast on radio to commemorate the fiftieth anniversary of Hiroshima, it also opened the permanent home of Northlight Theatre, which he served as artistic director for a decade. He lives outside Chicago and is a member of the Society of Stage Directors and Choreographers. The Fulbright Foundation sponsored his visit to Australia as a Senior Scholar.

Acknowledgements

Thanks to: Katharine Brisbane and Victoria Chance of Currency Press, Ian Brown of Playlab Press; Michael Earley, Eleanor Knight and Eugenie Boyd of Methuen; Dirk Pettigrew of the International Theatre Institute, Australian Centre; Steve Mullins of Northlight Theatre; David Zarefsky of Northwestern University; the Fulbright Scholarship Board; Len Berkman, Ian Dickson, Ron Elisha, Louise O'Hallaran and Mary Dilg.

Acknowledgements

The Isle is Full of Noises

The First Fleet of convicts and their keepers needed eight months to sail the 15,000 miles from Britain to Botany Bay, their new home in the penal colony now called Australia. The following year, 1789, George Farquhar's *The Recruiting Officer*, directed by a marine and performed by inmates, became the first theatre production in the new New World. Two centuries later, it takes less than a day to fly the 9,000 miles from Chicago to the same Botany Bay, now better known as Sydney.

Plays are still imported from the northern hemisphere, but the purpose of my visit, supported by a Fulbright Fellowship in 1996, was to experience indigenous work, which has proliferated in recent years. I saw dozens of productions over five months, attended conferences, visited festivals, and met theatre colleagues, especially playwrights. In addition, I devoured scores of play-scripts provided by my host, the performing arts publisher Currency Press. I had read Australian plays before as a dramaturg of American theatres. I had also produced Ron Elisha's *Two* at the theatre I served as artistic director. My purpose was not to read scripts, however, but to experience Australian theatre in its fleshy context in order to understand better the cultural currents that run through it. Like the foundation that sponsored my trip, I am committed to international exchange and global understanding, but pursuing these ideals is sometimes like working on a jigsaw puzzle whose border, like the universe itself, keeps expanding.

In 1970 Graeme Blundell, founding director of Melbourne's LaMama Theatre, complained: 'Australian theatre, for the most part then, still lives off imitative productions of safe West End successes, the odd classic run up without adequate rehearsal, the annual pantomime and musical from America.' Later that year, David Williamson's first full-length play was produced at the same LaMama. Days after arriving, I visited the Sydney Theatre Company for 'A Tribute to David Williamson: Celebrating 25 Years in the Theatre'. This fete of the most successful playwright in Australian history was also a fund-raiser for new Australian writing. Much had changed since Blundell's lament. Williamson's emergence in the 1970s, along with a generation of Australian playwrights, marked a turning point in their theatre. Collectively, they nudged the country beyond its dependence upon imports. Australians were ready to see themselves on the stage, to hear their own incarnation of the English language, to confront indigenous quandaries, and to laugh at Aussie follies. Playwrights were ready to oblige.

The readiness was not all, however, not quite. The benefit audience was reminded that Prime Minister Gough Whitlam, elected in 1972, had personally assumed responsibility for the arts ministry and that his Labor Government had tripled federal funding. With that, the former Prime Minister himself was introduced as three hundred celebrants applauded heartily. Their enthusiasm did not surprise me, but Whitlam's presence did. I could imagine a former president honouring an American playwright by sending a congratulatory telegram, or an effusive videotape, or even a loyal spouse in his stead. I could not imagine a former president dispatching himself.

Three months later, I attended the New South Wales Premier's Literary Awards. Premier Robert Carr delivered the citations and $98,000 to recipients in eight categories. He, too, was personally invested in the arts under his jurisdiction. Again, I could not imagine an American politician of similar stature, a governor for example, doing the same – either out of sincere interest in writers or because breaking bread with the literati would boost his numbers in the polls.

The dinner was held in the famous Opera House, Sydney's soaring civic symbol and, internationally, the icon of a nation. Until actually setting foot Down Under, I had not realised how appropriate it was that this young colony-turned-country was symbolised by a modern building that opened only in 1973, but that it also bore the name of an art form begun in seventeenth-century Europe. On previous trips abroad, I had been the refugee from an upstart culture eager to embrace the venerable past. Now, I was immersing myself in a culture younger than my own.

A few months is hardly long enough to comprehend a culture. However, it is sufficient for discrete observations to distil into patterns – despite a caution in Hannie Rayson's *Hotel Sorrento*. An editor complains, 'what is it that makes them think that living elsewhere automatically qualifies them to make sweeping general-isations about this place.'

(Multi)Cultural Backdrop

Britain's custom of deporting convicts took a new direction after 1776. The New World had provided an ideal dumping ground for jettisoned human beings, but revolutionary turmoil in America meant that English ships had to sail further south, to *Terra Australis*, 'Land of the South'.

As in America, thousands of men and women living on one continent were forced to inhabit another. Unlike slaves, however, the Anglo-Irish convicts herded into ships had passed through a legal system that found them guilty of something, even stealing bread. Convicts became forced expatriots because of something they did, not because of who they were.

As in America, European immigrants zealously displaced indigenous people while piously striving to convert and 'civilise' them. Upon landing in 1770, Captain Cook declared the land *terra nullius*, 'land of no one', and claimed it all for the British Crown despite its previous settlement and traditional use by Aboriginal peoples. Colonising the continent began.

And as in America, too, settlers found beautiful shores fronting inland wilds. Most newcomers remained in coastal cities around the perimeter, choosing to face the sea 'out front' while desolate bush lay behind them 'out back'. Intrepid explorers of these nether lands captured the imagination of settlers, who remained in town for safety. Bushrangers like Ned Kelly were romanticised despite their outlaw ways. Or was it because of them?

'Australian society was born in violence,' writes historian Ian Turner. 'The brutality of the convict system, the way in which it corrupted prisoners and jailers alike, are too well known to require detailing here . . . Australians have thought of themselves as a homogeneous society sharing a common culture and common social aspirations. The class war has been muted by economic well-being. The Australian people have assumed a

common objective: One Continent, One People, One Culture.'
Turner's views on domestic violence and monoculturalism appear
in an introduction to David Williamson's first success, *The
Removalists* (1972).

In the thirty years since, the self-perceptions of Australians
have changed radically. 'Multiculturalism' was uttered so fre-
quently during my visit that I felt at home. Temporarily. The first
seventeen productions I saw were written by white men, living or
dead. The actors were nearly as homogeneous, audiences too,
though they were markedly younger than back home. Australian
theatre practice has yet to reflect multicultural theory, at least in
the mainstream companies. Where was the multiculturalism so
many Australians lauded? Had I become obsessed with diversity
and race, the birthright every American inherits through slavery,
our collective original sin?

Australian multiculturalism refers to more than Aboriginal
peoples (estimated at up to 2% of the population) and Asian
immigrants (another 7%). It includes Greeks, Italians and
Ukrainians among others. Southern and Eastern Europeans
began immigrating to North America at the end of the nineteenth
century but to Australia only in the 1950s. After Japanese attacks
during World War Two forced the country to acknowledge its
vulnerability as a sparsely settled continent, 'populate or perish'
became a patriotic plea for procreation. Following the war, the
government assisted the huddled masses of ravaged Europe so
they could populate Australia's outback, but it was not until 1972
that a policy of non-discrimination replaced the Immigration
Restriction Act of 1901. It had made 'White Australia' the law of
the land. Since the 1980s, the country has embraced the fact that
the earth's geography, coupled with Second and Third World
industrialisation, makes Australia's fate tied more to the future of
Pacific peoples than the past of Atlantic ones.

Asian-Australians are evident on every Australian street and
campus, but they are seldom seen on any Australian stage. The
exceptions are one-person shows written and performed by
minority artists and productions by the country's few ethnic
companies.

Asked about this gulf between multicultural ideal and reality,
Jon Hawkes, a performer who later became Director of the

Australian Center of the International Theatre Institute, explained wryly, 'Our greatest progress has been with food. We didn't enjoy as many cuisines when I was a boy.' He might have mentioned body-piercing and tattoos, since they are also very popular and are borrowed from other cultures. If these signify Aussie multiculturalism, perhaps Turner's perception of 'One Continent, One People, One Culture' is not so dated after all.

Federation Day, 1 January 1901, marked a step towards autonomy from Great Britain, but Australians are only gradually ending their ties to imperial glory. They carried British passports up to World War Two, bought their groceries with pounds until 1966, and sang 'Rule Britannia' as their national anthem until 1984. In November 1999, Australians voted against becoming a republic. The Queen's Birthday is still a national holiday and the Union Jack remains part of the Australian flag.

Still, most Australians act as if they are independent. It is true they drink their beer cold as well as profusely; class distinctions are not evident although plutocracy is; instead of a maze of identifying accents, only slight differences, inaudible to an outsider's ears, distinguish the speech of urban and rural Australians; what's more, they enjoy calling Britons 'Poms' or, with more relish still, 'whingeing Poms' (complaining Brits). Nevertheless, fervent avowals of independence strike a visitor as overly insistent. Were they trying to convince me or themselves? I thought of this divorce between theory and practice every time I bought a newspaper: the coin is called a dollar, but its profiled head is regal.

Youthful Culture, Youthful Theatre

Instead of an opera house or kangaroo, Australia's national symbol could be a teeter-totter, a seesaw: an uncertain balance beam between adolescence and adulthood, a link from past to future. As in formative stages of the development of human beings, young nations discover that identity is fluid, security fleeting, and equipoise hard to maintain. The teeter totters. No matter how self-assured youngsters appear, they steal frequent sideways glances and wonder, 'How in the world do I appear to everyone watching me?' Like Gatsbys on the make, Australians seem eager to seize a world of opportunities. And like parvenus elsewhere, upstart Australians seem none too sure about their place at the banquet table. 'I wannabe' seems more pervasive than 'I am'.

Australia prides itself on being classless, especially as opposed to Mother England. Australian homogeneity extends so far beyond economics and heritage that it seems a national ideal. 'Cutting down tall poppies' is an anti-elitist phrase for putting people in place if they distinguish themselves too much. America, alternatively, exalts vast differences between individuals while blithely accepting gross disparities in, for example, income, medical care and public education. This follows naturally, although not inevitably, from the founding of America by contentious individualists who were bent on escaping their society, its religious persecution, and the pressure to conform to someone else's norm. Whereas American settlers arrived voluntarily from diverse European cultures, and involuntarily from Africa, Australian settlers were almost exclusively Anglo-Celtic. Even more importantly, their colony was founded by the state, run by the state, and its settlers have viewed the state benevolently ever since. Australia has never had a revolutionary war or a civil one.

Chauvinist signs are ubiquitous: 'Produced in Australia', 'Owned by Australians', 'Australian-Made Goods Proudly Sold Here'. Is this economic protectionism, youthful braggadocio, or insecurity? Once rare, new Australian plays now are everywhere. The increasing nationalism of the culture was both cause and effect of Williamson and his generation.

In Australia, it is hip to see a play. Theatre-goers are younger than in the United States. Nevertheless, speakers at the 1996 Australian National Playwrights' Conference sounded exactly like their counterparts in North America complaining that too few young people go to theatre, that the audience is old, and that soon it will be extinct. Theatre makes Chicken Littles of its partisans, but somehow the sky does not fall, the centre holds, and the Fabulous Invalid slouches towards another opening, another show.

The (relative) youthfulness of the audience is due, at least in part, to the teaching of Australian plays in secondary schools. Playwriting, especially of the last quarter-century, is part of the curriculum and is included in state exams. Also, 'Teenage Plays' is a sub-genre that attracts established playwrights. The pejorative connotation in America of 'children's theatre' is absent. Subsidised theatres offer discounts for students, as in other countries, but even full price is less than at home. The unemployed get discounts too. Australians do not assume that you need a job in order to need art.

The federal government also promotes art in novel ways beyond direct subsidies. Australian art is recognised as good for audiences, artists *and* the balance of trade. Exported art is twice as lucrative as exported wheat. To increase art exports, the Australia Council for the Arts sponsors a Performing Arts Market every two years. It is scheduled to coincide with important festivals (and fringe festivals) so that international presenters can gorge on Australian 'product' during their visits. Radio and television cover the Arts Market as well as the art being sold, which is startling to an American used to radio and TV stories limited to popular movies and music. Broad theatre coverage is common in Australia: a weekly television show that is broadcast nationally features productions *before* they open. It also includes work from alternative and rural venues as well as mainstream theatres.

Such wide, deep and steady exposure in all media and in the schools obviously supports Australia's theatre. It underlies the assertion by Aubrey Mellor, artistic director of Melbourne's Playbox Theatre Company, that 'per head of population, Australia is one of the most theatre-going countries in the world'. Affection for the stage clearly predates the emergence of indigenous playwrights in the last quarter-century. A guide to notable graves in Waverley Cemetery, just outside Sydney, lists more famous actors than any other profession. Some are a century old. The convicts performing *The Recruiting Officer* began a cherished tradition.

This history, coupled with sweeping defamation laws, helps explain why reviews are less critical than their foreign counterparts. Australians seem prickly about criticism of any kind as if it contradicts their sense of optimism. (Popular refrains uttered everywhere include 'no worries' and 'not a problem'.) Evaluating the tenor of theatre reviews may seem as subjective as, say, selecting plays for an anthology, but my impressions were confirmed the first time I tabulated the listings in the *Sydney Morning Herald*. Of ten productions noted, six had been reviewed already. Five of the six were recommended. In the history of American theatre, no paper in any city has lauded such a high percentage of productions.

Good reviews, then, are the Australian norm. They imply that many productions are worth attending instead of few and that theatre-going ought to be a regular habit rather than a rare treat. John Krummel, actor, director and head of suburban Sydney's Marian Street Theatre, noted another tendency of local critics: 'When it's an Aussie play and subject, it's treated more positively since we're still encouraging ourselves.' Like rooting for the home team, Australian nationalism takes another form.

In *Hotel Sorrento*, a novelist argues with an editor, 'I think that this so-called cultural renaissance is actually about patriotism. Which makes people like you very defensive.' Theatre is especially susceptible to confusing reality with make-believe. Canadian director John Hirsch was fond of noting, 'We're so proficient at creating illusion that we often fool ourselves.'

Theatre Culture

Australia is among the most urbanised countries in the world. Its nineteen million citizens cluster along the coast, especially in the south-east. Over twenty per cent of the population lives in metropolitan Sydney. (To equal this concentration of their national populations, London would be home to thirteen million, New York to fifty-nine million.) While urban density is generally a precondition for a thriving theatre, there are far fewer producing companies in Sydney than an equivalent-sized American city such as Chicago. Sydney, originally populated by convicts, and Melbourne, begun by settlers, are national rivals. A local wag describes the difference this way: 'In Melbourne, audiences leave the theatre talking about the play's themes and ideas; in Sydney, they talk about the actors. In Melbourne, if someone has a good idea, they start a magazine. In Sydney, they have a party.' This may helps explain the success of the recent Olympics.

Australians are infatuated with sports, prizes and international arts festivals. Every major city has one. Importing prominent artists and companies from around the world mitigates geographical isolation. Despite the impressive quality of these festivals, there is a lingering sense that foreign work belongs in these elegant ghettos from which it is released carefully, annually and in concentrated doses. Local audiences and artists get their overseas exposure, then return to mainstream, middle-class representation. It was not until 1991 that Australia had a nationally recognised, multi-ethnic theatre, the Black Swan in Perth, which is the country's most isolated city. Foreign cuisine has moved from enclaves in Chinatown and Little Tokyo to neighbourhood restaurants, but diversity does not exist in the major theatres, at least as an American understands the term.

Casting difficulties explain some of this. For example, Sydney's Ensemble Theatre had difficulty casting the role of Billie Holiday in *Lady Day at Emerson's Bar and Grill*, but this does not explain the paucity of Asian-Australians and other minorities on stage or in training programmes. Moreover, playwrights have created few parts for actors who are not Anglo-Saxon. Non-traditional casting is seldom evident.

What constitutes a classic in a young culture? Ray Lawler's *Summer of the Seventeenth Doll* (1955) is the play most Australians would call their first classic. Its air of romance suggests boulevard drama, but only momentarily: The characters are barmaids and sugar-cane cutters; their humour can be crude; the central couple are in love, but never marry; even more unconventional for the genre and the period, they separate at the end of the play instead of remaining together, happily ever after.

The sturdy construction of *The Doll*, its familiar title, and its individuated characters cannot alone explain its appeal to Australians. Critics of the original production provide some clues. Following the Melbourne premiere, one wrote that Lawler 'has written a play so superbly true to Australian thought and to the Australian scene that theatrical conventions disappear'. When the play opened in Brisbane, the *Courier Mail* sighed, 'What a relief it is to welcome an Australian play to town without having to apologize for it.'

What distinguishes *The Doll* from imported plays of that period must have been more pronounced to mid-century Australians than its similarities appear today. The characters are rugged, use Australian idioms and possess an Australian sense of humour. The men earn their living with their hands, and however tenuous their bond to the land might be, their tie to one another is inviolate: they are mates! According to one editor, the 1950s 'was a crucial period in the development of the Australian identity'. In this context, *The Doll* 'stands at the watershed of our national consciousness, answering at the time a need for something of our own, for some kind of self-definition, for a celebration of what is unique to ourselves'. Still, Prime Minister Menzies tried to prevent a London transfer. He thought the play's morality reflected badly on his country.

Australian self-definition has long been stunted, a malady A. A. Phillips diagnosed in an influential 1950 essay called 'The Cultural Cringe'. He defined this as 'an assumption that the domestic cultural product will be worse than the imported article ... The devil of it will be that the assumption will often be correct. The numbers are against us, and an inevitable quantitative inferiority easily looks like a qualitative weakness under the most favorable circumstances – and our circumstances are not favorable.' For example, the population of Australia is about 30% of the United Kingdom, 7% of the United States.

David Williamson, for one, believes that 'the Cringe' persists: 'Australians are terribly concerned about their cultural image overseas. They never trust their own writers, poets, artists until some form of recognition comes from a larger culture.' The 1996 Atlanta Olympics proved his point. The kitsch of its closing ceremony included a preview of the 2000 Sydney Olympics that was produced by Australians. Its prancing dances featured inflatable kangaroos and chirping kookaburras. Down Under was incensed. Embarrassed patriots expressed their chagrin on the nightly news. Letters to the editor berated the propagation of cutesy images that, Australians seemed certain, reflected poorly on their modern society and cosmopolitan ways. The most curious part of this episode was clear four years later: Australia looked terrific through the lens of the XXVII Olympiad. The people came across as good sportsmen and Sydneysiders as gracious hosts. In short, the anxiety and insecurity in 1996 had little bearing on Australian reality.

This hypersensitivity to the Atlanta preview demonstrates for me the vulnerability that attaches to an uncertain self-image. Australia's youthful self-absorption also helps explain the appeal of *The Doll*. The nation's need to see itself on stage remains powerful. Audiences expect playwrights to fulfil it. This has become a power that writers hold over their compatriots like a talisman.

Stages of Self

John Krummel, one of the earliest graduates of the National Institute of Dramatic Art, recalls that: 'Virtually all the teachers were English; ditto the repertoire. Theatres in the early 1960s were also run by Englishmen. All this began to change around 1970.' Introducing the first play published by Currency Press in 1971, Katharine Brisbane wrote, 'the new Australian school of playwriting has embarked upon a process of discovery both of the Australian character and its environment as though it had never been done before.' Since then, Currency has published over 400 Australian plays.

Both before and after *Hamlet*, actors have been 'abstract and brief chronicles of the time'. Elizabethan audiences implicitly accepted that a Danish prince of another era could embody their own interests. Australia's protracted colonial history seems to incline audiences to experience such stories as someone else's. They want Australian plays, new plays, ones with a literal connection to local life. There is no evidence that Elizabethan groundlings questioned the 'relevance' of *The Tempest* to their quotidian lives. That question went unasked until recent years in 'sophisticated' places like America and Australia.

David Williamson both celebrates and mocks what is familiar. His Shavian satires imply a shared perspective with his audience. Unlike Claudius in *Hamlet*, the public enjoys seeing itself as guilty creatures at the play. Beginning in the late 1960s, Australian playwrights liberated themselves from overseas models, subjects and trends. The outpouring of energy that followed is comparable, at least in one regard, to the pattern of first-wave minority writers: free at last to write about themselves, they are initially obsessed with writing *only* about themselves.

At what point does the freedom to dramatise the recognisable world of here-and-now become its own form of slavery? When do a phalanx of characters who reflect the experience, education, beliefs, habits, lexicon, society and worldview of both playwright and audience become anaesthetics, numbing the senses because they are so predictably similar? As Peter Brook warns, 'One goes to the theatre to find life, but if there is no difference between life outside the theatre and life inside, then theatre makes no sense. There's no point doing it.'

American artists and audiences benefit profoundly, and through no personal effort whatsoever, from the richness inherent in a large and diverse population. Even simple, representational art has the opportunity to represent enormous variety. With its relatively small population, historical settlement and (until recently) narrow spectrum of immigration, Australia is far less pluralistic. Aboriginal peoples have only begun to adopt Western art forms over the last thirty-five years. Nationalism and the patrimony of conformity make the spectrum narrower still. It is easy for any audience to see itself in an artistic mirror aimed at what is already familiar. It is more difficult for that audience to take the imaginative leap of seeing itself in someone else's mirror.

By 1980, however, playwrights such as Jan Balodis, Ron Elisha, Louis Nowra and Stephen Sewell had begun to distinguish themselves from first-wave playwriting of the 1970s through non-Australian settings. Director Neil Armfield writes: 'There has always been a problem for Australian playwrights whose work uses metaphor as a way of creating and commenting on reality.' Much as Australians yearn to be cosmopolitan, they seem to prefer characters, settings and subjects that are transparently local, if not parochial.

An outsider cannot comprehend the profound satisfaction that Australians must have experienced upon seeing themselves represented artistically for the first time, whether by Lawler, Williamson, or the few examples in between. Treacle and popshlock are still imported, but Australian verisimilitude is now an established alternative.

Resident theatres rely heavily upon Australian playwrights. Melbourne's Playbox Theatre Company is committed exclusively to new writing. In 1996, the South Australian Theatre Company in Adelaide announced that it would only produce revivals of Australian plays until the year 2000. European classics retain a place in the repertoire as well, often in new translations by Australian authors. Contemporary foreign plays, however, are primarily English, or American ones bearing the imprimatur of a recent London success. There is virtually no contemporary work from the Continent or Scandinavia to say nothing of Australia's newly embraced Asian neighbours. This dependence on London seems paradoxical given gentle Pommie bashing and the fervent assertion that Australia really is a wholly separate nation. Wayne Harrison, former artistic director of Australia's largest theatre, the Sydney Theatre Company, answers the paradox: 'English plays sell. American and those from other countries don't. We see so many American movies and television programmes that going out to see an American play doesn't particularly excite Australians. They don't assume it would be different from the films and television they already see.' Herein lies another lesson of the new economic order: as bad money drives out good, so American pop entertainment drives away serious American plays, at least from Australia's contemporary theatres.

An audience's fascination with seeing itself on stage is undeniable. The need underlying it may be insatiable. However, mainstream Australian theatre seems entrenched in projecting this self rather narrowly. The society is more diverse than the Anglo-Celtic, middle-class characters who remain ubiquitous on stage.

Initially, spectators recognise themselves within an actor's face, gesture, words, or temperament. When the actor and play are communicating more than home truths, however, those same spectators can see themselves in a different generation, gender, nationality, or race. They experience, in short, empathy. If a nation's eating habits can broaden beyond home cooking, so can its artistic taste. Rather than malls, movies and mobile phones, *this* is the true global village.

The plays that follow invite audiences to make imaginative leaps. Four are dramas, often suffused with humour. The fifth is a satyr play.

Downstage Australia: Five Plays

For much of the twentieth century, domestic realism has been drama's undernourished and overworked yeoman. While many of the greatest plays ever written have domestic cores, *Oedipus Rex* and *King Lear* are not tethered by the homefront or to a kitchen sink. Behind every Chekhov and O'Neill lie a thousand simply realistic playwrights with only enough ability to reveal that beneath every surface lies yet another surface. While one purpose of art is to make the strange familiar, and another to make the familiar strange, domestic plays are often content to leave the familiar familiar. Literalness is the genre's calling card.

In *Hotel Sorrento*, three sisters gather at the family homestead after the death of their father. Past events are resuscitated, closet doors flung open and dirty linen aired – all as mandated by the implied rules of domestic drama. However, Hannie Rayson never settles contentedly for life inside the Moynihan household. Rather, it is a crucible for life outside. As Rayson says, 'My central question was how far we had come in terms of our quest to articulate an Australian identity.'

Ninety per cent of Australians live along the coast, a reminder that their nation is an island as well as a continent. The seaside setting of *Hotel Sorrento* is a gorgeous peninsula just south of Melbourne. Unlike Chekhov's three sisters, this trio does not yearn for a metropolis beyond its grasp. Two have already moved abroad: Pippa to New York and Meg to London. Meg does not join her sisters back in Sorrento until the beginning of the second act, but even in her London scenes of the first act, her perspective is insistently homeward. The bond between Australia present and Mother Country past remains umbilical.

A respected writer as articulate in speech as she is in prose, Meg utters some of the play's sharpest barbs and most penetrating observations about Australia. Her recently published novel, *Melancholy*, is a locus for heated debate throughout the play. Meg sometimes sounds like Rayson's *raissoneur*, and like many writers Meg desperately wants approval, but the playwright intentionally undercuts her character's credibility: Meg insists she is not an autobiographical writer, yet her novel clearly is. Rayson cautions her audience against accepting anything at face value as if to warn: the author Meg Moynihan should not be confused with the author Hannie Rayson. More bubbles beneath the surface of *Hotel Sorrento* than is first evident. Rayson makes each character's perspective so convincing, however divergent from another character's, that the clash between their views becomes an engine of the drama.

Aubrey Mellor, who directed the play's premiere, notes: 'The four men's roles are all supportive ones and this is rare enough in the theatre as to be remarked upon by the male actors – suddenly they understand what female actors have been saying for years.' Each woman also has a distinct history with men: the sisters are widowed, married and single; the teacher they befriend is divorced. *Melancholy* has a different meaning for each woman too.

Psychologist Carol Gilligan describes one difference between men and women as the internalised images of human relationships that they possess: hierarchies for men, with the ideal position at the top; webs for women, the ideal location being in the centre. The dramatic structure of *Hotel Sorrento* is not linear and Aristotelian but contrapuntal and web-like. For example, Rayson creates three distinct circles of action at the beginning of the play: members of the Moynihan household in Sorrento; the teacher and her companion in other parts of Sorrento; the novelist and her husband in London. These circles and their characters remain absolutely separate until the final scene of the first act. Then, only two circles touch. In the first scene of the second act, two other circles meet. It is not until the middle of Act Two that all three circles are congruent and all the characters join together.

Hotel Sorrento is the most episodic play collected here. Sometimes such cinematic flow reflects loose structure or none at all, but *Hotel Sorrento* is meticulously crafted. Scenes interlock deftly to create cross-connections that resonate back and forth. The luncheon scene when the three circles finally overlap is one of the most sustained and powerful in this anthology. Its energy derives from a simple Shavian dynamic: articulate antagonists argue their views as if the fate of their souls hung in the balance. Perhaps they do. Their subjects are art, books and Australia itself.

Rayson's Moynihan sisters, like Chekhov's Prozorov sisters, must cope with the recent death of their father, endure betrayal and discover a meaning for tomorrow. The play ends with an auctioneer soliciting bids for the family home, 'Who'd like to give me a reasonable offer?' His words reverberate as much as the sound of an axe felling a cherry orchard.

Meg Moynihan is talented enough to be nominated for the Booker Prize, but it would be unfair to compare her with David Williamson's writer, the archetypal dead white male, William Shakespeare. *Dead White Males* is, among other things, a critique of excesses of the Left from the Left, which gives its satire a bedrock of credibility. The targets include multiculturalism, feminism, fashionable literary theory and more. In *Dumbocracy in America*, Robert Brustein writes: 'Just as it was possible in the past to struggle for more equitable distribution of wealth without becoming a Stalinist, so it should be possible today to resist censorship and support social justice without adopting the rigid dogmas of political correctness.' When Williamson's protagonist, a university student named Angela, declares, 'Australia's multicultural policy has been a huge success story. We've become the international showpiece of ethnic harmony,' her father knows why and rejoins, 'Total apathy.'

Angela leads the audience on an invigorating voyage of discovery as the play follows the journey of her mind. Curious, eager to learn, Angela moves from mouthing platitudes to doubting them. She is a true intellectual, at least in Harold Rosenberg's sense of the word, 'one who turns answers into questions'. The forum for her education turns out to be her home as much as her university.

As with *Hotel Sorrento*, the family nest is again a play's launching pad, not its target for splashdown. Although Williamson's play is far more linear than Rayson's, three generations are again represented and four mature women again have distinct relationships with men. When a lecturer suggests that Angela analyse 'the controlling ideologies' within her family for his Cultural Studies tutorial, she decides to interview each family member by turn. Confounding her easy expectations, they utter surprising truths instead of recycling pat assumptions. The Judd family, like the Moynihans, shows how a playwright can create family members without their identity within that family superseding their consciousness of the outside world. These characters often disagree about facts, let alone the meaning of those facts.

The Bard himself appears periodically throughout *Dead White Males*. So do sentiments from *The Taming of the Shrew* and a speech from *King Lear*. Incorporating an entire Shakespearean scene might invite invidious comparisons for a lesser playwright, but Williamson skirts the trap of hubris. His first act builds to an exhilarating *coup de théâtre*: the denouement of *As You Like It*. Through pointed doubling of characters, its gender battles cleverly parallel those of *Dead White Males*. As the audience heads to intermission, it has licence to entertain the possibility of harmony between men and women.

Following two hours of invigorating engagement with ideology and theory, *Dead White Males* draws to a close. A young man and woman go off together hand in hand, not into the sunset, but to a movie on a date. It is an optimistic, reaffirming, even conventional ending that echoes *As You Like It*. This is not, however, as old-fashioned as it first appears: Angela is the bright student, Steve the dullard preparing to trade a university education for a pragmatic apprenticeship.

Williamson wrote his earliest plays while lecturing on thermodynamics and social psychology. He has clearly retained an ear for academic cant. He has also admitted to half believing some preachments of Dr Grant Swain, the university lecturer who is his antagonist. However, Williamson sustains his own credibility longer than Swain, who turns smarmy quickly and is a weak foil to Angela throughout the second act.

Williamson's highly theatrical play engages issues that resonate around the world. Through his screenplays, in particular, he has reached an international audience, but he would like to do the same on stage. If it helps to do so, he endorses dispensing entirely with Australian accents, as some overseas productions have done. After all, Shakespeare sounds best in a British accent only when he's performed at home.

*

Ron Elisha's *Two* dramatises familiar Australian issues, immigration and the search for identity, but it does not contain any transparent references to the country. It is set in Germany in 1948. Immigration and identity merge in the quest of Anna to learn Hebrew and to become a Jew through Rabbi Chaim Levi. This will help her settle in Palestine, just then on the cusp of becoming Israel. Elisha himself was born in Jerusalem three years after statehood. At the age of two, he moved to Australia along with three and a half million other immigrants in the aftermath of World War Two.

His play begins as a series of language lessons between the rabbi and his student. According to Barbara Damashek, who directed *Two*'s American premiere, 'The Hebrew alphabet is a code that reveals a perception of the world. Traditionally, the letters are recognized as living things. They are energies. And every word that shares a root has a relationship with every other letter and word that shares that root.' Hebrew is an etymological playground, but the puzzle of letters and words is only one part of *Two*'s complicated mystery. When the rabbi says, 'I'm going to set you a riddle. And in the course of each lesson, I'm going to give you a clue to its solution,' Anna is hooked. So is the audience.

Two gradually unfolds like a detective story about what happened to its characters in the past, as well as what occurs to them in the present. These mysteries energise the drama, but this outer narrative is not the same as *Two*'s inner meaning. Such a distinction exists for all plays, but it is especially easy to mistake the skin of *Two* for its bones. The play seems to focus on Jews, the Hebrew language, and the aftermath of the Holocaust. Ultimately, however, *Two* dramatises the interconnectedness of apparent opposites: good and evil, music and language, man and woman, theist and atheist, German and Jew, Israeli and Arab. Chaim is a man of the book as well as a man of the cloth, and these ideas reverberate from the walls of his hovel as naturally as his music – and just as loudly. Everything is a forum for Socratic or, rather, rabbinical debate: chess, history, morality, language itself. Chaim's mordant sense of humour leavens the discourse; he delivers his ideas with epigrammatic pungency.

In *Anti-Intellectualism in American Life*, Richard Hofstadter writes, 'the case against intellect is founded upon a set of fictional and wholly abstract antagonisms'. In theatre, a prevailing fiction is the supposed antagonism between intellect and feeling, as if the mind threatened the experience of emotion instead of being its font. *Two*'s physical canvas is the smallest in this collection, two characters and a single set, but its intellectual ambition is the greatest. It is ostensibly a period play set long ago and far away. Nevertheless, the bipolarisation *Two* explores to reveal the unity of apparent opposites has hardly disappeared from our digital world, whether in Germany, Australia or the Middle East. Alas.

All of Elisha's plays are informed by his Jewish heritage. He is the only playwright represented here who was born outside Australia. At the other extreme, Williamson is a fifth generation Australian and the indigenous roots of Wesley Enoch and Deborah Mailman stretch back millennia. Like Elisha, their heritage infuses their art. They created *The 7 Stages of Grieving* for Kooemba Jdarra, a group founded in Brisbane in 1993 that is committed to indigenous performing arts. The name means 'good ground'. Enoch was then its artistic director.

The 7 Stages of Grieving is a one-woman show that blends traditional storytelling, music and movement with techniques of performance art. Like much performance art, it is ostensibly autobiographical, and it relies on visual images as well as poetic ones. Slide projections are used, and a block of ice that gradually melts throughout the show is suspended by seven ropes above a patch of red earth, which defines a recent grave.

The play's title melds Elizabeth Kubler-Ross's five stages of dying – denial and isolation, anger, bargaining, depression, and acceptance – with Michael Williams's seven phases of Aboriginal history – dreaming, invasion, genocide, protection, assimilation, self-discrimination and reconciliation. The grief following the death of her grandmother, a beloved but long-lived elder, is the catalyst for Mailman to consider family and friends who die young and under unnatural circumstances, including police detention. What is personal to Mailman becomes political and, of course, what is political is highly personal. A granddaughter's loss transforms into the pain of a people.

Australia's indigenous peoples could not vote until 1962, were not counted in the census until 1967, and had no claim to the earth recognised in court until 1992 when *terra nullius* ceased to be the law of the land. Among many indicators, much shorter life expectancy and vastly higher unemployment echo the disparity that is found on every continent between the colonised and their colonisers. Here, the ancestors arrived as long as 50,000 years ago. Reconciliation, the seventh phase of Williams's history, represents the hope of Aboriginal peoples that white Australia will some day apologise. The government refuses to do so, but some traditional lands are returning to Aboriginal hands. This shift from assimilation to self-determination includes Uluru, previously famed as Ayers Rock.

One way to evoke the stage imagery of *The 7 Stages of Grieving* is by describing the theatrical uses of a suitcase. Invisible at first, it is buried beneath the dirt of Nana's grave. It becomes the suitcase of Aunty Grace, who has lived abroad for fifty years. Before returning to England after the funeral, she replaces her personal contents inside the suitcase with dirt from Nana's grave. It is this soil that has nourished her from afar. For the play's poignant conclusion, the suitcase becomes a sacred vessel for reconciliation: the word itself appears inside the suitcase through a slide projection. When the performer shuts the lid, 'reconciliation' is locked inside. She places the suitcase and the metaphorical healing it contains at the feet of the audience. Having told her story, she exits the stage without her baggage. What happens next to reconciliation is up to the audience.

In the course of her journey, writer-performer Mailman revisits stages of her own grieving and reveals some of the pain of Aboriginal history. She moves her audience to catharsis, then to the possibility of peacefulness that can follow. *The 7 Stages of Grieving* reflects the generosity and grace of a people mistreated for centuries. Despite this history, Mailman opens her hands and heart to her countrymen and, through them, to the rest of humanity.

Such a personal and collaborative piece may seem odd at first in a book of plays, but performance-driven work like this transcends its creator-performers when it is good enough. Personal plays created by Eric Bogosian and Anna Deavere Smith, for example, are now performed by others. Athol Fugard, John Kani and Winston Ntshona were startled that *Sizwe Bansi Is*

Dead and *The Island* resonated outside South Africa. In the thirty years since they devised these plays, they have been performed by scores of actors.

Hotel Sorrento, *Dead White Males* and *Two* all stem from the literary tradition of playwriting. They were written autonomously, by single authors, in advance of a production, and then entrusted to a director and actors. *The 7 Stages of Grieving* and *The Popular Mechanicals* evolved from a different tradition, one in which playwrights are also writing for themselves as actors and in which the script is wrought through a heightened sense of performance.

In *Dead White Males*, Shakespeare is shot on stage. He is murdered in *The Popular Mechanicals: A Funny Old New Play*. Post-structuralism on campus is a hard act to follow, but the mechanicals certainly act hard; deconstruction has never been funnier. Keith Richardson and Tony Taylor devote an entire play to the rude mechanicals of *A Midsummer Night's Dream*. Their hard-handed and hard-headed characters are as rude as they can possibly be. Like their model, Richardson and Taylor expropriate backstage life and transform it into the cosmos for a hilarious, punny play. Originally inspired by the bawdy, scatological jigs that entertained audiences after Elizabethan performances, *The Popular Mechanicals* incorporates one of these, the story of Beryl the Widow, to climax Act I with a resounding air.

Geoffrey Rush, who directed the original production, credits the genesis of the play to the Elizabethan experiments of Philip Parsons and Wayne Harrison in Sydney (see Rush's 'Words Words Words', reprinted here on pp 301–302). Over a number of years they explored staging Shakespeare under his original conditions: with male actors only, performing in rep, without elaborate props or many costumes, without *any* intermission or much rehearsal, performing on a platform stage and surrounded by a standing audience. Subsequent discussions inspired the notion of a 'Shakespearean' Vaudeville: 'songs, sketches, dances – something to celebrate the traditions of theatre clowning'. The same experiments influenced Harrison's own direction of *Dead White Males*: 'For a play that moves so fluidly between real and imagined worlds, I needed an open, fast, presentational stage much along Elizabethan lines.'

The Popular Mechanicals uses all four mechanicals scenes from *A Midsummer Night's Dream*, lines from a dozen other plays by Shakespeare, and much more that Robinson and Taylor invented themselves. Even with Shakespeare as co-author, *The Popular Mechanicals* depends on inspired clowning. Maybe that's only fair since Shakespeare earned more from his share as a performer than as a playwright. Blunt and utterly without pretensions, *The Popular Mechanicals* knows exactly what it is: it stands with its feet set firmly in two centuries (sixteenth and twentieth), its head planted squarely between its legs. It is a puckish play without a single appearance by Robin Goodfellow. Since Plato defined art as an imitation of an imitation, it follows that *The Popular Mechanicals*, being a parody of a parody, a satire of a satire, must be art too. It appeals to the groundling in us all.

Foreign plays provide the same stimulation as foreign travel: an opportunity to visit never-neverlands, to encounter other people and places intimately, to experience the dislocation prompted by alien mindsets and worldviews. Foreign travel and engagement with overseas art can also lead to new insights about 'here' by comparing it to 'there'. Travellers are amateur anthropologists. They strive to comprehend the new adventures they may not understand by comparing them with the old ones they do. Before maps noted *Terra Australis*, they were marked *Terra Incognita*, Unknown Land. Before that, ancient cartographers simply wrote 'Beyond Here Are Monsters', an appeal to our primal fear of the unknown. Recent Australian films, often written by Australian playwrights, have been widely distributed overseas and have helped make Australia better known. So have novels by Thomas Keneally, David Malouf and Peter Carey. They help transform *Terra Incognita* into *Terra Recognita*. So can these plays.

The challenge of selecting plays for an anthology is comparable to that of picking plays to produce for a season. The difficulty is not finding five that are worthy, but in deciding which five. Each work may be experienced independently, but they also constitute a larger whole. Individual plays should not be too similar in style, tone, subject or point of view. Other criteria, prejudices really, include my instinct for diversity and eclecticism. Contemporary

plays and productions seem to me too concerned with verisimilitude. I side with Verdi: 'It may be good to imitate reality, but it is
better to invent it.'

I respond to plays that surprise me, that tell me what I don't
already know, that take me to places I've never been or times I
did not live, that possess enough subtlety and complexity to
require a second and third encounter. I admire plays that nurture
me. I prefer a deep, long-term relationship with a play to a two-
hour fling in a darkened room. I like plays that make me think as
well as feel, and I do not accept the assumption that the two are
diametrically opposed. 'Deep thinking,' Coleridge believed, 'is
attainable only by a man of deep feeling.'

A fundamental question to ask of every foreign play is whether
or not it translates. This has very little to do with the language in
which it was composed. Idiomatic phrases and topical references
are seldom problematic; brief explanations can be noted after the
text, as is done here, or substitutions made in production. A far
greater difficulty is non-verbal translation: do given circumstances
make sense, subtexts resonate, metaphors suggest, quandaries
transcend the topical, and characters escape the parochial? If not,
the play remains a captive of its originating culture. Because
theatre is only in part a literary art, it is highly mobile from one
language to another. This is self-evident in international festivals
when audiences are enthralled by productions in languages they
do not comprehend. Consider, too, the different cultures represented by master playwrights of the last century. Each is a dead
white male, but each also wrote in a different language: Ibsen,
Shaw, Strindberg, Pirandello, Brecht, Beckett. The greatest
challenge in translating Chekhov is not from Russian to English,
but from page to stage.

A perfect anthology, like a perfect season, production or
performance, is a Platonic ideal that exists only in theory. No
musical is included here, no play stylistically novel or formally
inventive. All the plays depend on language. They are carefully
structured. All five are narrative. They have beginnings, middles
and ends. They even occur in that order.

This is a collection of discrete plays, not necessarily of
representative playwrights. Were it otherwise, writers such as
Alma De Groen, Nick Enright, Michael Gow, Joanna Murray-

Smith, Louis Nowra and Stephen Sewell would be included too. Eschewing continuity, unity or national leitmotifs, I hoped instead to bring together five plays that are intrinsically interesting, but that also create additional heat by rubbing together between the sheets and covers.

Finally, an inherent paradox must be acknowledged about these plays, about all plays when published. They were written to be performed. In a book they reach people who may never have the opportunity to see them. However much I enjoyed quiet encounters with these texts, they were not selected because of their quality as two-dimensional squiggles upon a page, but because of the three-dimensional life they possess on stage in my mind's eye.

Convict colonies have an illustrious history of inspiring writers. *Democracy in America* immortalised Alexis de Tocqueville, but the purpose of his 1831 visit was to study American prisons for the French government. In 1890, Anton Chekhov wrote to his publisher: 'After Australia in the past and Cayenne, Sakhalin is the only place where you can study colonisation by criminals.' Chekhov's *The Island of Sakhalin* reveals the brutality of penal servitude. And in 1920, Franz Kafka published 'In the Penal Colony', his harrowing tale of torture and execution through the very act of writing: a prisoner's sentence is carved into his living flesh.

Australian plays have become richer and more self-assured over the past quarter-century. This period coincides with the nation embracing its past, including Aboriginal peoples and inmate ancestors. New convictions have replaced old embarrassment over 'convict stain' within the family tree. Australians have grown proud to discover thieves among their ancestors. After all, it was they who performed *The Recruiting Officer* in 1789. Two centuries later, the theatre tradition is stronger than ever.

Evanston, Illinois, April 2001

Hotel Sorrento

Hannie Rayson

Hannie Rayson is a graduate of Melbourne University and the Victorian College of the Arts (VCA) and has an Honorary Doctorate of Letters from La Trobe University. A co-founder of Theatreworks, her theatre credits include *Please Return to Sender* (1980), *Mary* (1981) and *Leave It Till Monday* (1984). *Room to Move* (1985) won an AWGIE Award, as did her next play, *Hotel Sorrento* (1990), which also won a NSW Premier's Literary Award and Green Room Award for Best Play. It has since had over 50 productions throughout Australia and overseas and has been translated into French, Japanese and Swedish. Other plays include *Falling From Grace* (1994, which also won a NSW Premier's Literary Award) and *Competitive Tenderness* (1996).

Rayson's television scripts include *Sloth* (ABC, *Seven Deadly Sins*) and two episodes of *SeaChange* (co-written for ABC/Artists Services). A feature film of *Hotel Sorrento*, produced in 1995, was nominated for ten Australian Film Institute Awards. Her most recently produced play, *Life After George* (2000), won the Victorian Premier's Literary Award and has been nominated for eight Green Room Awards and three Helpman Awards.

A Sweet Pensive Sadness

Hannie Rayson

With *Hotel Sorento* I wanted to write a play of ideas; something which would send an audience out into the night with all sorts of things to talk about over coffee. I also wanted to create a 'sweet pensive sadness' to pervade the experience, as there is something delectable about melancholy which seems to alter the way we see things.

To date, my plays have been a response to particular contemporary social phenomena which I want to understand more fully. I am interested in subject matter which is bursting with contradiction. As a playwright I am concerned with the task of posing questions, both in the process of writing and in the finished work. As a dramatic device it allows me to activate and engage an audience but perhaps more importantly it is a vehicle for both playwright and audience to embark upon a genuine line of enquiry together.

With *Hotel Sorrento* my central question was how far we had come in terms of our quest to articulate an Australian identity and what kinds of changes had taken place during the past decade. I was interested in how the experience of living elsewhere alters one's perceptions of home. And, conversely, for those who've stayed and contributed to the life of the culture from 'the inside', where is the line between a healthy nationalism and blind patriotism?

I decided to focus on the relationship between literature and cultural identity and to exploit the debate in critical/literary circles about Australian fiction. To merely hold a mirror to reflect ourselves and our culture does not automatically constitute great art, some argued. In our bid to be counted as a country with important cultural heroes and myths were we overstating the calibre of our cultural products? Could we really look for profundity and passion in our own literature?

My interest also was to try and weave themes of cultural identity through several layers of the narrative, so I could explore ideas about loyalty, for example, or betrayal, from the perspective of the expatriate's response to her country, her fiction and her family.

In 1986 I went to London on a research grant from the then Theatre Board of the Australia Council to do a series of interviews with expatriates. Peter Carey's face was in all the bookshop windows and on sandwich boards on the street. He had been nominated for the Booker Prize for his novel *Illywhacker*, and while he didn't win that year, Oz literature was a talking point.

In an interview in *The Times*, Carey said that he had lived in London for two years from 1968 and loved it like any other visitor. 'But one day I looked at the man at the local service station and suddenly realised that if I lived here ten years I wouldn't know that man any better. I decided to go home . . . What I missed was that ability to recognise instantly what people are, what they are thinking and feeling which comes effortlessly with your own kind.'

At this point, the idea of a novelist as my central character was born and that of her Booker-nominated novel forming the backbone of the play. I needed to create someone whose opinions were going to receive attention by the world press; someone passionate and outspoken about Australia so that the pendulum between my own sense of deep affection and frustration that this country can engender, could swing back and forth freely. In this way I could create a tension and interplay of often contradictory ideas. But at the heart of this play is the family and the sisters.

'Few other relationships can inspire such loyalty or such anger as sisters. Sisters can experience great closeness, but when they fall out, the conflicts go deeper too.' *Sisters on Sisters*, Jane Dowdeswell, Grapevine, UK, 1988.

Although I have no sisters, I used to think that the long-term bonds I've made with certain women friends were of the same ilk. But in writing this play and observing sisters over a long period, it is clear that sisters have something else. One thing that interests me is the volatility that is often a feature of the relationship: knowing intuitively and often unwittingly how to ignite a fuse and start a spot fire, which may rage out of control or be extinguished quickly. And yet despite this, families seem to have an astonishing capacity to endlessly postpone the settling of conflicts and old scores.

In the writing and subsequent production of this play, Playbox have been stalwart supporters. I am indebted to them for their encouragement and patience and to the Performing Arts Board and Literature Boards of the Australia Council, for their support.

I especially want to acknowledge the contribution of my friend and dramaturg Hilary Glow. With talk into the wee small hours, the patient reading of draft upon draft, and the constant challenge of her intellect, she has been a sustaining and inspiring force.

I also wish to express my gratitude to Aubrey Mellor who directed the play in Melbourne and Sydney and again with a new cast in Brisbane. He choreographed the movement of the play with such grace, elicited some very fine performances and with passion and delicacy, revealed the heart of the drama.

Finally, to my partner James Grant and our son Jack Grant for their love and encouragement, and to Kathy and Suzie Skelton who kept me entertained for years with their stories of Sorrento – thank you.

Collingwood, October 1992

Hotel Sorrento was first performed by the Playbox Theatre Company at the Merlyn Theatre, C.U.B. Malthouse, Melbourne on 27 July 1990, with the following cast:

Hilary	Elspeth Ballantyne
Marge	Julia Blake
Wal	Robin Cuming
Dick	Peter Curtin
Meg	Caroline Gillmer
Edwin	David Latham
Troy	Tamblyn Lord
Pippa	Genevieve Picot

Directed by Aubrey Mellor
Designed by Jennie Tate
Lighting by John Comeadow
Sound by Stuart Greenbaum

Characters

Marge Morrisey *is fifty-seven, a teacher, divorcee and mother of four. All of her children have grown up and left home. She has a holiday house in Sorrento, where she goes every weekend.*

Dick Bennett, *forty-three, the editor of the* Australian Voice. *His friendship with Marge dates back to the early seventies. He lives alone in a rented flat, and is a regular visitor to Marge's holiday house.*

Hilary Moynihan *is the eldest of the Moynihan sisters. She lives in Sorrento, in the family house, with her father and sixteen-year-old son. Her husband was killed in a car accident. She owns a small gourmet deli in the main street.*

Wal Moynihan *is sixty-nine, father to Hilary, Meg and Pippa. He is retired now, having been the proprietor of the local garage, Moynihan Motors. His family has been in Sorrento for generations, and as a result he is something of a local character.*

Troy Moynihan, *Hilary's son.*

Edwin Bates, *forty-five, an Englishman married to Meg. He is a partner in a successful publishing firm in London.*

Meg Moynihan, *the middle sister, is a novelist and expatriate. She has been in London for ten years. Her second novel,* Melancholy, *has been nominated for the Booker Prize.*

Pippa Moynihan *is the youngest sister, currently living in New York. She is well travelled and now a highly paid advertising executive.*

Setting

The play takes place in the present time.
In Act One, there are three households – Meg and Edwin's flat in London, the Moynihan family home in Sorrento and Marge's holiday house in Sorrento.
In Act Two, all action takes place in Sorrento.

Sorrento is a pretty coastal town on the Mornington Peninsula in Victoria, Australia.

for Kathy and Suzie Skelton

Act One

Scene One

Two figures sit on the end of the jetty. It is dusk. The man is fishing. There are remnants of fish and chips in white paper lying between them. She is reading Melancholy. *He is staring out to sea.*

Marge Listen,
'In the autumn, the dusk fell gently. She sat at the end of the jetty listening to the tinkling of the masts and the water lapping at the poles. The jetty creaked at the joints and the boats bobbed about, deserted now. There was a nip in the air.
'With the demise of summer, the town seemed to settle back on itself, to mellow. The breeze no longer carried the crackle of transistors, the call of gulls and the smell of fish and chips. With the summer visitors gone, there was a sense of quiet industry about the place. It was the business of getting on with things.
'From where she sat, she could see the quiet little foreshore with its white bandstand framed by Norfolk pine. Beyond that, the road swept up the hill into the township. She could see the rooves of the cottages, peeping out from amidst the straggle of ti tree. She focused on the tip of the tallest pine and counted across from the left. A red, a green, a red. The second red roof on the hill. "That's us," she whispered, and it was then that she felt it; the sweet pensive sadness, the melancholy, the yearning for something that she could not name.'

Marge *closes the book and looks up at* **Dick** *expectantly. She scrutinises his face for a response.*

Dick What?

Marge This is the jetty, I'm sure of it.

Dick *smirks unconvinced.*

Marge Look, the bandstand, the pines, the road sweeping up to the township. Everything. It's exactly as she describes it. It's Sorrento.

Scene Two

It is seven a.m. **Hilary** *stands on the balcony looking out to sea. She wraps her cardigan round her tightly and holds on to her mug of tea. She watches affectionately as her father,* **Wal**, *and son,* **Troy**, *come up the path.* **Wal** *strides forward with his towel slung over a shoulder.* **Troy** *scrambles behind huddled in his towel, shivering.*

Hilary   How was it?

Wal   Beautiful.

Hilary *laughs at her son, who is standing at the bottom of the verandah steps shivering and shaking his head to get the water out of his ears.*

Wal   Look at it will you. Looks like a plucked chook.

Troy   Get off!

Wal   Go on. Get into a hot shower.

Hilary   Get the sand off first.

Troy *disappears around the back of the house.* **Wal** *leans on the balcony.*

Wal   Look at that, eh? It's beautiful down there this morning. Clear as crystal that water. You ought to come with us.

Hilary *gives him a 'don't be stupid' look. He picks up a coat lying on a chair.*

Wal   What's this?

Hilary   It's Pip's.

Wal   Got more clothes than I've had hot breakfasts, that girl. Got a cup of tea on the go?

Hilary   Mm hm.

Wal She still asleep?

Hilary Yep.

Wal I'll take one into her.

Hilary No, don't. Let her sleep.

Wal Ah . . . missing the best part of the morning.

Hilary Dad. Let her sleep. They knock you about those long flights.

Wal Yea. S'ppose so. Bloody long time to be cooped up in one of those things.

Hilary You know she's only going to be staying for a week, don't you?

Wal Yeah. I know, I know.

Hilary She's got to go to Melbourne.

Wal Beats me why anyone would want to spend time in that stinkin' joint. Wouldn't get me up there if you paid me.

Hilary Yeah. Well that's why she's home. They're paying her.

Wal *says nothing, then breaks into an indulgent smile.*

Wal She's glad to be home, eh? I knew she would be. Well . . . better get a wriggle on. I promised Lorna Watson I'd clean out her guttering.

Hilary Oh, Dad! What about her son-in-law? Lazy bugger. Why can't he do it?

Wal Oh, he's got a crook back or some other bloody thing.

Pause.

Hilary I was thinking, we need a coat of paint on this place. (*She pulls a flake of paint off the wall.*) Look at this.

Wal Yeah. Thought we might get Tracker Johnston to

give us a hand. I got a few tins of that red paint left. That oughta do us for the roof.

Hilary   Yeah. I've always liked the red. Looks nice when you're looking up from the jetty.

Wal   Mm. Bit o' colour on the hill.

Scene Three

A London flat. Evening. **Meg** *opens the door to find* **Edwin** *in the kitchen making a cup of tea. He has the tea cosy on his head.*

Meg   Edwin!

Edwin   Ah, Meg, you're home.

She stares at him, a smile playing on her lips.

Well, you know what they say. Leave an Englisman alone in a room with a tea cosy . . .

Meg *goes over and kisses him.*

Meg   Actually, it's terribly becoming.

Edwin   Thank you. You've had twelve telephone calls.

Meg   Oh, God.

Edwin   The price, my dear, of becoming suddenly enormously famous. How was the new Aussie play?

Meg   Awful.

Edwin   Oh, dear.

Meg   Why do Australians always have to be so obvious? (*Pause.*) Am I obvious?

Edwin   Let me see . . . 'Hello, how are you, would you like to have sex here, or at my place in Fulham. I don't mean to appear hasty but if you do want to have sex in Fulham we'll have to go now because the number fifteen leaves in ten minutes.' I don't know. Would you call that 'obvious'?

Meg   I never said that.

Edwin   Perhaps not in those exact words . . .

Meg   I never lived in Fulham.

Edwin   Ah, Chelsea. I beg your pardon.

Pause.

Meg   Anyway, you needed a bit of prodding.

Edwin   Englishmen are notoriously coy about things of this nature.

Meg   Backward. Let's face it. Anyway I'm not talking about that. I'm talking about my book. When you read it did you think, 'God that is so obvious!'

Edwin   No. Why?

Meg   I was beginning to wonder whether it was a cultural handicap.

Edwin   Being obvious?

Meg   Yes.

Edwin   Well let's face it, you lot like to call a spade a spade, don't you, which is all very admirable in real life . . . but if you think about it, it doesn't make for great drama does it?

Meg *looks at him curiously.*

Edwin   Well take *Hamlet.* An Australian could never have written that. You'd have Hamlet walking on stage saying, 'Cut the bullshit. I don't believe in ghosts.' And the whole thing would've been over in a couple of minutes.

Meg *is only vaguely listening. She is flipping through some mail on the table.*

Edwin   You see, I think as a people you appear to be very suspicious of subtext actually.

Meg   Jesus, Edwin.

Edwin   It has something to do with an unwillingness to deal with the emotional texture of things.

Meg   Really?

Edwin   Mmm. It's like the English chatter on ad nauseam and quite inadvertently we blunder into revealing things about ourselves. But your lot seem to do either of two things. They say exactly what's going on. Or else they're dead silent. Oh, no, there's a third thing. They do a lot of grunting. The men.

Meg *laughs despite herself.*

Edwin   So it's not like Australians are less complex emotionally.

Meg   Oh, Edwin . . .

Edwin   Well I used to think it was. I thought that was why I was so attracted to them – being so inordinately repressed myself as a human being – but I've realised it's all to do with the way it's expressed. You see, if you take . . .

Meg   Who was on the phone?

Edwin   There's the list. Journalists mostly.

Meg   What are they doing ringing me on a Friday night?

Edwin *shrugs.*

Edwin   Nothing much on the telly I s'ppose. (*Pause.*) One chap rang from Australia. He said he used to go out with your sister.

Meg   Which one?

Edwin   Pippa.

Meg   That's hardly a claim to fame.

Edwin   That's what I said to him. 'You and the rest of the male population.'

Meg   You didn't!

Edwin I did.

Meg What did he want?

Edwin Same as everybody else. An exclusive. The Meg Moynihan story. The unknown Aussie novelist makes it to the Booker shortlist with her second novel.

Meg *sighs and briefly scans the letter she is holding.*

Meg Jesus Christ!

She flings it on the table.

Edwin What is it?

Meg The London Book Council. They're organising a forum on women and autobiography. They want me to give the opening address.

Edwin What do you know about autobiography?

Meg Exactly. (*Pause.*) But you must understand, I'm a woman writer. And as such I don't have any frame of reference beyond my own immediate experience. Didn't you know all novels written by women are merely dressed-up diary entries?

Edwin So your novel is *really* about the adventures of Meg Moynihan en famille. That's quite funny really.

Meg Hilarious.

Edwin I wonder what your sisters would make of that?

Meg They'd think it was ridiculous. Do you know, at that play tonight, Carmel refused to speak during the interval in case anyone recognised her accent. I can't tell you how much that irritated me.

Edwin I would have thought it was quite affirming for you. Seeing something really bad. Then you can say to yourself – isn't it good. I don't live there any more.

Pause.

Meg Edwin, where did you get that shirt?

Edwin I bought it at the Camden Market on Sunday. Seventy-five p. Not bad eh?

Meg I think you got ripped off.

Scene Four

Hilary *is ironing. From the ashtray placed on one end of the ironing board we see a single stream of blue smoke.* **Troy** *is sitting at the kitchen table reading the paper.* **Pippa** *enters looking decidedly the worse for wear. However, despite her dishevelled appearance she looks stylish in her silk robe.*

Hilary Ah . . . good afternoon.

Pippa What time is it?

Hilary Eleven.

Pippa Oh, is that all. My tongue feels like it's got a sock on it. Did we drink a huge amount last night or am I imagining things?

Troy About a dozen stubbies, half a dozen bottles of champagne and then you two got stuck into the whisky.

Hilary Thank you, Troy.

Pippa You're kidding?

Hilary Yes. He's kidding. (*To* **Troy**.) Put the kettle on, Troy.

He leans over and plugs it in.

Pippa Not for me. (*He pulls the plug out.*) I think I'll just sit for a minute. (*Pause.*) Why aren't you at the deli?

Hilary Well, it's not every day that your little sister comes home.

Pippa You know no one over there drinks much these days. Not in New York anyway. I'm out of practice. What are you grinning about?

Troy Nothing.

Hilary *plonks a glass of water down in front of her and an aspro.*

Hilary Probably jet lag.

Troy I doubt it.

Hilary Put the kettle on, Troy.

He puts the plug back in.

Pippa Ugh, that cigarette stinks. (*Disapprovingly.*) You're still smoking, Hilary.

Hilary No, Pippa. I gave it away. (*To her son, warning against further nagging.*) And don't you start.

Troy Did I say anything?

Hilary *makes a face at her son.*

Pause.

Pippa Is that old thing still going? (*Indicating the iron.*)

Hilary Mm hmm.

Pippa I thought so. Poor old Mum. Outlived by her iron. (*Pause.*) Yeah. Life sucks, when you think about it. What d'you reckon, Troy?

Troy Mm hm.

Hilary Troy?

Troy What?

Hilary She just proffered an extremely contentious philosophical point of view. You don't just say mm hm.

Troy Why not?

Hilary Well you either agree or disagree . . .

Troy I agree.

Hilary You do not. You're sixteen years old. When you're sixteen years old life does not suck. Life is . . . brimming with . . . excitement and . . . purpose. Isn't it, Pippa?

Pippa *giggles.*

Troy   She can't remember.

Pippa   I can so.

Pause.

Hilary   Poor ol' Mum.

Pippa   She'd be here night after night on her own, wouldn't she? Always got the rough end of the stick, our mum.

Troy   Where was Pop?

Pippa   Out fishing.

Hilary   Or in the pub. But mostly they'd be out in the bay. Dad and Ernie Mac, Tracker Johnston, Jock Farrell. All that lot.

Pippa   Mick Hennessey.

Hilary   He wouldn't get in till after midnight some nights. Remember? We'd hear him coming down the hall, banging against the walls. He'd throw the fish in the sink and crash into bed. Drunk as a skunk.

Pippa   Yeah.

Hilary   It's cruel I reckon.

Pause.

Pippa   What do you mean?

Hilary   Well he was a bastard to our mother. Hopeless father, all of that. But when it all boils down, he's the one that everyone loves. We all love him. Don't we?

Pippa   Yeah.

Hilary   More than we ever loved her.

Pippa *looks dubious.*

Hilary   It's true. And yet she was the one that kept it all together.

Silence. The flywire screen door slaps. They exchange looks, hoping their father didn't overhear. **Wal** *enters. He is carrying a bag of fish.*

Wal   Ah, you're up?

Pippa   Yeah.

Wal   Good. Ernie Mac gave us a few flatties. He said to say g'day by the way.

Pippa   Oh, yeah.

Wal   Thought we might scrub 'em up for tea. What d'ya reckon?

Pippa   Beauty.

He chucks them in the sink. The others smile at the sound.

Wal   What are you laughin' at?

Pippa   Nothing.

Hilary   Don't look at me. I'm not gonna clean 'em.

Wal   All right. No one's askin' ya. (*He grins.*) Troy here's not doin' anythin'.

Troy *makes a face.*

Troy   No. I'm just sitting here brimming with life and purpose.

The girls burst out laughing.

Hilary   What do you do with a kid like that?

The kettle starts whistling.

Wal   What's that kettle doin'. Turn it off will ya.

Troy *leans over and pulls the plug out again, shaking his head.*

Troy   I don't believe this.

Pippa *laughs and leans over ruffling his hair affectionately.*

Wal Well ... I got a bit more news. (*He pulls a little piece of torn-up newspaper from his pocket.*) Last Thursday's *Herald*. I was up at Lorna Watson's.

Pippa Lorna Watson? God. She still alive?

Wal Yeah. An' doing very nicely if you don't mind. Any rate, she was sayin', 'Wal, those girls of yours have done very well for 'emselves.'

Hilary Meaning you and Meg.

Wal Nah. Come on. Meaning all of yous. What with you (**Pippa**) bein' in the States makin' more money than Rupert Murdoch ...

Pippa Yeah, come on, get on with it.

Wal And Meg winnin' that book prize.

Pippa She hasn't won it yet, Dad.

Wal Yeah, I know. Still ... Any rate we got talkin' and she showed me this. (*He opens out the piece torn from the paper and hands it to* **Troy**.) I haven't got me glasses. Read it out will you, Troy.

Troy 'AAP. London. Expatriate Australian novelist Meg Moynihan has been nominated for the prestigious Booker McConnell Prize. Her novel *Melancholy* was included on the shortlist announced yesterday. With literary heavyweights like Fredrico Kutz ...'

Pippa Koetz.

Troy 'Koetz, and Johnathon Drewmore as contenders, insiders are speculating that a win for the Australian seems unlikely.'

Hilary Sounds like a horse race.

Wal Ssh. Go on.

Pippa They take bets on it, you know.

Hilary Bullshit.

Pippa   They do.

Troy   You right?

Wal   Come on. Get on with it.

Troy   'Moynihan's novel, which deals with the rites of passage of a young woman growing up in an isolated coastal town in the fifties, is a contentious choice. Her central argument is that in the brutalising male culture of Australia in the fifties, a woman's survival was conditional on the extent to which she was prepared to betray her sisters.' (**Troy** *pauses momentarily. An awkward silence descends.*) 'The novel has been described as displaying a disappointing lack of stylistic ambition by London critics whereas Lucinda Brampton of the *New York Book Review* hailed it as containing one of the most exquisitely executed scenes of recent English-language fiction.'

Troy *looks up.*

Hilary   Is that it?

Troy   Mm hm.

Wal   Not bad, eh? (*To* **Pippa**.) Never thought your own sister'd be a celebrity, did you? Eh?

Pippa   Yeah. I knew.

Hilary (*to* **Wal**)   I reckon you're the one that's most surprised. It would never have entered your head that a daughter of yours'd be anything out of the bag.

Pippa   Well you gotta admit, 'being a daughter of his', that's the weird part. (*They laugh.*)

Scene Five

Marge *and* **Dick** *on the jetty.* **Marge** *is looking at the cover of the book lovingly. She is obviously quite transported by it.*

Marge   *Melancholy.* Such a lovely title. (*Sighing.*) And to think that you hated it.

Dick   I didn't hate it. I told you, I just find it hard to believe that it's been nominated for the Booker Prize. I mean it's all right: a very nice, sentimental, lightweight piece of fiction. A good read, all that stuff, but it's certainly not great literature.

Marge   You know what I think? I think that melancholy is something that men don't understand. Australian men, dare I say it.

Dick   Bullshit.

Marge   No. You confuse it with depression. Which is different. See, I know exactly what she's talking about. There are certain times when I feel overcome by this immense sadness. But it isn't depressing. It's tender and gentle . . . I don't know how to describe it . . . It's very female, I think.

Dick   Is this before you went through the change, Marge?

Marge   Don't be cheeky, you! (**Dick** *laughs*.) Anyway, what's great literature supposed to be? If I may be so bold as to seek definition?

Dick   Great literature. Let me see. Great literature awakens us to our humanity. Like fishing. (*He chuckles.* **Marge** *rolls her eyes*.) It certainly isn't about gender politics, that's for sure.

Marge   This isn't about gender politics.

Dick   Ah, but you're trying to explain my indifference by arguing that I can't really appreciate its true worth because I'm a man.

Marge   Not because you're a man, my dear. Merely that you have blunted sensitivities. Obviously.

Dick   No. Don't wheedle your way out of it. 'Men don't experience melancholy.' That's what you said.

Marge   Well. Do you?

Dick   Yes. I do, as a matter of fact. And I have. (*He* *smirks.*) When I've been feeling particularly self-indulgent.

Marge   Ah, why do we women bother?

Dick   I didn't think you did.

Marge   Well that's true. 'Cept for a few old mates. How long have we known each other?

Dick   Footscray High. Staffroom. '72.

Marge   Twenty years. Tsch. Long time to have a friendship when you don't share the same sensibilities. What do you think is the basis of it?

Dick *shrugs. They are both smirking.*

Dick   The Cause?

Marge   Which neither of us is committed to any more.

Dick   Well, I wouldn't say that. We've just 'modified' our political thinking haven't we?

Marge *laughs.*

Dick   Maybe it's to do with the fact that you have a weekender in Sorrento which I'm rather fond of visiting.

Marge   Oh, don't say that.

Dick   You should know about the folly of acquiring property.

Marge   Humph. A place where the ideologues can come and enjoy the view with a clear conscience.

Dick *laughs.*

Marge   Anyway, what happened about that house you were going to buy?

Dick   Oh, I think I missed the boat, somewhere along the line, Marge.

Marge   Tsch. Forty-two years of age and you're still living in student digs.

Dick   Forty-three actually.

Pause.
Her tone becomes more serious.

Marge   You've invested quite a lot in the paper, haven't you?

Dick   With its circulation dropping at a rate of knots every week. (*Silence.*) Australians don't really want to hear an independent voice telling them that they're being duped. But I suppose any fool could have told me that.

Scene Six

The kitchen. **Troy** *is doing his maths homework on the table.* **Pippa** *is sitting on the stool.* **Hilary** *is reading.*

Pippa   Have you heard from Meg recently?

Hilary   Not for a while.

Pippa   Do you write?

Hilary   Of course.

Pause.

Pippa   Bloody awful title, *Melancholy*. She needs a marketing manager.

Hilary   She doesn't seem to be doing too badly.

Pippa   I suppose it could've been worse. She could've called it 'Depression'.

Troy   I think it's a good title.

Hilary   Concentrate on your homework, Troy.

Pippa (*looking over at* **Hilary**'s *book quizzically*)   What *are* you reading? *The Canterbury Tales?*

Hilary   Mmm hmm.

Pippa   Chaucer! At your age?

Hilary   Thank you.

Pippa   Oh, well, no accounting for taste, is there, Troy? (*Pause.*) I'm thinking of coming back at the end of the year.

Hilary   Really?

Pippa   Mmm. My contract finishes in December. I mean I could renew it, but . . . I dunno.

Hilary   What about Martin?

Pippa *shrugs.*

Hilary   Oh, Pip. I thought it was serious between you two.

Pippa   Yeah . . . so did I. But it doesn't seem like anyone wants to take me *that* seriously.

Hilary   What do you mean?

Pippa   Well, I'm kind of . . . entertainment value, but not a serious contender. (*Pause.*) He wants a nice Jewish girl.

Hilary   I thought he'd come to terms with that.

Pippa   Yeah. He has. He found a nice Jewish girl.

Hilary   Oh, no, Pip.

Pippa *shrugs.*

Pippa   If it wasn't that, it'd be something else. (*Pause.*) It always is. (*Pause.*) Did I tell you about going to visit his parents?

Hilary   No.

Pippa   I was so nervous I dropped a lump of mozzarella cheese into the fish tank.

Hilary   Oh, no.

Wal *enters.*

Pippa   Yeah. And I'm not just talking about a little lump of cheese. This thing was huge. When it went in, the water went out in a big way . . . along with about fifty tropical fish. They kind of dived onto the carpet. All I can remember is turning around and seeing Martin's mum standing on a chair screeching, 'Get the cat out.'

Hilary   Oh, I am sorry, Pippa . . .

Pippa   Yeah, things seemed to take a turn for the worse after that.

Silence.

Wal   You're a silly bugger.

Scene Seven

Meg *is sitting on the lounge-room floor reading aloud excerpts from a letter from* **Hilary**.

Meg   Listen to this bit . . .

Edwin   This is still from Hilary?

Meg   Yeah . . . (*She reads aloud.*) 'I'm doing an English course with the Council of Adult Education. We are studying Chaucer at the moment. It's very interesting.' See what I mean? Chaucer is not interesting. Chaucer is very, very dull.

Edwin   So, she finds it interesting.

Meg   She does not. She just thinks she *should* find it interesting, because that's what being 'cultured' is all about.

Edwin   Being conversant with things that are irrelevant and dull.

Meg   Exactly. That's what the whole middle class is like back home. They go off and memorise Shakespeare's date of birth and a few rhyming couplets so they can sprinkle it in conversation around the barbie. 'D'you think Kylie'll bring the coleslaw.' 'Ah, To bring or not to bring. That is the question. Shakespeare, you know. Born in 1564, strangely enough.' 'Yes. Died in 1616. Poor thing. Such a tragedy. Terrific bean salad, Val.'

Edwin Ooh, you're such a snob.

Meg No, I'm not. I don't care two hoots about Shakespeare, you know that. In fact I've often thought that my idea of purgatory would be an everlasting subscription to the Royal Shakespeare Company.

Edwin I'll never forget the look on Peter Hall's face, the night you told him that you thought *Othello* was dreadfully overwritten.

Meg Ah, you see, that's one thing I really regret about ageing. I resent having to mellow. I'd never say that sort of thing now.

Edwin Well, that's just as well I should think. I can just see *The Times Literary Supplement*. 'Booker-Prize nominee Meg Moynihan says that Shakespeare's plays are dreadfully overwritten.'

Meg But that's what it's like at home. For all that obsessive nationalism, people still equate 'culture' with Shakespeare and Chaucer. (*Pause. She sighs.*) I just wish she'd say something about my book. (*She wrinkles her nose.*) It's silly isn't it, 'cause on one level I don't give a damn what she thinks of it – as a piece of 'literature'. I just want a reaction. Anything. 'Dear Meg, I found your book excruciatingly turgid.'

Edwin Maybe she hasn't read it yet. Too busy swotting up on Chaucer.

Pause.

Meg If you'd written a book, you'd expect your family to read it wouldn't you?

Edwin Oh, not necessarily. I suspect the last book that Gareth ever read was probably *Biggles*. Might be expecting too much.

Pause.

Meg I bet she has read it. She's just not saying anything.

Pause. **Edwin** *looks at her appraisingly. She looks away. Pause.*

Meg   She says . . . 'You'll be pleased to hear that Dad is much better. I think the fact that Pippa is arriving has cheered him enormously.' (*She sighs.*) Why does she always do this?

Edwin   What?

Meg   Oh, make me feel so damn guilty about everything.

Scene Eight

Hilary *and* **Pippa** *are walking arm in arm along the jetty. They stop and lean on the railing looking out across the bay, oblivious to the couple at the end of the jetty.*

Pippa   D'you remember the time I drank Mum's liquid foundation?

Hilary   That was Oil of Ulay wasn't it?

Pippa   No. It was brown. I think I must have thought it was chocolate milk.

Hilary   Poor ol' Mum. She'd probably saved up for months to buy that stuff. And then her daughter drinks it.

Pippa   God. I must have been seriously defective. Why did you take the blame for it?

Hilary   I didn't. Meg did.

Pippa   Meg? I thought it was you. You told Mum you spilt it in the basin.

Hilary   No. Meg took the blame.

Pippa   Really? (*Pause.*) Why would she have done that?

Hilary   I don't know.

Pippa   God! She's weird that woman. (**Hilary** *laughs.*) Well she is. That's just another example of it. It shits me.

Hilary   You should write to her and tell her. 'Dear Meg,

I feel compelled to tell you that I'm still deeply angry about
the Liquid foundation incident in 1961.'

Pippa   You don't understand.

Pause.

Hilary   I do.

They muse privately.

Pippa   It's odd isn't it, all these bits and pieces turning up
in Meg's book. I felt . . . cheated or something. (*Pause.*) It
makes me feel that my childhood, well, our childhood has
been . . . sort of . . . raided. Not that anyone's going to say,
'Oh, that's Pippa' or, 'that's Hilary' or whatever, but it
kind of does something to your own memories. Not that
there's anything deep and meaingful in there . . . about us
. . . It's just the little things. It's almost as if they're not
ours any more.

Pause.

Hilary   I don't care about the little things.

Scene Nine

Marge *and* **Dick** *are relaxing in easy chairs in the garden of*
Marge*'s holiday shack in Sorrento.*

Marge   When you were growing up . . . ?

Dick   Mm?

Marge   Did you think that you were ordinary or did you
think that you were special?

Dick *frowns and shrugs.*

Dick   I don't know. What? You mean did I think I was
going to be . . . one of the great minds of my generation?

Marge *smiles.*

Dick   For a while there, I thought I might be a famous

detective; I remember that. Then when I was about fifteen
I modified it a bit and thought I might run a crime
bookshop. There was this bloke who ran one of those
bookshops in the city and I used to go down there with my
dad every so often. I used to think there was something
really good about that bloke. He was a complete slob. He
was about fifty and he was open all weekend. He was
totally into it. He had none of the trappings of the
suburban shit that my family went on with. He used to
chain-smoke Gauloises and then he'd stub 'em out in the
left-overs of his Chinese take-away.

Marge   Oh, yuck.

Dick   I used to think there was something really . . .
magnificent about that! It was a statement really.

Marge   Oh, Dick!

Dick   It was! It was a statement about anarchy. And I
remember reading it as such.

Marge   Anarchy?

Dick   I thought my mother, my sisters, they'd never
understand this. My mother would not be able to hold
herself back. She would have to get a plastic bag and put
the whole contents of his desk (his life work I might add) in
the rubbish. She would have to impose her suburban
mentality. She would have to stamp on this . . . this . . .
simple gesture of . . .

Marge   It didn't occur to you that the simple gesture of
stubbing out the cigarette in the empty contents of his take-
away . . .

Dick   It wasn't empty. It had stuff in it.

Marge   Right. Sorry. The simple gesture of stubbing the
cigarette into a container of cold, congealed, sweet and sour
pork . . .

Dick   It was noodles actually.

Marge   Noodles, OK . . . could also have been read as

the act of a pathetic human being who had no grasp of the simple concept of personal hygiene, because ... wait ... he expected his mother or some other female figure to clean up after him. That never occurred to you?

Dick No.

Marge Well, there you are, you see. Therein lies the great tension between feminism and the Left. (**Dick** *laughs*.) I would have read it very differently of course.

Dick You would have read it like my mother, who believes there is great virtue in a clean sink.

Marge I agree with her.

Dick I know you do. It's just that you've developed your personal philosophies a little more over the years, I think.

Marge Thank you, dear. Mind you to what end I'm not so sure. Is she happy your mother?

Dick Don't be silly. Why waste time being happy when you could be cleaning the venetians.

Marge You must be a great disappointment to her. That's all I can say.

Dick That I am. It's a small achievement, I know. But I've spent years working on it.

Marge *shakes her head. They muse.*

Marge You know when I asked you before about whether you thought you were special? Listen, (*She reads aloud from a section of the book. Lights come up on* **Hilary**, *working at her desk in her own space.*) 'There was something very ordinary about Helen. Ordinary and sensible. She had an ordinary face. People would stop her in the street. "Don't I know you from somewhere?" It used to happen a lot. She'd shimmer with pleasure, shrugging it off for our benefit of course, but inside she held on to that hard little nugget of hope that there was something distinctive about her. Something that would single her out in a crowd. A permissible vanity. After all what good would it do to know that you were indistinguishable from a thousand others. But then again, it is a country which honours ordinariness above all else. She might have taken heart that she'd always be cherished for it.'

Dick (*nodding*)   Yeah?

Marge   That really touches me. I keep going back to it. (*Pause.*) Do you think this is a country that honours ordinariness?

Dick   No. It might have been like that in the fifties, but not any more. See that's what irritates me about that bloody book. There are hundreds of 'em. Every Tom, Dick and Harry's writing one. Growing up in the fifties. My childhood in Toowoomba, my tortured adolescence in Kalgoorlie, or Woy Woy or some other bloody place. And you know what it is? It is essentially culturally reactionary stuff. I mean sure, the fifties was a time when it was impossible to be ... different ... if you like. Anyone with any nouse packed up and cleared out. But it's not like that now. And to keep harking back to it ... it's just very safe territory. It's not going to shake anyone up.

Marge   It's shaken me up. (*Pause.*) Maybe you don't read between the lines. There's nothing safe about this ...

Dick   I despise nostalgia.

Marge *scoffs.*

Marge   It's not nostalgia.

Dick   Where are the people who are writing about the big picture. Hmm? Who's tackling the big issues? Who's trying to come to grips with some sort of contemporary vision about this place? Can you think of anyone?

Marge   Yes, I can think of lots. But ... Meg Moynihan comes to mind. Off the top of my head. (*She smiles.*)

Dick   Oh, Jesus!

Marge   You're looking for the big, broad brush stroke. Aren't you? I know you are. But Australia can't be

contained in the sort of broad sweep that you're asking for.
Great big visions make very empty pictures if you don't
attend to the details.

Scene Ten

Troy *comes into the kitchen switching on the overhead light. He
pours himself a glass of milk.*

Troy   You still at it, Mum?

He downs the glass of milk and pours another one.

Hilary   Books won't balance themselves.

Troy   You know, I've been thinking . . .

Hilary   Good God.

Troy   Mum!

Hilary   Come on, what were you thinking? I have an
inkling that it involves money.

Troy   Yeah.

Hilary   Yeah. You know how I know. I have this
involuntary sensation of my stomach kind of turning over.

Troy   Really?

Hilary   Mmm hmm.

Troy   Well you know how I know that you know?

Hilary   How?

Troy   Your lips go really thin and mean and they
disappear inside your mouth.

Hilary   They do not.

Troy   They do. They make a little round hole like a
chook's bum.

Hilary   That's nice. Thank you for that.

Troy   Wanna hear my idea?

Hilary   No.

Troy   I'll tell you anyway. OK. If we had a *lot* of money
. . . quite a lot of money.

Hilary   Mm.

Troy   So as we could be . . . not rich . . . but . . . fairly
rich.

Hilary   Come on, come on. Let's be filthy rich.

Troy   Right. We could buy a flat. In St Kilda.

Hilary (*laughing*)   I thought you hated Melbourne.

Troy   Yeah. But St Kilda's something else. (*Pause.*) Brett
Williams's dad's got a flat in St Kilda and it's really good.

Hilary   Has he just.

Troy   He goes every second weekend. They go to the
footy and the movies and have their tea in restaurants.
Stuff like that.

Hilary   His parents separated, are they?

Troy   Yeah. They hate each other's guts.

Hilary   Oh, charming.

Troy   I reckon you should . . . you know, get together
with Brett's dad.

Hilary   Oh, yeah. Sure, Troy. (*Pause.*) What's he got to
offer? Apart from the flat in St Kilda of course.

Troy (*shrugging*)   He plays a pretty mean game of golf.

Hilary   Wow, quick, get me his number.

Troy   What have you got against golf?

Hilary   I don't have anything against golf. I am just
repulsed by people who play it.

Troy   Mum.

Hilary   I bet he wears SLACKS . . . !?

Troy   Get out.

Hilary   You know when somebody runs their finger down a blackboard. That's the feeling that white slacks give me.

Troy   You've never even met the guy.

Hilary   I know. He's probably got a very nice personality.

Troy   Not really. He's a dickhead.

They laugh. **Hilary** *looks at her son, her eyes shining with affection.*

Hilary   What would I do without you. Hey?

Pause.

Troy   I'm sort of glad you're not divorced Mum, (*Pause.*) Sometimes I think it's better . . . this way.

Hilary *says nothing. She does not look up. There is a long pause.*

Troy   Brett's got this . . . stutter. Not all the time. He had to go to this shrink in Melbourne. He reckons it's because his oldies got divorced. D'you reckon that's true?

Hilary *shrugs. Pause.*

Hilary   Oh . . . kids bounce. That's what they say, isn't it?

Troy   What d'you mean?

Hilary   They cope. Sometimes I think they cope better than adults. Look at you. You've coped. But maybe it's different for you because your father's dead. Sometimes I wonder whether a death isn't easier to deal with. Because it's final. And because it's nobody's fault. I don't know, Troy. (*Pause. Her tone lightens.*) If things'd been different and your oldies had got divorced, never know what might have happened to you. Might have been a dribbler. That'd be nasty.

Troy *does not respond to the joke. There is an awkward pause.*

Hilary *lights a cigarette.*

Hilary   It was only a joke.

Troy   Yeah. Well it wasn't very funny.

Hilary   Sorry.

Troy   How come you can't be serious.

Hilary   About what?

Pause.

Troy   Have you read Aunt Meg's book?

Hilary (*snapping*)   What made you think of that?

Troy   I dunno.

Hilary   I mean how come you said that, Troy? Just out of the blue, like that?

Troy   I don't know. (*Pause.*) Have you read it?

Hilary   Yes. I've read it.

Troy   Do you mind if I read it?

Hilary   No. Why should I mind? (*Pause.*) I didn't think you'd be interested.

Silence.

Troy   'Course I'm interested.

Hilary   Well read it then. (**Hilary** *gathers up her book work.*) I'm going to bed. Good night.

She kisses him lightly on the forehead. **Troy** *stands alone in the kitchen, looking disgruntled.*

Scene Eleven

Exterior, London flat. **Meg** *storms up the stairs to their flat,* **Edwin** *in tow.*

Meg   'Ors-tralians are just like their country. Big and empty.' Ha! Ha! That is the last time, Edwin. He is a pompous old bore and I'm not going to put up with it.

Edwin   He was only trying to get a rise out of you.

Meg   Well he succeeded.

Edwin   Oh, come on, Meg. He's seventy-one.

Meg   Since when was age ever an excuse for anything.
Anyway, it's not only your father. What about Gareth?
He's as bad as that other little prick you work with. 'We
used to dread arriving at parties too early. Imagine being
the only one there in a room full of Or-stralians.'

Edwin   Well, Gareth's a prick. That's well documented
... but Dad doesn't mean any harm.

Meg *is rooting around in her handbag for the keys to the flat.*

Meg   He's so fucking patronising towards me.

Edwin   Look, I've told you. Dad's like that with everyone.
Either tell him you find all this Australian rubbish he goes
on with ... offensive. Or else quit being so sensitive. It's
getting tedious.

Meg *has tipped her handbag onto the step in search of her keys.*

Meg   Oh, tedious, is it? Well, you try being an outsider in
this dump of a country and see how you like it.

Edwin   You're hardly an outsider, Meg, for Godsake.

Meg *raises her voice.*

Meg   How would you know what it's like?

Edwin   Ssh ...

Meg   You've never set foot off home turf for more than
two weeks except for some cruddy little package holiday in
Spain.

Edwin   Sssh.

Meg   No, I will not sshhh. You have no understanding of
what this is like. The minute I open my mouth I'm an
outsider. There's more prejudice in this shithouse place ...

Edwin   Give me the keys.

Meg   No I will not!

She flings them on the ground.

Edwin   For Chrissake, Meg. You've almost been given the most prestigious bloody honour that this country could bestow on anyone and you're behaving like they've taken your sodding pension cheque away. Outsider? What rubbish! If you'd stayed in Australia you'd be a fucking school teacher.

Edwin *picks up the keys and proceeds to unlock the door.*

Meg   Bullshit!

Edwin   You've said as much yourself, Meg!

Meg   That's crap.

Edwin *pushes the door open.*

Edwin   Well go home then.

He slams the door behind him. **Meg** *sits down on the step outside. She looks up suddenly as someone is watching her from the window of the flat opposite.*

Meg (*yelling*)   What are you looking at? Why don't you go and feed your fucking gas meters?

Scene Twelve

Troy *and* **Pippa** *are fishing together on the jetty where* **Marge** *and* **Dick** *were sitting earlier.*

Troy   Pippa?

Pippa   Mm?

Troy   Have you read Aunt Meg's book?

Pippa   Yeah.

Troy   What d'you think?

Pippa Have you read it?

Troy No.

Pause. **Pippa** *looks uncomfortable.*

Pippa Well it's good. Very well written. (*Pause.*) I mean that's what everyone is saying. The critics and everyone.

Troy Yeah. I mean did you like it?

Pippa Mmm. (*She takes a deep breath. Pause.*)

Troy I read this letter that Meg sent to Mum. (*He steals a glance at* **Pippa**. *She gives him a disapproving look.*) Yeah, I know. Anyway she said that people might think that the 'Helen' character was . . . Mum. But that she shouldn't worry because it wasn't supposed to be . . . or something like that.

Pippa What else did she say? Did she say anything about the Grace character?

Troy *shrugs.*

Troy Does it make Mum out to be . . . an idiot or something?

Pippa No. Nothing like that.

Troy Well, what is it then? How come everyone just goes silent. (*Pause.*) Is it about my dad?

Long pause.

Pippa Why don't you read it. You read it . . . and make up your own mind? It's sort of about all of us. In a way . . .

Troy Make up my mind about what, Pippa? I didn't even know him.

Pause.

Pippa Yeah.

Pippa *nods sympathetically, however, we sense that she is feeling deeply uncomfortable.*

Troy You know ... the guys at school reckon I'm really lucky. 'Cos they reckon you can talk to my mum about anything. All the guys I know reckon she's really ace.

Pippa She is.

Troy Yeah. But you can't talk to her about everything. Not everything. I can't anyway. I don't even know how it happened, Pippa. I know he had a car accident. But there's more to it than that, isn't there?

Pippa *stares resolutely out to sea. The question lies hanging.*

Scene Thirteen

Interior of the London flat. **Edwin** *is pouring himself a Scotch, when* **Meg** *comes into the room.*

Meg What do you mean by that – go home! What's that supposed to mean?

Edwin Exactly that. Book yourself a flight and go home for a while.

Meg Oh, sure. Forget about the Booker. Just go and have a holiday.

Edwin Yes.

Meg *scoffs incredulously.*

Meg You can't be serious. I've got to be in London till the twenty-sixth of October. I've got publicity appearances lined up ...

Edwin Cancel them! It's turning you into a screaming ratbag.

Meg Oh, thank you, Edwin.

Edwin You've said as much yourself! And you've been talking obsessively about Australia and your family for weeks now. Just go for a month. And then come back.

Meg Thanks a lot for your support! (**Meg** *picks up the paper.*)

Edwin   Oh, don't.

Meg   Why not?

Edwin   It's that interview you did, and you're hardly in the right frame of mind to read it at the moment.

Wal *calls to* **Pippa** *and* **Troy** *at the end of the jetty.*

Wal   Pippy! Troy! Come up and get your tea.

Scene Fourteen

Marge *skips up the steps of her holiday house, carrying a string bag full of shopping. She is obviously pleased with herself.* **Dick** *is perusing the papers on the verandah.*

Marge   Dick? Oh, Dick, guess what? I was right. I knew I was. I knew from the moment I read that first chapter. It's Sorrento all right! I've just been speaking to the people who run the paddle boats down on the beach during the summer. They've been here for years. I knew they'd know. And sure enough, the Moynihan family has been in Sorrento for as long as they can remember. Apparently they used to run a garage on the Back Beach road and a little café next door. The Neptune Café. So I walked back that way on my way home and blow me down, there it is. It's not used as a garage any more but you can still see the sign 'Moynihan Motors'. They have mini golf or something in there now. Isn't that incredible. I'm so thrilled. I can't tell you.

Dick   Are they still here?

Marge   The old man apparently and one daughter. She runs the deli in the main street.

Dick   Oh, yeah.

Marge   But Meg, the writer, she lives in London, of course.

Dick   Yes. I know. She did an interview with the *Guardian* recently.

Marge   Oh.

Dick *takes out a sheet of paper from his briefcase. He hands it to her.*

Dick   Special delivery for you. Hot off the fax from work.

Marge   Oh, thanks.

Dick   Mm. I'll be interested to hear what you think, but as far as I'm concerned she sounds like a pain in the arse.

Scene Fifteen

The London flat. **Meg** *is in a state of agitation. She is waving the* Guardian *having just read a feature article about herself.*

Meg   I sound like such a pain in the arse.

Edwin   Don't let it get to you, Meg.

Meg   I tell you, that is the last time. I am never going to do another interview. Never!

Edwin   The guy's a prat. The whole article's completely disjointed.

Meg   I'm not cut out for this. I can't stand it. All this hype and carry-on. I hate it and I can't handle it any more.

She starts to cry.

Edwin   Oh, sweetheart. Sweet heart.

Meg   My family sound like morons. What would they think if they read this at home? They'd be so angry and hurt.

Edwin   Hey, come on. That's the one thing you don't have to worry about. Who's going to read the *Guardian* in Sorrento? Hmm? They probably don't even have it on the news-stands.

-Long pause.

Meg   They don't even have a news-stand.

Scene Sixteen

On the verandah at **Marge***'s place. They sit drinking coffee.*
Marge *has the* Guardian *article in her lap.*

Dick   These bloody smart-arse expatriates. I mean what is
it that makes them think that living elsewhere automatically
qualifies them to make sweeping generalisations about this
place. A culture isn't static for Godsake. Things change.
The woman hasn't lived here for ten years. Look what's
happened in that time.

Marge   Yes, it is a bit disappointing, I have to admit.

Dick   Disappointing. Jesus! The woman's an idiot.

Marge   No, she's not. She's not an idiot.

Dick *scoffs.*

Dick   I might seem like an idiot, talk like an idiot. But
don't be deceived. I *am* an idiot!

Marge   Well, I think some of the things she says are
quite true. I love this bit,
'If you ask the average Brit what he knows about Australia,
he'll probably say Foster's and vomit. The trouble is that
your average Aussie bloke on the loose in London,
regardless of whether he's backpacking or wheeling and
dealing, does nothing to dispel that image. When I meet
Australians over here I take some comfort in the fact that it
is only a minor outbreak. At home we're talking epidemic!'

Dick   Oh, very funny. What about this statement – 'this is
a country that's rife with xenophobia and anti-
intellectualism'? Like that bit too, did you?

Marge   No. But the media force them to give an opinion.

Dick   No. No. Look, if she has any intelligence, any common sense, she makes it abundantly clear to her interviewer that her perceptions about a place (that she hasn't lived in for ten years), are obviously going to be outdated. And all that stuff about the father.

Marge   But she's right! There's a whole generation of old boys like that.

Dick   Yeah, there is. But they do not represent 'the spirit of Australian life' or whatever she said. Not any more. That's the whole point. The woman's out of touch. (*Pause.*) OK if I ring Kelly at the office?

Marge   Why?

Dick   I think I'll get her to track down this Moynihan woman in London. I've got an idea for a piece on Australia's image problem abroad. This could fit in very nicely.

Scene Seventeen

The kitchen. **Troy** *is doing homework on the kitchen table.* **Pippa** *is perusing a newspaper.* **Hilary** *is ironing.* **Wal** *comes in searching for his lost glasses.*

Wal   Can't find those bloody glasses anywhere. Aw . . . What's the use of the damn things. Can't see to find 'em and when I got 'em I can't read a bloody thing anyway.

Hilary   Dad! You'll have to go and get yourself another prescription. This is stupid.

Wal   Yeah, yeah, yeah . . .

Troy   You'll have to get those real thick milk bottles.

Wal (*chuckling*)   I knew a bloke once, used to drink with 'im down the Koonya. His missus used to call him MILK BOTTLE. She reckons he was always full on the front porch in the morning. (**Pippa** *and* **Troy** *laugh.* **Hilary** *rolls her eyes good-humouredly.*)

Hilary   That's as old as the hills.

Wal   Still funny. Gotta admit! Troy! Come here for a sec will ya? Out here.

He goes out onto the verandah. **Troy** *follows him out.* **Pippa** *shakes her head.*

Pippa   You know, sometimes I have to pinch myself. Just every now and again ... I see you and I think ... It's Mum standing there.

Hilary   Yeah, ordinary and sensible. Thanks. Thanks a lot.

Pippa   Oh ... don't be offended. It's nice. It's kind of comforting.

Hilary *makes a face.* **Wal** *and* **Troy** *stand out on the balcony.*

Wal   Listen, I been thinkin'. How 'bout you and me have a go at that book o' Meg's.

Troy   How d'you mean?

Wal   Well ... I thought you could read it out to me ... you know ... just a few chapters at a time. I'm blowed if I can read m'self these days, 'less it's in bloody great big print. What d'ya reckon? Would you do that for us?

Troy *mulls this thoughtfully.*

Troy   Yeah. OK, OK.

Wal   Good on yer. Hey, Troy ... (*He winks.*) Just between the two of us, eh? She'll harp at me about goin' up to that eye bloke in Frankston. (**Troy** *looks reproving.*) Aw ... Can't stand the little bastard. (**Wal** *leaves.*) Milk bottle. Hah! Still funny!

Pippa   Hilary?

Hilary   Mmm?

Pippa   Troy asked me a few things the other day . . . about Meg's book. (*Pause.*) He asked me if it was about . . . his father.

Hilary *becomes terse.*

Hilary   What gave him that idea?

Pippa   I dunno.

Hilary   What did you say?

Pause.

Pippa   I told him it was sort of about all of us.

Hilary   Why did you say that? Why did you say that, Pippa?

Pippa   Because he asked me straight out and I wasn't going to lie to him.

Troy *stands in the doorway.*

Hilary   Lie? Oh, God, Pippa. What is the poor kid . . . Oh, Jesus. You told a sixteen-year-old boy that some character in a book is his father. His father who he can't even remember. He was only six years old. What gave you the right to say that?

Pippa   He needs to talk about it, Hilary.

Hilary   Oh, I'm sure he does. I'm sure he needs to talk about it now that you've thrown that into the works.

Pippa   Hil . . .

Hilary   What is there to talk about, hmm? Didn't anyone ever tell you about fiction? You know, make-believe . . . Did you get confused somewhere . . . because it was written by your own sister? Or are you angry about something because you may have seen a bit of yourself in it that you don't particularly like. Because if that's the case, I'm sorry. But don't put that on me. And don't put it on my son.

Wal (*off*)   Who left their bicycle leaning against the bloody garage door?

Troy Coming, Pop.

Scene Eighteen

The London flat.

Meg You know, I keep wondering what Dad would make of all of this business – the London press having a field day with the book and me being grilled about my upbringing, my family life and everything. I reckon he'd say 'Meggy, there are two things you oughta know about the Poms. The first is that they're not real keen on gettin' wet and second, they're whingeing bastards. So all this hoo-hah about your book. I wouldn't take a jot o' notice. Just sour grapes.'

Edwin A genuine Antipodean Socrates, your dad.

Meg (*smiling*) It's all so simple. His whole way of looking at things . . .

Edwin Mmm. Xenophobia and prejudice usually are.

Meg Oh, don't be such a stuffed shirt. You'd like him. If you met him. Everybody does.

Edwin Mm.

Pause.

Meg I wish you could meet him.

Edwin Mmm. (*He begins to peruse the paper. He becomes aware of* **Meg** *looking at him.*) I will. I'll get to meet him. (**Meg** *begins to look sullen.*) Don't start. Please. (*Long pause.*) I must say I'm not so keen on this last bit. 'Moynihan cannot foresee that she would ever return to Australia to live. "I am married to an Englishman," she says, "who is terrified of flying, could not swim to save his life, and has a morbid fear of mosquitoes and sunburn."' Is that what you said?

Meg Mm hmm. It's the only thing he got right.

Scene Nineteen

Marge *is painting at her easel in the garden. She has a still life set up on a table, some fruit and a glass vase, etc.* **Dick** *comes out.*

Dick   There goes that bright idea. Our Ms Moynihan is not available for comment apparently. Shit. Shit. Shit.

Marge   She's a novelist remember, not a political commentator.

Dick   Well then, she should stick to discussing literature.

Marge   Why are you so defensive, Dick? I think that's the more interesting question myself.

Dick   Defensive! It's not a personal issue, Marge.

Marge   Isn't it?

Dick   What are you getting at?

Marge   I'm wondering why you're so resentful?

Dick   All right. OK, I am 'resentful' if that's the word you want to use, that this kind of shit (*he waves the newspaper clipping in front of her*) is perpetuating – on a global scale – the impression that we are still a colonial outpost. That is the source of my resentment.

Marge   I understand that. I think, maybe, there might be something else in there, that's all.

Dick   Like what? (*Pause.*) Marge?

Marge   Well, it seems to me that your own work doesn't get the attention that you'd like it to. That it deserves.

Dick   So your little theory is that I'm envious. Is that it? Because I haven't 'made it' like Ms Moynihan?

Marge   No.

Dick   Good. I'm glad of that, because I'm well enough read in social theory to understand that anyone who adopts a radical position is not going to have currency in the mainstream. I think I've come to terms with that. I don't think my essays are going to be published in extract form in *The Women's Weekly*, if that's what you're suggesting. I have accepted this.

Marge   Yes, I'm aware of that, Dick.

Dick   Good. And be aware of another thing that makes me feel 'resentful'. People like her – they piss off as soon as they can, their ignorance about their own country is breathtaking and they have no qualms whatsoever about dumping on it and yet . . . in her case, the fact that she grew up in this country is at the very heart of that novel. It's the life source. Now doesn't that strike you as hypocrisy?

Marge   I hear what you're saying.

Dick   Don't 'hear what I'm saying'. I can't stand that shit.

Marge   OK, I don't hear what you're saying. Why should I? Stupid me! It's not as if you ever bother to actually *hear* what I'm saying or anyone else for that matter.

Dick   Oh, for God's sake, Marge. It's just the language – that crappy psychological jargon. I can't stand it.

Marge   Funny about that. I'm getting pretty sick of your crappy sociological jargon. But in this instance – it's not just the language I can't stand. It's the fact that you don't have any *other* language. (*He picks up an apple distractedly from* **Marge***'s 'arrangement' and bites into it.*)

Marge   Dick!!!!

Scene Twenty

London flat. It is late at night. **Meg** *is getting ready for bed.* **Edwin** *comes in sleepily in his pyjamas. He collapses into an armchair.*

Edwin   I'm exhausted.

Meg   Me too.

Edwin   It's such a terrible drag having to visit one's parents isn't it? I quite like Brighton otherwise. I mean I like the seaside.

Meg   Seaside. You're so quaint sometimes. Still, you could hardly call it the beach could you?

Edwin   We have been known to use poetic licence on occasions.

Meg *laughs. She looks over at* **Edwin** *with affection.*

Meg   I love you.

Edwin   Nah, it's just lust. It's these pyjamas. They have that effect on women.

Meg *laughs.*

Meg   You know, after today I was thinking . . .

Edwin   I know. You're never going to come to a family dinner in Brighton again. I don't blame you. I wish I could decide that.

Meg   Oh, come on. You love those dinners. Everyone yelling at each other. You're in your element.

Edwin   Yes, I suppose I do quite like that part.

Meg   Of course you do. You've got the loudest voice. I was looking at you all this afternoon. It's like being at an exhibition of oil paintings. All hanging on separate walls, screaming at one another. But when I'm there, I always feel like this pale little watercolour hanging behind a cupboard.

Edwin *roars laughing.*

Meg   I do. I think it must be your father. He has this effect on me. (*Long pause.*) He's so hell bent on being certain about everything isn't he? I suppose most men are. It's probably the one true emblem of masculinity. The central ideal to which every man aspires: to be certain about his ideas, his actions and his place in the world.

Edwin What's wrong with that?

Meg What's wrong with it is if you're preoccupied with a need to be certain, you don't allow yourself to see the contradictions in things. And when you don't see contradictions, your perceptions are totally blunted. I'm not the least bit interested in being certain about anything.

Edwin So I've noticed.

Meg Ah! Listen, your family always have to take up a position. If you proffer the slightest whisper of an idea it gets pounced upon and moulded into something unbelievably weighty. And before you know it, you find yourself desperately committed to something and you spend the rest of the night under siege.

Edwin You're just apolitical and making excuses for it.

Meg No I'm not. I'm just trying to understand why I feel so odd every time I go to Brighton.

Edwin The pale little watercolour. I must say I've never thought of you as that.

Meg *smiles.*

Meg I miss it, you know. Being part of a family.

Edwin Look, believe me. They think you're the best thing since sliced bread. As far as they're concerned, you're absolutely one of the family.

Meg I mean my own family.

Edwin Oh, well . . . that's different isn't it?

Pause.

Meg I was thinking that I might go home. Just for a bit. It's what I need. I realised after today . . . I actually need to go home.

Edwin I know.

Meg But I can't go without you, Edwin.

Edwin   Oh.

Meg   Is that pathetic?

Edwin   Really pathetic.

Meg   Please come with me. Just this one time. Please?

Scene Twenty-One

Hilary *and* **Pippa** *come home late at night.* **Hilary** *comes into the sitting room to discover* **Wal** *asleep on a chair.* **Troy** *has crashed out on a cushion on the floor.* **Troy** *has a copy of* **Meg**'s *book open at his chest. They are positioned in such a way that we may assume* **Troy** *has been reading to his grandfather.*

Hilary   Oh, my God. Look at this.

Wal   Ah . . . must have nodded off.

Troy *sleeps on soundly.* **Pippa** *comes in.*

Hilary   What's he doing here?

Wal *grins.*

Wal   Sleepin' by the looks of things.

Hilary   Oh, Dad . . .

Wal *leans down and surreptitiously slips the book under his seat.*

Wal   Well . . . d'you paint the town red.

Pippa   Yeah, sure, Dad. This place's really jumping.

He chuckles.

Wal   What time are you off tomorrow?

Hilary   I'm driving her up to the train at half past one.

Wal   Ah hah. What are you doin' up there any rate?

Pippa *sits down on the arm of his chair. She strokes his hair lovingly.*

Pippa   Do you know that's the first time you've asked me anything at all about what I'm doing here. Do you realise that you haven't asked me one thing about my work since I've been here?

Wal Yeah, orright. Well I'm askin' you now aren't I?

Hilary Come on, let's get to bed. It's late. I've got to go to work in the morning.

Wal Hang about. Got something to tell you. Come on, Pippy.

Hilary *leans against the chair.*

Pippa Well . . . I've landed this big account . . .

Wal Yeah.

Pippa The agency I work for in New York's got this client and they want to start marketing their product in Australia. So they've sent me over here to liaise with their Australian office, so that we can come up with a concept.

Wal What's the product?

Pippa *grins.*

Pippa Margarine.

Wal *roars with laughter.* **Troy** *wakes.*

Wal Trust the bloody Septics, eh? Floggin' Yank margarine to the Aussies. An' I s'ppose you've got to come up with something that cons us poor suckers into thinkin' this is the real McCoy. Dinky di Aussie margarine we're buying here.

Pippa Yep. Got it in one.

Wal Aw . . . make your socks rot wouldn't it?

Hilary Come on Troyby. Bed.

Troy (*sleepily*) Did he tell you about Meg?

Hilary No.

They turn to **Wal** *who is grinning smugly.*

Wal   You better sit down for this.

Hilary *sighs, looks at her watch and plonks herself on the arm of the couch.*

Hilary   Come on. Spit it out.

Wal *and* **Troy** *exchange looks. Being the purveyors of exciting news they want to spin it out.* **Wal** *indicates for* **Troy** *to tell.*

Troy   She's arriving next week.

Pippa   What? Here?

Troy   Yep.

The two women greet this news in astonished silence.

Pippa   Jesus. (*Pause.*) How come?

Wal   Well, she's missin' out, isn't she? Us all bein' here. And she knows it. Not a real family. Without everyone.

Wal*'s eyes begin to smart with the sentiment.*

Hilary   Oh, Dad.

Hilary *goes over and hugs him.*

Wal   Not before time eh? (*To* **Pippa**.) And you took your time too.

Pause.

Pippa   Is Edwin coming?

Wal   Yeah. She's finally convinced him. That's what's been holdin' her back, you know.

Hilary *laughs.*

Hilary   Oh, Dad!

Wal   True. Silly whacker.

Troy   You don't even know him.

Wal   Hmm. I know enough.

Troy   Rubbish. It's just that he's a Pom. Isn't it?

Wal Got nothin' to do with it.

Troy That's bullshit, Pop.

Hilary *notices* **Pippa** *leaving the room.*

Hilary Pippa?

Troy Pippa?

Troy *gets up to follow her.* **Hilary** *holds up her hand.*

Hilary Hang on, Troy.

Wal What's goin' on? I thought she'd be as pleased as punch.

Hilary *shrugs.*

Hilary I'm going to bed.

Silence. **Wal** *sighs.*

Wal Let's hit the sack eh? Come on. (**Troy** *says nothing.*) Thought we might take off down the back beach in the morning. Get in a swim before breakfast. What d'ya reckon? Bring your board? (**Troy** *nods, distractedly.*)

Troy OK.

Scene Twenty-Two

Marge *and* **Dick** *sit at a table of a small coffee shop/gourmet food deli. This is* **Hilary**'s *shop. She comes out to take their order.*

Hilary Hello. How are you?

Marge Good thanks.

Hilary (*to* **Dick**) Hi. What can I get you?

Dick Hi. Just two cappuccinos please.

Hilary Okey-doke.

Hilary *goes behind the counter.*

Marge Er . . . excuse me, I hope you don't think this is presumptuous, but er ... I was wondering ... whether you were Hilary Moynihan.

Hilary   Yes, I am. Well I was.

Marge   Related to Meg Moynihan?

Hilary *laughs.*

Hilary   Yep. She's my sister.

Marge   Uh. Well, I just wanted to say ... er ... I am sorry, my name's Marge Morrissey ... I have a holiday house down on the Back Beach road. And this is a friend of mine, Dick Bennett.

Hilary   Hi.

Marge   I'd just like to say that ... I loved your sister's book. I think ... it's one of the most beautiful books I've ever read. And I ... just wanted to tell you. That's all.

Hilary *smiles warmly at* **Marge**.

Hilary   Thank you. Well, thank you on her behalf. She'd be very touched by that. I'll tell her.

Marge   Would you?

Hilary   Sure. She'll be here next week as a matter of fact.

Marge   Oh.

Dick   Sorrento?

Hilary   Yeah. Oh, you're not from the press I hope?

Dick   No.

Pause.

Marge   No.

Hilary   Oh, good. It's supposed to be a secret. She doesn't want the place crawling with journalists apparently.

Hilary *laughs and shakes her head a little disbelievingly.*

Dick   No. Good idea.

Marge   She's coming home to her family.

Hilary   Yeah. Next Wednesday.

Marge   How lovely.

Hilary   We haven't seen her since ... well I met her in Italy in ... '85 ... so that's six years ago. But she hasn't been home for ... years.

Marge   Oh, that'll be wonderful. A lovely family reunion.

Hilary   Yeah.

Marge   We won't tell anybody. Will we?

Dick   Er ... no. We certainly won't.

Hilary *laughs. The phone rings.*

Hilary   Ah! Excuse me. Won't be a moment.

Hilary *leaves.*

Dick   You bloody beauty. This is my lucky day. You little bloody beauty. The woman is going to be in town and no one else from the media knows. (*He looks skywards.*)

Marge   You are not from the press, remember?

Dick   We'll work something out.

Marge   Don't you dare. I mean it, Dick. People are entitled to their privacy ...

Hilary *suddenly bursts into the room.*

Hilary   Oh, my God. (*She stands in the room in a state of near hysteria and panic, looking around her frantically, moving from one spot to another, looking for keys, anything.*) Oh, no. Oh, no. I'm sorry. I'm sorry. Oh, no. I have to go. Oh, God. I'm sorry.

Marge   What, dear? What?

Hilary *stands staring at* **Marge** *in a state of utter panic.*

Hilary   My father. He's gone missing. In the sea.
Blackout.

Act Two

Scene One

The three sisters are sitting at the end of the jetty. Over to their right, **Edwin** *is paddling in the shallows. The atmosphere is infused with a sense of melancholy.*

Hilary Do you remember the Sorrento fair? (*Both* **Pippa** *and* **Meg** *nod in recollection.*) Remember the year the fortune-teller came?

Meg He wasn't a fortune-teller, was he?

Hilary What was he then?

Pippa He was a 'world renowned' palmist and clairvoyant. Punditt Maharaji.

Meg That's right. It was written on the caravan. Punditt Maharaji.

Hilary What did he tell you? Do you remember?

Meg Not really. Something like 'You are going to be rich and famous and travel vast distances across the sea.'

They smile.

Hilary What about you, Pip?

Pippa Er . . . rich and famous and travel vast distances. Something highly personalised like that.

Hilary Do you know what he said to me? He said I was one of three.

Pippa That was a good guess.

Meg What else?

Hilary That was it. The Rixon kids threw stones at the caravan and he went off after them.

Pippa I don't think you got your shilling's worth.

They muse over the memory. In the distance **Pippa** *sees* **Troy** *walking alone at the top of the cliff. He is looking out to sea.*

Pippa   There's Troy.

The other women look in that direction. They watch silently. There is a change in mood.

Still looking for Pop.

Silence.

Meg   Poor kid. The sea will never give up its dead.

Hilary   He's a different boy isn't he? He's just clammed up. He loved Dad so much. They had something very special those two. It's not fair is it? (*Silence.*) People are always dying on him.

Pippa   He's a survivor, Hilary. He is.

Hilary   Yeah . . . but at what cost?

Pause. **Meg** *looks at her penetratingly.* **Hilary** *looks away.*

Pippa   What do you mean?

Hilary   He feels responsible this time.

Silence.

Meg   Yes. I know what that's like. (*They stare out to sea.* **Meg** *waits for a response. None is forthcoming.*) I think I'll go for a walk. (**Pippa** *and* **Hilary** *say nothing.* **Meg** *makes her way over to* **Edwin**.)

Pippa   She can't concede can she, that anyone else could be hurting as much as she is? She's like a child. (*Silence.*) You think I'm still an angry young thing, don't you? You may think this is bullshit, but I'm different when I'm away. I'm a different person. If you met any of my friends in New York and you said, 'Pippa's such a cot case isn't she?' they wouldn't know what you were talking about.

Hilary   I don't think you're a cot case.

Pippa   Oh, I am. I know I am. But only when I'm here.

Hilary   Must be in the water.

Pippa   I really did want people to see how much I'd changed. I was really looking forward to coming home you know. But people don't want to see that do they? They don't want to see what's new about you. They're suspicious of that. It's like you've reneged on who you are. And that's fixed. That's immutable. You are who you are and if you try and change, you must be faking. Bunging on an act. But over there Americans think differently. In fact, if you're not working to make positive changes in your life, they think you're in deep shit.

Hilary   Yeah. So I hear.

Pippa   You're cynical about that, aren't you?

Hilary   No. I'm just not so sure that people actually *do* change.

Pippa   Everybody has the potential. It's just whether we choose to take up on it or not.

Hilary   Sounds like propaganda to me. I think I'd rather be saying, 'OK, this is who I am. Like it or lump it. May as well get used to it, and make the best of it.'

Pippa *makes no response. She looks out to sea.*

Scene Two

In the shallows.

Edwin   What's up?

Meg *sighs.*

Meg   'We shall not cease from exploration.
　　　And the end of all our exploring
　　　will be to arrive at where we started
　　　and know the place for the first time.'

Edwin   T.S. Eliot.

Meg   Mm. I had hoped that I would know the place for the first time. But I'm not sure that I know it any better than when I left.

Edwin   Things change in ten years, Meg.

Meg   No. They haven't. That's just it. It's like there's this highly elasticised thread that's tied around us three and it stretches from Australia to Britain and to the States and all of a sudden it's just given out and thwack we're flung back together again. And we're just the same little girls, but this time in women's bodies. And we don't know any more than when we started out. (*Sighing.*) I'm beginning to feel quite middle-aged.

Edwin   I'm not surprised. This town feels like everyone in it was born into middle age. D'you know, the only conversations I've had since we arrived have been about children and compost.

Meg   People don't know what to say to us. Grief makes people realise how inadequate they are.

Edwin   Yes. (*Pause.*) Tell me, does anything ever happen here?

Meg   No. People live out quiet prosaic ineffectual lives and then they die. And the other people spend the rest of their lives utterly emotionally crippled by the experience. That seems to be the pattern.

Silence.

Edwin   I must say, Hilary is quite a remarkable woman isn't she?

Meg   Why do you say that?

Edwin   The way she copes with things.

Meg   Oh, yes. Hilary copes. She 'copes' because she shuts down. That's the way she lives her life. She doesn't let herself feel. She doesn't think about things too deeply. It's like she made a decision a long time ago that she was done with crying. Nothing or nobody was ever going to hurt her again. So she 'copes' magnificently and people think she's so strong, so remarkable. I don't. I think she's a coward.

Silence.

Edwin I think you're being very unfair. I can't imagine what it must be like for her. She's had to deal with three deaths. All of them tragic. I can't even begin to think how one would ever really deal with that.

Meg No, perhaps you can't.

Edwin And I don't think you can either.

Meg They were my parents too, Edwin . . .

Edwin I know.

Meg And I was here, remember, when Gary died.

Edwin I know. But he wasn't your husband, Meg.

Meg No, he wasn't my husband. But I loved him. That's what you don't understand. I loved him too.

Scene Three

Hilary *and* **Pippa** *make their way up the path to the house. They stop for a breather and take in the view.*

Hilary I dreamt last night that I married Edwin.

Pippa Whoa, that was nasty.

Hilary I forgot to shave my legs.

Pippa Oh, Hilary. That was an oversight.

Hilary I know. I was wearing a short white dress and these terrible hairy legs. I just couldn't enjoy myself.

Pippa I can imagine. Did he wear pyjamas?

Hilary No. He was wearing a purple suit.

Pippa *bursts out laughing.*

Pippa   I mean afterwards, you dill.

Hilary   I didn't get that far. I woke up about halfway through the reception.

Pippa   That was lucky. You know, I can't get my head around the possibility that anyone could actually lust after Eddie.

Hilary *laughs despite herself.*

Hilary   Oh, Pippa. You're dreadful. He's not that bad.

Pippa   He is. He's ridiculous. Look at him down there. 'Paddling'. God help us. Anyway, I've always found Enlgishmen rather ridiculous. Well, can you imagine it. Grown men referring to their penises as their 'willies'. It's very off-putting.

The two women walk up the path to the verandah. **Troy** *comes out of the house.*

Hilary   Troy?

Troy   Yeah.

Hilary   Who was that, driving off?

Troy   That guy Dick Bennett.

Hilary   What did he want?

Troy *holds up a single rose in a cellophane cylinder.*

Troy   He left this.

Hilary   He must be down for the weekend.

Pippa   Who?

Hilary   The guy who drove me to the beach . . . that day.

Troy   I think he's got the hots for you.

Hilary   Don't be silly, Troy. (*She takes the rose and reads the* *card.*) What makes you say that?

Troy   He asked me if I wanted to go fishing.

Pippa   Uh-huh? That makes sense. A way to a woman's heart is a bucket of fresh flathead.

Troy   You'd be surprised the number of boring old farts that come round here with flowers asking me to go fishing.

Hilary   Oh sure, Troy. They're bashing down the doors.

Pippa   Maybe they've got the hots for you. Nice young boy like you. Anything's possible.

Troy *gives her a 'don't be smart' look.*

Hilary   What did you say anyway?

Troy   'No', of course. I don't want to go fishing with him.

He gets up to leave.

Hilary   Why don't you go over and see one of your mates?

Troy *shrugs and goes indoors.* **Hilary** *and* **Pippa** *exchange looks.* **Hilary** *sighs.*

Pippa   What's the card say?

Hilary   'With deepest sympathy.'

Pippa *nods.*

Pippa   Do they really come round here asking him to go fishing.

Hilary   What do you reckon?

Silence.

Pippa   You know what I reckon. I reckon you ought to pack up and leave.

Hilary *stops in her tracks.*

Pippa   You're marking time Hil. You've been marking time for years. Now's your chance.

Scene Four

Meg *is wandering alone through the cemetery. A light rain is beginning to fall.* **Troy** *hovers some distance away, unseen by* **Meg**.

Troy   Meg? Aunt Meg?

Meg *looks up and smiles wanly.*

Troy *approaches gingerly. He hands her a coat.*

Troy   Thought you might need this.

Meg   Thank you. (*They stand together silently for a while.*) I used to come here when I was a kid. Just wander around and read the tombstones. I still remember the names. Charlotte Grace Phelps and Frederic Ernest Phelps. See, September 12, 1890 and October 1, 1890. He died three weeks later. Lottie and Fred. D'you think he died of a broken heart? I used to imagine that he found life intolerable without her. Can you imagine loving someone so much that you just couldn't go on?

Pause.
Troy *shrugs.*

Troy   I just wanted to say that we read your book, Pop and me, but . . . we didn't finish it.

Meg *nods.*

Meg   It's only a book.

Troy   He asked me to read it to him. We used to read it on the verandah when Mum was at work. We only had two chapters to go. (*He sighs.*) I tried to read them last night . . . but . . . (*He shakes his head. Pause.*) D'you know the part I liked best?

Meg   No?

Troy   When Helen and Grace meet in Italy.

Meg   That's the thing you have to be careful about with fiction. It leads us to believe that reconciliations are possible.

Troy   What d'you mean?

Troy *looks at her intently, obviously wanting a response.*

Meg   People coming together . . . reconciling their differences. It doesn't always happen.

Troy   It doesn't happen in real life, you mean?

Meg   Not always. No.

Troy   Well, why did you write it then?

Meg *makes no reply.*

Scene Five

Edwin *stands on the balcony of the verandah looking out to sea.* **Pippa** *is sitting on the steps.* **Hilary** *comes out. They both look down at* **Meg** *walking alone along the beach.*

Edwin   'Lost Angel of a ruin'd Paradise!
   She knew not t'was her own; as with no stain
   She faded like a cloud which had outwept its rain.'

Hilary *and* **Pippa** *exchange looks.*

Edwin   Shelley.

Hilary   Ah. (*Long pause.*) I thought you might like a beer.

Edwin   Yes. Thank you. That'd be nice.

Hilary *hands him a can. He expects a glass, but as none is forthcoming, he pulls the ring off the top of the can and sips tentatively.*

Edwin   It's really very beautiful, isn't it. It grows on you, I think.

Hilary   Mm.

Edwin   Poor Meg. She looks so fragile doesn't she?

Pippa *rolls her eyes, unseen by* **Edwin**.

Edwin   Well, I don't suppose you know where Troy is, do you?

Hilary *shrugs.*

Hilary   I think he might be in his room.

Edwin   I thought he and I might go fishing tomorrow.

Pippa *bursts out laughing.* **Hilary** *suppresses a grin.* **Edwin** *looks vaguely hurt.*

Pippa   Sorry, Eddie. Bit of a private joke.

Edwin *manages a weak grin. He goes to leave, then turns to* **Pippa**.

Edwin   By the way, if you could manage it . . . I'd really rather be called Edwin.

Pippa   OK, Edwin it is.

Edwin   Thanks.

Once out of earshot.

Pippa   No wuz, Eddie ol' bean! (**Hilary** *gives her a withering look.*) Shelley.

Hilary   Pip.

Pippa   She looks so fragile.

Hilary   Don't be a bitch.

Pippa   I'm not. It just turns my stomach that's all.

Hilary   He loves her. God! I'd give my eye-teeth for someone to love me like that. Wouldn't you?

Scene Six

Marge *and* **Dick** *are sitting on the verandah of* **Marge**'s *holiday house.*

Marge   I saw her on the jetty today. She's quite plump really. That's odd isn't it?

Dick   What?

Marge   Well, her being a rather large, big-boned sort of woman.

Dick   What's odd about that?

Marge   I don't know. I suppose I expected her to be fragile. You know, rather slight with fine bones and long fingers.

Marge *smiles, not without irony. Pause.*

Dick   I thought I might wander over there this afternoon.

Marge *looks at him sideways.*

Marge   Oh.

Dick   Yeah, just to see how they're getting on.

Marge   Hilary, you mean.

Dick *shrugs. Pause.*

Marge   Were you wanting to see Hilary? . . . Or Meg?

Dick   Well, Hilary, I suppose. I haven't met 'Ms' Moynihan.

Marge   Don't you think that's a bit intrusive?

Pause.

Dick   Well, we got a bit involved.

Pause.

Marge   Don't use that please.

Dick   What do you mean?

Marge   I'd just hate to think that you'd use the situation to get your interview with Meg. That's all.

Dick   What do you think I am?

Marge   A journalist.

The muscle in his jaw is twitching.

Dick   Ah. Well, that's very telling isn't it?

Dick*'s anger is imploding. He stands. He leans on the balcony. He doesn't know what to do with himself.*

Marge   I'm sorry if I've . . . hurt your feelings.

Dick   Oh, don't worry about it, Marge. I don't have any feelings. Remember? I'm a journalist. We're the lowest of the low. I'm just sorry I didn't have my camera with me. I could have got some really good snaps. I mean I was first on the scene, remember? I could have got the sister and the nephew. The whole damn page one horror story.

Scene Seven

Meg *comes into the kitchen where* **Pippa** *and* **Hilary** *are sitting.*

Pippa   Meg, we were just talking about the estate. We have to make an appointment with the solicitor. You free tomorrow?

Meg   He didn't have any money to speak of, did he?

Hilary   Not much. But there's . . . the house. We have to decide what to do about it.

Meg   What d'you mean?

Pippa   Whether to sell it or not.

Meg   Sell it? You can't be serious? (*Pause. She looks from one to the other and fixes on* **Hilary**.) It's your home. Why would we want to sell it?

Hilary   It belongs to the three of us now.

Meg   So what? You live here. I mean that's fine by me. Isn't that fine by you, Pip?

Pippa   She's thinking of moving up to Melbourne. Which I think's a very good idea.

Meg (*to* **Hilary**)   You didn't tell me this.

Hilary I haven't made up my mind . . . yet. And I'm only one of three. I suppose I wondered how you felt about it.

Meg I feel terrible.

Pippa Why? You don't live here. You haven't lived here for ten years. And the way I see it, is that Hilary has been the one to look after Dad for all these years while you and I have been able to do exactly as we please. So I think it's up to her to say what she wants.

Meg And what do you want, Pip?

Pippa I want what Hilary wants. And since she's the one who's made the sacrifice . . .

Meg Please don't tell me about Hilary's sacrifice. She is the one who made the choice. Hilary. You made the choice.

Pippa There was no other choice.

Meg She made the choice.

Pippa What was the choice? That we had a nurse for the two years after he had the heart attack. Got in a housekeeper. Meals on wheels. Don't be ridiculous, Meg. There was no choice. Were *you* prepared to come here and look after him?

Hilary Pippa, please.

Meg No. I was not prepared to come back here. You know that. But other arrangements could have been made.

Pippa Like what?

Meg I don't know because it didn't come to that.

Pippa Because Hilary said she'd step in.

Meg Yes. She made a choice.

Pippa *is fuming.*

Hilary It's OK, Pip.

Pippa   No it's not OK. I think we owe you something. I think we owe you a great deal. And I'm sorry that Meg doesn't feel like that. In fact I think it's disgusting.

Meg   Well you're a child.

Pippa   Is that all you can say?

Meg   It's our home. Our family home.

Pippa   Not any more.

Hilary   It is, Pip.

Pippa   It's not. You live in England for Godsake. It's not your home.

Meg   And you're doing your best to make me feel like that.

Pippa   Jesus Christ.

Scene Eight

Edwin *and* **Troy** *are fishing off the jetty.*

Troy   Did you ever meet my dad?

Edwin   No. I met Meg after she came to London.

Troy   Oh, yeah, that's right.

Silence.

Troy   How come she went. Do you know?

Edwin   Well, I suppose she wanted to travel. Most Aussies have the travel bug don't they?

Troy   Yeah. Pop used to say that he couldn't understand why people wanted to do it. 'Why would anyone want to leave a place like this?' He was always saying that.

Edwin   Perhaps he had a point.

Troy   He said people only travelled when they needed to run away.

Pause.

Edwin Well two of his daughters did travel. What did he say about that?

Troy He said they were running away.

Edwin Oh, I don't really believe that. Do you?

Troy *shrugs.*

Troy I don't know what to believe. I don't think there's much use staying put. Just for the sake of it. (*Pause.*) There's nothing much to do here. Not any more.

Scene Nine

Hilary *sits alone on the beach.* **Marge** *approaches.*

Marge Hilary?

Hilary Oh, hello. How are you?

Marge I'm OK. How are you – more to the point?

Hilary Oh ... bearing up. By the way – I've been meaning to write you a note – I'm sorry I just haven't got around to it.

Marge Of course you haven't. Don't be silly.

Hilary I wanted to thank you for all your help. That day and everything. You and Dick.

Marge I just feel so sorry. I can't stop thinking about you all.

Hilary Yeah. (*Pause.*) Do you want to sit down?

Marge You don't want to be on your own?

Hilary No. I think I'll go potty if I spend too much time on my own. So, how's it going at your place?

Marge Oh, pretty good. Dick's down again this week.

Hilary Yeah.

Marge   He's been coming down quite a bit lately. Driving me nuts.

She laughs. **Hilary** *smiles.*

Hilary   I thought you two were the best of mates.

Marge   Oh, yes we are, I suppose. He's just been getting on my quince a bit lately.

Hilary   Really?

Marge   I can't be bothered with men much these days! Terrible thing to say isn't it? But I'm afraid it's the truth.

Hilary *laughs.*

Marge   He's such an idealogue. It's a bit like having lunch with a textbook.

Hilary   Is he a teacher too?

Marge   No. Used to be, but no, now he's a writer. He writes political stuff, cultural analysis, that sort of thing.

Hilary   I think I'd be out of my depth there.

Marge   No, not necessarily. Anyway he's totally out of his depth when it comes to relating to women. Anyone probably. I used to find him quite intimidating you know, because he seemed so clever and articulate. But now . . . (*She scoffs.*)

Hilary   You should be at the dinner table at our place. With Meg and her husband. I'm sure they must think I'm a complete dummy.

Marge   I doubt it.

Hilary   You know, I used to think that when my sisters had children they'd have to stop for a bit. And that'd be my chance to catch up. So when they were up to their elbows in nappies and all that business, I'd be out there doing all the things that they've been able to do. But it doesn't work like that does it?

Marge *smiles.*

Hilary They'd be able to have their children without the slightest hiccup, those two girls.

Marge Hard to say. They might be totally bamboozled by it.

Hilary I doubt it. They're so competent in every other way – motherhood isn't that hard.

Marge Millions'd disagree of course. (*Pause.*) You sound like Helen.

Hilary Who's Helen?

Marge Helen, in the book.

Hilary Oh, yeah. That'd be right. The parochial one. That's me.

Marge She's my favourite character actually.

Hilary Is she?

Marge Oh, yes. (*She smiles. Pause.*) I was so much like Helen . . . (*She pauses, lost in thought. She glances at* **Hilary** *who looks at her questioningly.*) . . . except that I don't think I was betrayed quite so terribly as she was. My husband left me for another woman when the children were little. Oh, years and years ago now. And I behaved just like Helen – so 'adult' about it all. Well I had to be I suppose. I was always seeing them because we were constantly ferrying the children back and forth between the two households. (*Pause.*) I was so nice to them, you know. I had such little self-esteem that I was able to completely understand or at least rationalise why he'd want to team up with her. She was everything I wasn't. And because I wanted the children to be able to cope with the divorce and the split households, I kind of promoted them as a couple. I told the children they were lucky to have her. She'd be able to show them and tell them things about the world that I couldn't. I gave her such good publicity . . . and it worked. And I paid for it. Not that the children lost respect for me, necessarily . . . and I think they've always loved me . . . but I don't feel as though they know me. (*Pause.*) I'm not a known quantity.

To my children. And I know exactly why I did it. I couldn't bear my children to see me being so resentful and bitter. Which is exactly how I felt. (*Pause.*) So I suppose that's why I understood Helen. She couldn't really vent her spleen ever, could she? She had too much to lose. Or at least that's how she saw it. So, she just went on coping . . . and everyone thought she was strong.

Scene Ten

Meg *is in the garden,* **Pippa** *comes out.*

Pippa   Meg?

Meg   Mm?

Pippa   I'm sorry.

Pause.

Meg   Pip, I've been carrying guilt for too long. I don't need you to lump it on me again.

Silence. **Pippa** *looks frightened.*

Pippa   I haven't lumped anything on you.

Meg   Haven't you?

Pippa   Look, I don't want to talk about all that.

Meg   You never want to talk about it. You never have and you never will.

Pippa   It's in the past, Meg.

Meg   You ask Troy whether he thinks it's in the past. I don't know what to say to him, Pip. Do you know? Or do you just change the topic? Or perhaps he doesn't ask you about Gary, because he asks me.

Pippa *says nothing.*

Pippa   What do you want me to do, Meg? What do you want me to say? Hmm?

Meg *closes her eyes. Long pause.*

Meg   I think I hurt his feelings this morning.

Pippa   Well you're a shit!

Meg   Oh, God, Pippa. Don't you have any softness about you at all? Do you have to cut at everything?

Pippa *is cut to the quick. She says nothing. Silence.* **Meg** *goes to touch her arm.* **Pippa** *flinches.*

Pippa   He's only a boy remember. I don't want him to have to hurt any more than he is already. That's all.

The flywire screen bangs and **Troy** *comes out onto the verandah. He comes over to where the women are standing.*

Pippa   How are you, ol' bean?

Troy   Mum said to say that she's asked that guy Dick Bennett and Marge someone or other over for lunch. That OK with you guys?

Pippa / Meg   Shit.

Pippa   She's always been the sociable one of the family.

Scene Eleven

The lunch. **Edwin** *and* **Dick** *are on the verandah. The sounds of chatter and laughter are heard from the kitchen. It is as though they are waiting for the women to come out. There is an awkward silence. They drink from cans of beer.*

Dick   So, you're in publishing?

Edwin   Yes. It's just a small concern really. I'm in partnership with another chap and we do about twenty books a year.

Dick   What sort of stuff?

Edwin   Oh ... coffee table books mostly. (*He laughs self-deprecatingly.*) We do a lot of art books. Architecture, historic buildings. That sort of thing. We've done the occasional cookery book. Against my better judgement I might add.

Dick I wouldn't have thought the English had much of a culinary tradition.

Edwin Ah ... no. That's not strictly true. There's quite a resurgence of interest in it at the moment – it's highly fashionable to know about food and wine. The art of entertaining. Among certain sections of the community of course.

Dick I don't suppose you've ever considered grubbying your hands with anything more political?

At this moment **Troy** *comes out.*

Edwin I don't think it's a question for grubbying one's hands actually. I think it's merely a matter of expertise. Ah Troy. You know ... er ... Dick? Dick Bennett – Troy.

Troy Yeah. G'day.

Dick How's things.

Troy OK.

Edwin Traditional Australian gathering by the looks of it. Men in one room, women in the other. Isn't that how it goes?

He grins.

Troy Yeah.

Edwin I've never really been able to understand that, you know. I mean as far as I'm concerned, I've always thought that Australian women were amongst the loveliest in the world. And yet the men – your average Aussie bloke – doesn't seem to be all that interested in them. That's always struck me as being very peculiar.

Dick I think that's a bit of a cliché, actually.

Troy You reckon?

Edwin Well I've got a bit of a theory about this. I'd be interested to hear what you think. I suspect all this mateship business is quite possibly a way of disguising a deeper stratum of misogyny in the Australian male. (*Pause.*) What do you think, Troy? (**Troy** *shrugs.*) You see, I don't find it at all surprising that the feminist voice is at its most strident in Austrlaia. It's always struck me that this is a very male culture and as a result the struggle for women is by necessity more vehement here.

Dick Compared to where? Britain?

Edwin Yes. I think so. Well, for example, in Britain, there are so many women moving into top executive positions these days.

Dick That may be so, but your lot has just dumped a woman prime minister who wasn't exactly a paragon of liberal enlightenment. Look, if feninism is only about women making it – then it's a crock of shit as far as I'm concerned. What matters is what women actually do, when they have made it.

The two men drain their glasses. **Troy** *aware of the tension finds this slightly amusing.* **Hilary** *and* **Pippa** *enter carrying food.*

Hilary OK. Everyone. Food.

Troy *seizes the opportunity to make a getaway.*

Troy Great, I'm starving.

Everyone assembles in the living room. **Troy** *pinches a piece of bread.* **Pippa** *slaps his hand.*

Pippa Starving, are you? Could you eat a horse?

Troy Yes.

Pippa Good.

Pippa *She lifts the lid off the casserole and* **Troy** *looks in. He looks dubious.*

Pippa That's all he had. The butcher. I begged and pleaded but . . .

Hilary   Shut up, you two. It's chicken cacciatore. Sit anywhere you like.

Meg   This looks great, Hil.

There is general assent.

Marge   Who did this painting?

Referring to a painting on the wall. The family members all smile at the mention of the painting.

Pippa   A bloke called Clarrie Evans.

Hilary   He was a local. He's dead now.

Pippa   He was such a whacker. That's him on the far left.

Meg   Dad gave him a hand building a chicken coop in his backyard and Clarrie was so grateful he did this painting 'specially for him.

Hilary   Dad was so funny about it wasn't he? He wasn't real keen on the idea of having one of Clarrie's works of art, but as soon as he laid eyes on it . . . he loved that painting. It was his pride and joy wasn't it?

The family members all nod their assent.

Marge   It's this house isn't it?

Troy   Yeah.

Marge *squints at the picture, reading the sign hanging from the verandah.*

Marge   Hotel Sorrento?

Hilary   Dad and all his mates used to sit out on the verandah and have a few beers. They called it Hotel Sorrento.

Pippa   They're all dead now. Every one of those blokes. (*Referring to the figures in the painting.*) Clarrie, Mick Hennessy, Jock Farrell, Grabber Carmichael.

Edwin   Grabber?

Hilary   Best full-forward Sorrento's ever had.

Pippa   You know, when I'm away, and I'm thinking about home – that's the thing I remember. Those summer evenings, they'd all be out there, listening to the cricket. Drinking and laughing.

Meg   And drinking and drinking . . .

Pippa   I was thinking about this the other day . . . If I had to say what my dad taught me . . . as a kid . . .

Hilary   Never back a two-year-old in the wet.

They laugh.

Pippa   Yeah. (*Pause.*) I grew up believing that the penultimate sign of weakness in a man was when he couldn't hold his grog. The ultimate sign was if he ordered lemonade in a pub. That kind of man was highly untrustworthy. Funny isn't it?

Meg   Pathetic really. Considering they were all drunks.

Pippa   Our mum used to run around after them. Taking out trays of cold meat and cheese and tomatoes and stuff. There was never any room in the fridge. Remember? It was always full of bottles.

Meg   She couldn't even afford to buy herself a dress at Christmas.

Hilary   She wouldn't have had it any other way.

Meg   You reckon? She never had any friends of her own. It was all right with the blokes, because they wouldn't notice. But with women – I think she felt terrible.

Hilary   What do you mean?

Meg   I think she was ashamed of her house, her clothes, the state of the backyard. She never went out visiting and she certainly never invited anyone back here. I think she was desperately lonely.

Pause.

Marge   And I suppose she never complained?

Hilary   Oh, no. She complained all right. Loud and clear.

Pippa   She harped and whinged and nagged. All the time. And in the end it killed her.

Meg   She got cancer. (*Long pause.*) What do you do, Dick?

Marge *and* **Dick** *exchange looks.*

Dick   I write.

Meg   Oh, really? Fiction?

Dick   No.

Meg   What then?

Pippa   Non-fiction.

Troy *laughs.*

Dick   Essays.

Meg   Mmm.

Edwin   Essays. I've always thought that was a very honourable pursuit. I like essays. I think it's one of the most delicious of the literary forms.

Hilary   Everybody got everything. Salad, Marge?

Marge   Oh, no thanks, dear.

Edwin   It comes from the French. 'Essayer', to try, to attempt. Thank you. What's your subject?

Dick   Australia. Contemporary Australia.

Edwin   Right. Fairly vast I would have thought.

Dick   I edit a bi-monthly paper.

Everyone stops and looks at **Dick**.

Troy   Which one?

Dick   *The Australian Voice.*

Troy   Oh, yeah. Pop used to buy that.

Pippa   No he didn't.

Troy   He did.

Hilary   Oh, that pink paper.

Dick   That's the one.

Hilary   So you're the editor?

Dick   Yeah.

Hilary   Well then, you'd better own up, Troy.

Troy   What?

Hilary (*to* **Dick**)   Remember that article on the motor industry. Beginning of the year. Did you write that by any chance?

Dick   No.

Hilary   Phew. That was lucky.

Troy   Mum!

Hilary   Troy got an 'A' for an essay on the motor industry.

Pippa   Hey, good on you, Troyby.

Hilary   Word for word, was it, Troy?

Troy   Get off. I changed it around ... Sort of.

Everyone laughs.

Meg   Fancy Dad buying it.

Hilary   Dad said it was the only paper that gave the working man credit for having a brain.

Meg   What about the working woman?

Hilary / Pippa / Troy   If you're a woman and you got any brains – you don't work!

Pippa   Big champion of the feminist movement our dad!

Troy   He was coming around.

Edwin 'Let us sit and mock the good housewife
Fortune from her wheel, that her gifts may
henceforth be bestowed equally.'

Meg What are you talking about?

Edwin Shakespeare. (*Pause.*) Terrific bean salad, Hil.

Meg *gives him a look.* **Edwin** *grins impishly.*

Dick If he was down on feminism, what did he make of
your book?

Pause.

Meg I don't know. I didn't have a chance to ask him.

Silence.

Troy He liked it. What he read of it. (*Pause.*) But he said
he didn't think you understood about loyalty.

Pause.

Meg Loyalty to whom?

Troy He just said that loyalty was the most important
quality a person could have.

Silence. No one quite knows what to say.

Marge Do you think he would have argued that loyalty
was more important than truth?

Hilary Yes. I think he would have. Loyalty was a big
issue for him. Sticking by your mates . . . all of that.

Silence.

Edwin I think people hold on to these things, like the
notion of loyalty, or truth, as if they were unassailable,
which means that they lead fairly unexamined lives I would
have thought. Er . . . with respect to your father. I was just
speaking generally.

Marge Oh, I agree absolutely. It's like religion. It makes
life so easy. Once you've signed up, you don't have to ask
so many questions.

Meg   Exactly.

Dick   I suppose as a writer, this sort of thing must come up for you quite a lot.

Meg   What sort of thing?

Dick   The issue of loyalty. Writing as you do, so autobiographically . . .

Edwin *scoffs.*

Meg   I don't write autobiography. I write fiction.

Marge   There is a significant difference.

Dick   All right. Fiction. It's just that the connection with Sorrento is fairly obvious . . .

Marge   I don't think it was *obvious*. In fact I don't think you would have made any connection, would you, unless I'd pointed it out?

Dick *sighs. He is irritated.*

Dick   I don't actually think that's the point, Marge.

Edwin   What is the point?

Dick   Well, just this business about loyalty. OK, you don't write autobiography as such, but to me your writing has a very personal feel and I wonder if people ever take offence.

Meg   It hasn't come up.

Dick   So it's not an issue for you?

Meg   Oh, yes, it's an issue. But it hasn't come up. (*Pause.*) No one's ever raised it. That's what I mean. In fact, I've been home for ten days and this is the first time the book's been mentioned.

Troy   No it's not.

Meg   Oh, yes. Sorry. You and I had a bit of a talk about it, didn't we? (*To her sisters.*) But you two haven't said a solitary word about it. I don't even know whether you've read it.

Pippa   'Course I've read it.

Meg (*to* **Hilary**)   Have you?

Hilary   Mmm.

Meg   Well, why haven't you said anything to me?

Edwin   Meg. Come on. That's a bit unfair.

Meg   Why is it unfair? Talk about loyalty.

Pippa   There have been a few other things going on, Meg.

Silence.

Dick   Well I'm quite happy to talk about it.

Marge   Dick.

Meg *ignores* **Dick** *and continues to address her sisters.*

Meg   It *has* been nominated for the Booker Prize. It's not a completely insignificant piece of work. Not that you'd bloody know it round here. (*Pause.*) You know, Dick, people used to ask me why I stayed in London. Why I didn't come home. And I used to say it was because the artist has no status in this country. Why make art when you can make money? That's Australia for you. But I'm talking ten years ago. I was sure things would have changed . . .

Marge   But they have. There's been significant changes . . .

Meg   Look, there's all this talk about the new renaissance in Australian culture. The literature, the cinema, the theatre. Aboriginal art, taking the world by storm. Australian novelists getting huge coverage in the *New York Book Review*. All of that. But the fact is, in this country there is a suffocatingly oppressive sense that what you do as an artist, is essentially self-indulgent.

Dick   How do you know? You've only been here for ten days but you've been away for ten years.

Meg   I know because I lived here for thirty years. I went away. And now I'm back. *Nothing* has changed.

Dick   See, I think you're wrong. And I can't for the life of me see how you can feel so authoritative about this. Like that interview in the *Guardian*.

Marge   Dick.

Dick   I'm sorry but I found that highly offensive. What you said was cliché-ridden and misinformed. Look, you're entitled to your views . . .

Meg   It doesn't sound like it.

Dick   Well, I'm entitled to disagree with you, all right. But the issue for me is why you, as an expatriate, feel compelled to dump on this place. Because in effect you're dumping on the people who are actually trying to do things.

Meg   So one can only be critical from the inside. Is that it? Or perhaps one can't be critical at all?

Dick   You're missing the point.

Meg   The point is, I think that this so-called cultural renaissance is actually about patriotism. Which makes people like you very defensive.

Dick   That's bullshit.

The following dialogue occurs simultaneously.

Pippa   I think you're the defensive one in this instance. I didn't read the *Guardian* . . .

Edwin   It wasn't worth reading, I think that's the point.

Dick   It was a highly contentious set of opinions.

Edwin   Which actually misrepresented everything that Meg was on about.

Dick   So you're going to retract that now, are you? That's not what you meant at all. It was the media's fault.

Meg   No, I'm not retracting anything. I stand by what I said.

Hilary   What did you say?

Meg   I said that Australians are terrified of any expression of passion. Unless of course the passion is about hedonism and making money. Oh, and sport. Then that's all right. The cultural heroes, the real cultural heroes are good blokes who make a lot o' dough, don't take themselves too seriously and have no pretensions whatsoever about their intellect. You see, you all think I'm terribly pretentious because I take myself seriously. Because I referred to myself as an 'artist'. You think that's pompous bullshit, don't you?

Marge   No. I don't.

Dick   I do.

Meg   (*turning to her sisters*)   And you do too, don't you?

Pippa   Yeah, I do. 'Cause you're trying to lay a claim that what you do is more important than anyone else.

Meg   I'm doing no such thing, Pip.

Dick   You are. You're mythologising the role of the artist. And that is precisely what the cultural movement of these past two decades has been about. *De*mythologising it. Cutting away all the rarefied, ivory tower thinking. Making 'culture' accessible to ordinary people.

Meg   And you're suggesting that I'm not. You don't think *Melancholy* is accessible – to 'ordinary' people?

Marge   Oh yes, of course it is. Absolutely accessible . . .

Pippa   It's just your attitude, Meg.

Meg   Oh, now I have an attitude problem do I? (*Pause.*) Well let's talk about attitude shall we? What about when someone writes a novel and gets no response from the people she knows. What can we understand from that? That the novel itself is no good? That novels per se are not really all that relevant? Or is it something to do with the *attitude* of the other people? Something to do with selfishness? Or what about cowardice?

Pippa Cowardice? Jesus Christ, Meg. What about the cowardice of someone who can't talk about stuff openly so they have to go and put it in a book.

Meg Pippa. I can't believe I'm hearing this. From you.

Hilary What do you want us to say, Meg? You've spent the whole time telling us that you don't write autobiography. You write fiction. Now I've had to sit here and listen to all that when you know as well as I do that the only difference is, you haven't used our real names.

Scene Twelve

Meg *sits alone on the verandah in half-light.* **Troy** *approaches.*

Meg Troy? What are you doing up?

Troy I couldn't sleep.

Meg It's cold. You should go in.

Troy Meg. (*Pause.*) What happened the night my father died?

Meg I can't tell you.

Troy Why not?

Meg Because I promised. (*Bitterly.*) It's called loyalty. Keeping a promise even when you know it's wrong.

Troy Who did you promise?

Meg Your father.

Silence.

Troy Were you having an afffair with him?

Meg *shakes her head.*

Meg Tell me something, Troy. Just tell me this first. When Pop said to you that he didn't think I understood about loyalty . . . ?

Troy Yeah.

Meg Do you think he meant it as a writer or as a person?

Pause.

Troy I don't know.

Pause.

Meg The problem with loyalty is that you can keep on and on, living a lie. And you don't even know you're doing it.

Troy *doesn't understand.*

Meg I don't know whether you'll be able to make sense of any of this. But I'll tell you anyway. It's not fair otherwise. (*Pause.*) For quite a long time, I was very much in love with him. Your dad. I never admitted it. In fact I only admitted it to myself when I was halfway through my book. He was such a wonderful man. He was loving and warm and generous. And so funny. He used to make us laugh. Hilary and me. We'd be on the floor, holding our stomachs. Absolutely weak with laughter. (*She smiles at the memory.*) He was also very sensual. Very affectionate. For those last two years before he died, I thought that he wanted to have an affair with me. I'd got it into my head that he was quite infatuated. And maybe he was. A little bit. But I was resolved that nothing could happen. He was married to my sister. You don't do that. Still, I think if I'm honest . . . I did want something to happen. Anyway that night, I was staying with Dad. The phone rang about midnight and it was Gary. He said he had to meet with me urgently. Somewhere private. So I agreed to meet him on the pier. I got there first and I waited and after a while he came walking up the pier huddled in his jacket. It was very cold and he stood there trying to roll a cigarette and his hands were shaking. He was really agitated. He said,

'Meg, I've done something really stupid.' He was finding it impossible to get the words out. And then he said it, 'I'm having an affair with Pippa.' (*Long pause.* **Meg** *daren't look at his face.*) I'm sorry, Troy. I'm sorry it's so shoddy.

Troy   Pippa?

Meg *nods. Silence.*

Troy   What did you say?

Meg   I asked him whether Hilary knew and he said he didn't think so ... and then he asked me what he should do. And I said 'End it obviously', and I turned my back and walked down the pier and I never saw him again. I just turned my back. And that was the night he drove his car into a tree. A month later I went to England ...

Long silence.

Troy   Do you think he did it on purpose?

Meg   No. You must never think that. It was an accident.

Troy   Does Mum know?

Meg   I don't know what she knows, Troy. She thinks it was me, I think.

Troy   That's what everybody thinks.

Meg   I know.

Troy *puts his head on* **Meg**'s *shoulder. She puts her arm around him.*

Meg   I'm sorry, Troy.

Scene Thirteen

Hilary *is alone in the garden.* **Dick** *comes by.*

Dick   Anyone home?

Hilary   Hello.

Dick   I just wanted to drop by and thank you for lunch yesterday.

Hilary   I'm sorry that it got so tense. It wasn't much fun.

Dick   I . . . er . . . wanted to apologise actually. I think I opened a can of worms and . . . well, I didn't let up. It was very . . . insensitive and . . . I'm sorry.

Pause.

Hilary   You weren't to know.

Dick   Well, I think I behaved pretty boorishly. Which no doubt confirms Meg's picture of Australian men.

Hilary   I think she was acting pretty boorishly herself. (*Pause.*) Lethal combination really. Expatriates and Australian men.

She looks up and grins.

Dick   Marge isn't speaking to me.

He grins sheepishly. **Hilary** *laughs.*

Hilary   Want a cup of tea?

Dick   No, I'm right thanks.

Hilary   She's gone for a walk. Don't worry. You're safe.

Dick *laughs.*

Dick   I sat up last night and reread *Melancholy*.

Hilary   Oh, no. Please.

Dick   This is the last time I'll mention it, OK? I promise.

Hilary   Good.

Dick   You really are an extraordinary family, you know?

Hilary   Is that the word for it.

Dick   Browning said this thing, 'When I die, the word "Italy" will be engraved on my heart.' I couldn't get that out of my mind last night. I kept thinking, 'When I die, what the hell'll be engraved on my heart? Glen Waverley? All the miserable dumps I've lived in?'

Hilary *is looking at him not understanding.*

Dick See, I realised last night that Meg actually does know what she's got here . . .

Hilary You mean Sorrento?

Dick No. Not even Sorrento. I mean this house. This family. I feel quite envious of you all. Stupid as it may sound. But I do.

Hilary You're a funny fish.

Dick Yeah. That's what Marge always says.

Scene Fourteen

Marge *has set her easel up on the pier facing diagonally across to the beach.* **Meg** *stands behind appraising the painting. There is a slight awkwardness about them after the events of the preceding evening.*

Meg I didn't know you were a painter.

Marge A weekend painter, I'm afraid.

Meg *looks carefully at the painting.*

Meg Oh, it's lovely. It's very lovely actually.

Marge *blushes slightly. Silence.*

Meg Full of yearning.

Silence.

Marge 'Yearning for something that she could not name.'

Meg *smiles at the reference to her book.*

Marge My relationship to this place has changed so

much since reading *Melancholy*. (*Pause*.) I didn't get the chance to talk about it with you yesterday, but what I wanted to say was that reading *Melancholy* was just like the experience I had when I first read Helen Garner. I remember reading *Monkey Grip* and thinking, 'This is the place where I live and I've never seen it like this before.' It was as though she'd given me the summer in the inner suburbs. Like it hadn't existed until I read her book. And all of a sudden, everything became meaningful – going down to the Fitzroy pool – Aqua Profunda – and walking to the shop on one of those hot evenings and smelling the asphalt. Watching those young women in their cotton dresses riding their bicycles through the park. She gave it to me. She gave it life.

Meg   Mmm. I know exactly what you mean.

Marge   I feel the same about Sorrento. It's not just the pretty little place that I come to every weekend for a bit of R & R. Not any more. I've started to feel that I *need* to come here. I take that walk often you know – from the back beach across the headlands towards Portsea. And I think I've found the place Grace calls 'The Great Rock'. '. . . perched on the farthest point, with the steepest fall, a place for glorious departure.'

Meg *smiles*.

Marge   It's so wild, with the wind and the surf smashing around over the rocks. Way down there at the foot of the cliffs. I feel as though you've awakened something in me. It's like a yearning, a real yearning . . . to . . . feel again. (*Pause*.) One closes down on one's passions so much. I suppose I always used to choose the sheltered spots . . . (like Helen) but now . . . I feel this urgency . . . to be part of it all, part of the expanse.

Meg *is deeply touched by* **Marge**'s *outburst*.

Marge   I always used to paint with watercolour, you know, but now I've started to use oils.

Scene Fifteen

Pippa *is wandering restlessly around the living room.* **Edwin** *enters.*

Edwin   I was looking for Meg.

Pippa   So was I.

Edwin   Oh, by the way, I finished that book you lent me.

Pippa   Uh, huh.

Meg *enters, unseen by* **Edwin**.

Edwin   Yes, I realised that I have a bit of a problem with Australian novels. They're so hampered by an obsession with the vernacular. It utterly constrains them. I don't know. The Australian language – it's really a language for such tawdry dreams. (**Edwin** *realises* **Meg** *has been present.*) Oh. I was just off to bed.

Meg   OK.

Edwin   Will you be long?

Meg   I don't know.

Edwin   Mmm. All right. I'll see you later. I haven't seen that much of you lately. I thought perhaps we could go for a little walk. Before bed. But perhaps tomorrow.

Meg   Yeah.

Pause.

Pippa   Good night, Edwin.

Edwin   Oh. All right.

Edwin *leaves.*

Pippa   I think we need to talk about a few things.

Meg   Yes. We do.

Meg *looks up at the painting. She moves over to it and straightens it up.*

Pippa   What are you doing?

Meg   Oh, just looking at this. (*She smiles.*) It's a bloody awful painting isn't it? We really should take it down . . .

Pippa   No. Leave it . . . Sorry. Please leave it. (*She takes a deep breath and talks in a measured way.*) I know you think that this house means nothing to me. You think I don't feel things as strongly as you do . . .

Meg   That's not true.

Pippa   I don't think that you believe I feel any real sentiment about this house. But you're wrong. I do. Regardless of what I feel, I think we should encourage Hilary to move out. (*Pause.*) This place is dying, Meg. The heart and soul of this house, this town, disappeared with Dad. Vanished – presumed dead. But it's not dead yet. It's just dying. Don't you feel it? We're living with the dying because there's no body. No burial. And there will never be a burial until we sell this house. For Hilary's sake . . . I'm really begging you . . . Meg . . . she will shrivel up here – like Mum, and it's not right. She has to salvage her life . . .

She starts to cry, heavy sobs. **Meg** *puts her arms around her.*

Meg   Oh, Pippy. Pippy Long Stocking.

Meg *hugs her, stroking her hair until* **Pippa** *pulls away.*

Pippa   Please? Meg? Will you talk to her?

Meg *stares at the floor. Her heart is in turmoil.*

Meg   I'll only talk to her . . . if you will.

Silence.

Pippa   She doesn't want to know, Meg. Believe me. She doesn't want to know.

Meg   I want her to know.

Pippa   It just makes things worse, Meg. Don't you see? And it's not going to bring him back.

Scene Sixteen

In the pitch black there is a scream. **Hilary** *sits on the edge of* **Troy***'s bed. He has woken in a sweat after a nightmare. She tries to console him.*

Troy   I got cold, Mum. I had to come in.

Hilary   I know. Ssh.

Troy   I went to get my towel. And when I turned back . . .

Hilary   Ssh.

Troy   He was gone.

Hilary   I know, darling.

Troy   I just turned my back. I turned my back. And now . . . every night . . .

Hilary   Oh, my darling boy . . . my dear, darling boy.

Troy   And it's the same one. I'm talking to someone. And I turn my back and when I look around . . . they're gone. They disappear. Oh, Mum. Mum. I can't stand it.

Hilary   They'll stop. They will. I promise you.

Troy   Every night . . . I'm standing on the sand, Mum. And I look out to sea and I search and search the waves and I try and see him. And I think I see him. (*He starts to sob.*) But I didn't do anything. I just ran away.

Hilary *takes him firmly by the shoulders.*

Hilary   Troy, listen to me. You didn't see anything. By the time you looked back there was nothing there. If there was something, Troy . . . if he'd been calling you, or waving his arms . . . if you'd seen anything, you would have gone back in there. I know you would. And not because you're brave – even though you are – you're the bravest kid I know. But you would have done it, Troy. Just on instinct. I know that more than I know anything in the whole world. But you didn't, you see, because there was nothing there. There was only the sea. (*Pause.*) One day, Troyby, one day . . . we'll walk along the back beach and we'll look out at the sea and we won't be frightened by it any more. We'll say, 'This is what happened.' (*Pause.*) We don't know why, but what we do know is that it didn't happen to you and it didn't happen to me. We're the lucky ones. (*Pause.*) We've got a lot to feel sorry for – you and me. God knows. But I'm buggered if I'm gonna go under. And I'm not gonna let you either.

Scene Seventeen

Edwin *stands looking out to sea on the jetty as* **Marge** *paints.* **Meg** *wanders up the jetty towards them.*

Edwin (*to* **Marge**)   Sometimes I have this very strange feeling of having been here before. It all seems so familiar. Then at other times it's not at all like what I imagined. It's very odd.

Marge   How is it different to what you imagined?

Edwin   It isn't as harsh. The light. In fact it's very gentle . . . very mellow.

Marge   Rather melancholy?

Edwin   Yes. (*He smiles.*) I suppose that's why I feel I know the place. Odd isn't it?

Marge   No, not at all. It's a very powerful evocation of the place.

Edwin   Yes, it is isn't it? I hadn't really appreciated that before I came. She writes with such a potent sense of place and I haven't really understood before just how central it is to her writing.

Marge   It's the life source of the novel I would have thought.

Edwin   Yes. (*Pause.*) I wonder whether it's the life source for the novelist.

Marge *nods thoughtfully. There is a pensive silence.*

Edwin   You know . . . the great irony is that she's being accused here of 'borrowing' from real life, at least that's what her sisters are suggesting, and yet in London there are certain critics who've argued that it's derivative of other fiction.

Meg *wanders up.*

Marge   British critics?

Edwin *nods.*

Marge   That'd be right. They can't conceive that anything original could be produced here; that something of beauty, profundity or passion could arise from an experience that's essentially Australian.

Edwin   I don't think it's a question of a lack of originality.

Meg   No, it's only a question of quality isn't it? Being written in a language of such tawdry dreams?

Silence.

Marge   You could hardly put *Melancholy* in that category.

Meg   Oh, perhaps you could. Perhaps it's all about tawdry little dreams.

Edwin   Oh, come on, Meg.

Silence.

Marge   Edwin, could you imagine yourself living here?

Edwin *is non-commital. Silence.* **Meg** *looks at him wanting him to take the question seriously.*

Meg   Could you?

Edwin   Here? In Sorrento? I don't think so.

Marge   What about Australia?

Long pause.

Meg   Could you? You haven't answered the question.

Marge   And you, Meg? Have you?

Scene Eighteen

Hilary *sits by the window of the sitting room.* **Pippa** *enters. She gives* **Hilary** *a small pile of clothes.*

Pippa   Here, you can have these if you want. I can't fit them in. (*Pause.*) I don't care what you decide about the house now. It's up to you. It doesn't affect me. It's really about you and Troy. What you want to do in the future. But I want to take this. (*The painting.*) That's all I want. You can have everything else. And I want to take it with me now, because I might never come back.

She attempts to unhook the painting.

Hilary   Leave it! None of us might ever come back. But until we decide, that stays where it is.

Pippa   You successfully manage every time to divest me of any sense of belonging, don't you? You won't say it, you won't admit it but you really believe that this house and this family is yours . . .

Hilary   What family? What family are you talking about? There is no family any more.

Pippa   No. Because you won't share it. You want to own it!

Hilary   I've never owned anything in my whole life. Damn you! I never even owned my own marriage. Damn you. Damn you . . .

Meg *stands at the door.*

Hilary   And damn you!

Meg *is silent.*

Meg   It's about time you started. It's about time we all started. To own what's happened to us.

Pippa Why, Meg? So we can all write best-sellers?

Meg Yes. All right, let's talk about best-sellers. I wrote that book. And I didn't steal anything from you or you or anyone else who wants to lay claims to ownership.

Hilary But you don't, Meg. You don't own what's happened. Don't you see that?

Meg No. I only own my story. And that's a very small thing.

Pippa Oh, yes it's your book. Your story all right. It's got your name written all over it. But it's our integrity. That's what you've stolen.

Silence.

Meg Is that what you think? Do you really believe that I have robbed you of your integrity? Because if I'm guilty of that, I'll recall every single copy of that book from every publisher and every bookshop in the world. I'll withdraw it from the Booker Prize right now . . . if that's what you think. (*Pause.*) But I always thought that integrity was something that couldn't be given or taken away. That it was the only thing a person could own. (*Silence.*) D'you know why I came home? Because I wanted to see if I could fit into this family again. I wanted to see if the three of us could be together. I want to know now, whether you two think it's possible? (*Silence.*) You'll never forgive me, will you, for writing about something that we couldn't talk about.

Hilary Did we ever try? Did we ever really try?

The three women maintain their position in a freeze. Music plays.

Scene Nineteen

Music continues as the three women maintain their freeze.

Auctioneer (*voice-over*) Ladies and gentlemen. I'd like to take this opportunity to welcome you all to the auction of number one Ti-Tree Road, Sorrento. It's not often that a property in such a glorious location as this comes on to the market and we're very pleased indeed to be offering it to you today. We've sold many, many properties on the peninsular and I can assure you that prices are escalating every week. Investment opportunities like this one don't come your way very often. This is a holidaymakers paradise. And with this beautiful location the possibilities are endless: holiday flats, guest houses, even a luxury hotel. What a beautiful site for a hotel. Ladies and gentlemen, I offer you number one Ti-tree Road, Sorrento. Who'd like to give me a reasonable offer?

End.

Glossary

10	chook	chicken
11	get a wriggle on	hurry up
16	stubbies	small bottles of beer
17	aspro	brand name, asprin
19	flattie	flathead, a common fish on the New South Wales coast
20	AAP	Australian Associated Press
21	out of the bag	special, out of the ordinary
23	Footscray High	secondary school in a suburb west of Melbourne
24	dropping at a rate of knots	dropping fast
26	barbie	barbeque
27	*Biggles*	a famous series of 1950s books about a World War Two pilot
32	Toowoomba	a town in Queensland
	Kalgoorlie	a mining town in Western Australia
	Woy Woy	a town north of Sydney
	nouse	know-how, inside knowledge
34	St Kilda	a Melbourne suburb
	footy	Australian Rules Football
35	oldies	parents
40	ratbag	despicable, disreputable, hopeless person
42	prat	idiot, jerk
45	Frankston	a satellite city of Melbourne
47	the Poms	the British
	whingeing	complaining
53	Septics	Americans
54	whacker	peculiar, eccentric person
60	cot case	so highly strung as to be confined to bed
61	bunging on	putting on
64	dill	idiot (affectionate)

68	No wuz	No worries, no problem
73	potty	crazy
74	getting on my quince	getting on my nerves
	nappies	diapers
81	full-forward	position at the goal mouth in Australian Rules Football
93	Glen Waverly	a Melbourne suburb

Dead White Males

David Williamson

David Williamson's first full-length play, *The Coming of Stork*, premiered at the La Mama Theatre, Carlton, in 1970 and later became the film *Stork*, directed by Tim Burstall. *The Removalists* (winner of an AWGIE award and the London *Evening Standard*'s Most Promising Playwright award) and *Don's Party* followed in 1971, then *Jugglers Three* (1972), *What If You Died Tomorrow?* (1973), *The Department* (1975), *A Handful of Friends* (1976), *The Club* (1977) and *Travelling North* (1979). His success continued with *Celluloid Heroes* (1980), *The Perfectionist* (1982), *Sons of Cain* (1985), *Emerald City* (1987), *Top Silk*, (1989), *Siren* (1990), *Money and Friends* (1991), *Brilliant Lies* (1993), *Sanctuary* (1994), *Dead White Males* (1995), *Heretic* (1996), *Third World Blues* (an adaptation of *Jugglers Three*), *After the Ball* (both 1997), and *Corporate Vibes* and *Face to Face* (both 1999). His most recent works have been *The Great Man* (2000), *Up For Grabs* and *A Conversation* (both 2001).

Williamson has won the Australian Film Institute film script award for *Petersen* (1974), *Don's Party* (1976), *Gallipoli* (1981) and *Travelling North* (1987), and eleven Australian Writers' Guild AWGIE Awards. He lives in Queensland.

Deconstructing Human Nature . . .

David Williamson

The genesis of *Dead White Males* occurred at a literary conference some years ago when a young male academic gave a paper on deconstruction and post-structuralism to a roomful of writers. No one in the room understood a word he said. When one writer rose at the end and asked for a plain English translation, we were told that it was a very difficult theory and that we shouldn't bother ourselves with it. 'Just keep writing,' was the response, 'and we'll tell you what you've done.' The writers weren't happy at all. The tendency of academics to treat writers as *idiots savants* who scribble away without knowing in the least what they're doing, has always been a source of tension, but this new wave of theory, which appeared to take the language of criticism totally out of the common domain, seemed something else again. Perversely, I became determined to find out what the post-structuralists were talking about.

Despite the fact that I have made Dr Swain the villain of this social satire, on a personal level I don't believe all his theory to be nonsense. Like all ideas that have impact, post-structuralism would not have flourished if it did not have some insights to offer. There is no doubt that Nietzsche, the intellectual precursor of post-structuralist thought, was on to something when he pointed out that humans find it very hard to be objective and rational. Most of us have been guilty of reconstructing our own history in a way that makes us the hero and the other party the villain and there have been many instances in which so-called historical, philosophical and scientific 'truths' have turned out to be heavily distorted. Power elites in every society have used the slipperiness of language to try and foist their 'constructed' version of the 'truth' on to minorities, but this doesn't mean that there is no *real* truth nor that literature is just another source of misinformation. While ideology can certainly be discerned in literature, it's not all that can be discerned. It is my belief, shared by the young protagonist of *Dead White Males*, Angela Judd, that the great writers can still speak to us across the ages because they do offer us wisdom and insight about our common human nature.

Which brings me to Shakespeare. When I told my friend, the academic Don Anderson, that I was thinking of satirising the excesses of the post-structuralists, he alerted me to the controversy that had raged in the *London Review of Books* not long before. Called by the *LRB* 'Bardbiz' it had been initiated by Terrence Hawkes, a post-structuralist professor of English at Cardiff University, who had declared that Shakespeare was a 'black hole' into which we fed our own needs and desires, and that his eminence in literature was not because of any special genius, but was due to the fact that his writings served conservative interests.

For the play, I decided that the central academic issue in Angela's mind would be over the literary status of Shakespeare and whether, in particular, his works were vehicles of sexist patriarchal ideology, a theory propounded by her lecturer, Dr Grant Swain.

I sent an outline off to my director Wayne Harrison. The story at this stage didn't include the physical presence of Shakespeare. Wayne rang me some days later and told me that while he was sitting in a theatre enduring 'an extremely boring play' he had had a vision of our play opening with Shakespeare being shot by Dr Swain. I raced to the word processor. With Shakespeare up there on stage, however, I thought it would be a pity to get rid of him immediately. We could kill him and still bring him back to defend himself, through Angela's consciousness, against the attacks of Dr Swain.

Paradoxically, the inclusion of Shakespeare enabled me to take the play's concerns beyond the narrow focus of post-structuralism and literary theory to the play's real concerns, the relationship between males and females in the last ten years of the twentieth century.

In the play, Shakespeare (who is not an attempt to recreate the real historical Shakespeare but is the Shakespeare Angela needs in order to make sense of her life) becomes an representative of his era, who believes that male and female natures are biologically different. Dr Swain, in contrast, believes culture is all-important and that biology plays no part.

Angela is not sure, and to the end remains unsure, but in other areas of her life her certainty and wisdom grows.

Angela learns in unexpected ways when she adopts Dr Swain's suggestion that she examine her family in order to discern its 'controlling ideologies'. She finds a grandfather who has behaved with a quiet heroism which belies his status as the chauvinist monster the family has 'constructed'; she finds a courageous mother wracked with guilt and exhaustion over the mother/career tug of war, and a father who loves both her and her mother, despite apparent layers of resentment. Angela, in short, finds that human nature *does* often break out of the strictures into which ideology tries to constrain it.

The play is partly a satire aimed at the political correctness enforced on society by the 'holy' ideologies of post-structuralism, radical feminism and multiculturism. The tone of the play is one of wryness rather than belligerent anger. It is an attempt to suggest to the adherents of those ideologies that they *are* ideologies and not 'truths', and that while ideologies typically contain truths they also contain untruths. It is not helpful to claim that all men are rapists or potential rapists. It is also, frankly, not true. It is also not true that all artistic products of minority groups are necessarily brilliant. It is also, surely, still faintly possible that heterosexual family life, despite its complications, can still be one interesting and valid way to live, and males and females are still capable of needing and loving each other.

I would like to thank Wayne Harrison, not just for the play's opening scene, but for his invaluable dramaturgical input during the play's development, and John Senczuk, Nick Schlieper, Tony David Cray, Tony Bartuccio, Marion Potts and the cast, John Howard, Michelle Doake, Henri Szeps, Anna Volska, Simon Chilvers, Patrick Dickson, Maggie Blinco, Kelly Butler, Glen Hazeldine, Barbara Stephens and Babs McMillan, for realising what I consider to be one of the finest productions I have ever been given in the theatre.

Sydney, May 1995

Dead White Males was first performed at the Drama Theatre, Sydney Opera House, on 9 March 1995, with the following cast:

Angela Judd	Michelle Doake
William Shakespeare	Patrick Dickson
Grant Swain	John Howard
Melissa	Kelly Butler
Steve	Glenn Hazeldine
Col Judd	Simon Chilvers
Grace Judd	Maggie Blinco
Martin Judd	Henri Szeps
Sarah Judd	Anna Volska
Jessica Squires	Barbara Stephens
Monica Judd	Babs McMillan

Director Wayne Harrison
Designer John Senczuk
Lighting Designer Nick Schlieper
Assistant Director Marion Potts
Composer Tony David Cray
Choreographer Tony Bartuccio

Characters

Angela Judd, *nineteen, a university student.*
William Shakespeare
Grant Swain, *a university lecturer.*
Melissa, *nineteen, Angela's friend and fellow student.*
Steve, *a student.*
Col Judd, *seventy-seven, Angela's grandfather.*
Grace Judd, *seventy-four, Angela's grandmother.*
Martin Judd, *forty-eight, Angela's father.*
Sarah Judd, *forty-six, Angela's mother.*
Jessica Squares, *forty-six, Angela's aunt.*
Monica Judd, *forty-four, Angela's aunt.*

Setting

The action takes place on the campus of New West University and in the Judd home.

Act One

Angela's Room

Angela Judd, *an engaging young woman with a sharp mind, sits reading a volume of Shakespeare's plays. She looks up.* **William Shakespeare** *materialises, looking around him, puzzled at the modernity of the furnishings.* **Angela** *walks up to him nervously.*

Angela   Mr Shakespeare?

Shakespeare *looks up and smiles.*

Angela   I hope I'm not interrupting, but I just felt I had to say – how much I admire your work.

Shakespeare   I thank you.

Angela   How is it that you know – so much about us?

Shakespeare *is just about to answer when a* **Man** *in his thirties, dressed in fashionable casual clothes, appears behind him.*

Man   He doesn't you know.

The **Man** *pulls out a pistol and shoots* **Shakespeare** *dead.* **Angela** *looks at the* **Man**, *horrified.*

Man (*smiling*)   Hi.

Angela   Why did you do that?

Man   These are exciting times, Angela. Dangerous and exciting times. You must know your enemies.

The **Man** *leaves.* **Angela** *is left staring at the body of* **Shakespeare**.

Lecture Theatre – New West University

The **Man** *who just shot* **Shakespeare** *stands at a lectern smiling at us. He is charismatic, articulate and animated by the intense certainty that he has a supremely important message to communicate* *and that he is enormously well equipped to deliver it.*

Swain   My name is Dr Grant Swain. Welcome to the English and Cultural Studies Department and to my course, Literary Theory 1A. Most of you have always assumed that there are certain eternal 'truths' about 'human nature', that perceptive writers reveal to us. This course will show you that there are no absolute 'truths', that there is no fixed 'human nature' and that what we think of as 'reality' is always and only a manufactured reality. There are in fact as many 'realities' out there as there are *ideologies* which construct them. Christian ideology constructs a 'reality' which includes a gentleman called God ticking off your good deeds and your bad. Conservative ideology constructs a 'reality' which includes the belief that most humans are inherently dishonest and lazy. As a prerequisite to entry to this course I asked you to write a short paragraph on what you regard as the essential 'thinking' you. I have selected one of these to read to you.

He takes a sheet of paper in his hands and reads.

'I am sceptical of all ideologies, and try to weigh all the available evidence in order to make informed choices.' Would you indicate if you wrote that passage or wrote something that contained significant elements of that passage?

He notes the hands.

A lot of you. That statement, in fact, was written by me. It sounds as if it is a credo that warns against ideology, but in fact it is the defining statement of liberal humanism, one of the most powerful ideologies to have ever appeared in Western thought, liberal humanism. Liberal humanism, pictures you, the individual, as rational and free. Free to make your own choices. Free to control your lives.
But the fact is none of us are free, or can ever be, free of ideology. All of use are conditioned by inbuilt and often unconscious mindsets to act in certain predictable ways. Our life scripts, in fact, are written for us. By whom?

He looks closely at his audience.

Largely by legions of well-paid 'experts' – economists, politicians, journalists and so on, who tell us the 'Truth' about 'The World', but it's not really 'Truth' we're being given, it's a series of ideological assertions. And the vast bulk of these assertions support the aims of the Western world's dominant ideology, the patriarchal corporate state. The project of patriarchal corporate ideology is simple. Keep corporate profits high and women in their place. Liberal humanism, in naively depicting us as capable of free and rational choice, is in fact the ideological handmaiden of the patriarchal corporate state. In encouraging us to believe we *are* in control of our lives it prevents us questioning the massive injustices to which most of us are subject. It is the aim of this course to show you how complicit the 'masterpieces' of liberal humanist literature have been in the process of depriving women, people of colour, people of non-normative sexual orientation, and people of the non-industrialised world, of power. The issues we will face go to the very heart of our undertanding of ourselves and of the world. They are perhaps the most critical issues of our times.

Outside the Lecture Theatre

Angela *talks to her friend* **Melissa Doherty**, *who is extremely attractive, knows it and flaunts it.*

Melissa   Do you believe any of that rubbish?

Angela   It made me think.

Melissa   What? That you haven't got a free will, that you are totally manipulated by the evil patriarchy?

Angela   The patriarchy's real. My mother has to fight it every day. And I wrote that Liberal humanist credo almost word for word. I thought at first it was mine he read out.

Melissa *looks over her shoulder and turns excitedly back to* **Angela**.

Melissa   Those guys over there are talking about us.

Angela *glances over her shoulder.*

Angela   They're talking about you.

Melissa   Don't always put yourself down, Angela. You've got that fresh sort of beauty you don't need to spend time on.

Angela   How come *guys* don't seem to want to spend time on it either.

Melissa   You look fine. It's just you scare them off.

Angela   How?

Melissa   Frankly, Angela, you're not good on signals of availability. Relax.

Angela *looks over her shoulder again, more carefully this time. A particular young man,* **Steve,** *who's not conventionally handsome but who is appealing in a run down sort of way, waves at her.* **Angela** *quickly looks away.*

Melissa   He's cute.

Angela   Melissa, he's *hopeless*.

Melissa   He's cute.

Angela   Would you go out with him?

Melissa   Aren't you interested in men at all?

Angela   Yes, but formed men, mature men, intelligent men.

Melissa   Angela, even *I* can't get one like that. Come and we'll chat him up.

Angela   No, Melissa. No.

Melissa   Check the body on that one.

Angela   The one picking his nose?

Melissa   You'll never get anyone, Angela.

Dr Swain's Tutorial

Swain, **Angela**, **Melissa** and **Steve** are present and we assume a few others are too.

Melissa   But literture *must* contain truths about human nature, otherwise why would people bother reading it?

Swain   Because they *think* they *are* learning 'truths' about 'human nature', but all they're really getting is the version of 'human nature' that accords with the power interests of its author.

Angela   Literature has *no* wisdom to offer?

Swain   Literature is *never* about wisdom, Angela. At its base it is always about power. At base, as Foucault, Althusser and Eagleton have shown us, all communication is ideological.

Angela   Surely we can step outside ideology?

Swain   Into what, Angela?

Steve   Reality.

Swain   Which particular version of reality, Steve? Patriarchal ideology constructs a reality in which women can only feel normal if they're married and heterosexual, radical feminist ideology constructs a reality in which women can only feel normal as separatist lesbians.

Melissa   No one 'constructs' my reality. I'm not becoming a lesbian and if I get married it'll be because I *choose* to be.

Swain   Your free liberal humanist autonomous self will make that choice?

Melissa   Yes.

Swain   Why have you already ruled out the lesbian option?

Melissa   Because I'm not attracted to women.

Swain   Could that possibly be because the dominant patriarchal ideology has constructed you to feel guilt and disgust at the very thought.

Melissa   No one has 'constructed' me. I'm not a puppet!

Swain   Is it also possible that the dominant ideology has also constructed a female gender stereotype which includes words like 'emotional', 'tactful', 'unassertive', 'caring' and 'supportive', which it just so happens prepares females *extremely* well for heterosexual marriage.

Angela   Are you saying that all that's left for us is to choose our ideology?

Swain   Most people don't even have that luxury. They accept the dominant ideology as their 'reality'.

Steve   By what criteria do you 'choose' an ideology?

Swain   On the basis of its social implications. I don't support radical feminism because its project is separatism, and I don't support the dominant ideology because its project privileges white middle-class Anglo-Celtic males.

Angela   Which ideology *do* you support?

Swain   My current subject position is non-essentialist feminism and multiculturalism. Its project is the equal coexistence of us all.

Col and Grace Judd's Living Room

Three generations of the Judd family are gathered. **Angela** *is there together with her grandfather and grandmother* **Col** *and* **Grace Judd**, *her father and mother* **Martin** *and* **Sarah Judd**, *her aunts,* **Jessica Squires** *and* **Monica Judd**. *It is meant to be a birthday celebration for* **Col**'s *seventy-seventh birthday but, apart from a party hat that sits forlornly on* **Col**'s *head, there seems to be* *little in the way of celebration going on.* **Monica** *has tears in her eyes.*

Grace Why did you ever believe him, Monica?

Jessica Because she's a fool.

Monica He was going to leave her. He really was.

Sarah Monica, I have to say that I think it's absolutely tragic that you spent eighteen years waiting around for a bastard who by the sound of it never had any intention of leaving his wife.

Monica He did.

Sarah Twenty years ago you were on top of the world. I'd just got you reading Shulamith Firestone and you were starting to understand the feminist agenda, when you went and –

Monica I fell in love, Sarah.

Jessica You're not a schoolgirl! If I ever hear one more woman, let alone my sister, say 'I fell in love,' as an excuse for some life-wrecking piece of total insanity, I will vomit! Will you stop that wailing!

Sarah Jessica, I know empathy is not one of your psychic priorities, but your sister is in some pain.

Jessica When has she ever *not* been in pain. I grew up with her. She pursues pain like a pig after truffles!

Monica You think I wanted this to happen?

Jessica Monica, anyone who wasn't deeply masochistic could have seen this disaster coming seventeen and three-quarter years ago.

Monica Someone like you with a heart made out of nickel alloy might've, but some of us do fall in love!

Jessica Fine, then you had eighteen years of wild illicit passion, so think yourself lucky and *move on*!

Monica We aren't all emotionally equipped to dump our

husbands and have a new lover every month like some
people around here. (*Bitterly.*) Pig after truffles.

Jessica   It was just a figure of speech.

Monica   Why that one?

Jessica   Monica, it was just –

Monica   Because I'm fat and ugly and I was lucky to
hang on to him for eighteen years, even as a part-time
mistress, eh?

Jessica   I'm sorry. I chose the wrong figure of speech.

Monica   You chose the one you meant to choose.

Sarah   Monica, please don't torture yourself. You made a
foolish mistake, but don't let it blight your life.

Martin   For God's sake.

Sarah   For God's sake, *what*!

Martin   If you're lonely and you need love you don't
always make brilliant choices.

Monica   Especially if you're fat and ugly!

Martin   I didn't mean that.

Monica   Stop treating me as if I'm pathetic. I didn't
come to Dad's birthday to be pitied!

Sarah   We don't pity you, Monica. I just think it's sad
that thirty years after the birth of the women's movement
we are still allowing ourselves to believe that happiness
requires us to have a man.

Martin   Sarah, the women's movement surely hasn't
altered the fact that men need women and women need
men.

Sarah   The one thing the women's movement has
established beyond doubt is that *men* need women, but
women certainly don't need *men*.

Martin   Excuse me while I slip out and kill myself.

Sarah Don't be so defensive. I wasn't talking about us.

Martin Oh great.

Sarah I was talking about men who still cling to patriarchal attitudes. You don't.

Martin No, I'm a certified wimp.

Sarah You're as near as a male can be to non-sexist, and given your background I think that's something you can be very proud of.

Sarah *looks pointedly at* **Col**. **Grace** *catches the look and reinforces it with her own glare of disapproval at her husband.*

Grace Ran this house as if he was bloody King Kong, and tried to teach Martin exactly the same habits.

Col *looks at his wife, but says nothing.*

Grace Nothing but a bloody bully. I was the best saleswoman in Haberdashery in David Jones before the kids came along and Maggie Shortland wanted me to start up a shop with her but Boss Cocky here said no. She asked Carol Sheedy and the two of them made a fortune. We could've been rich instead of ending our life in this bloody dump.

She glares at **Col**. **Col** *says nothing.*

All it would have needed was a ten thousand investment and we would've been rich. And the headmistress at Randwick said Monica and Jessica *both* should have gone on to university but His Holiness here said no. Martin had gone and that was all we could afford. Where did all the money he earn go, that's what I'd like to know? On the bloody horses?

She glares at him. **Col** *says nothing. She turns to* **Angela**.

When you get married, Angela, make sure it's not a bully like your grandfather.

Sarah I think marriage is the last thing on Angela's agenda, Grace.

Jessica   Good.

Sarah   A young woman these days would be crazy to even contemplate it.

Martin   Why?

Sarah   *Why?*

Martin   Sorry, but it's not quite so self-evident to me as it is to you.

Sarah   Because unless she's unusually lucky, the best she can hope for is a man who will expect her to work full time, *and* to function as a concubine and housekeeper and whose skills of communication will be such that she'd be better off sharing her life with a golden retriever.

Martin   Thank you, dear.

Sarah   Martin, I'm not *talking* about you. Will you please stop taking it so personally.

Martin   It's just a tiny bit hard not to, dearest.

Sarah   You went and did something about yourself.

Grace   What?

Martin   Sarah.

Martin *looks at his father, embarrassed.* **Sarah** *catches the look.*

Sarah   You don't have to be embarrassed. You should be proud.

Martin   I just don't –

Sarah   It saved our marriage. Why don't you tell your father. Admit you had the courage to seek help.

Martin   I don't want to talk about it.

Sarah *turns to* **Col**.

Sarah   Martin was in therapy for three years.

Martin   Sarah!

Sarah And the therapist said that his total inability to express himself emotionally was directly related to . . . (*Looks at* **Col**.) . . . a deficit of paternal warmth.

Col *says nothing.*

Martin Sarah, will you just shut up! It's Dad's birthday.

Grace It's a wonder Martin ever recovered. Even during his exams Clint Eastwood here had him up at five o'clock each morning loading wooden battens on his truck. (*She glares at* **Col**.) The girls could get away with murder, but he worked Martin like a dog.

Martin He needed help.

Grace He could've hired an assistant. He was just too mean.

Martin At least it taught me –

Sarah It taught you that powerful males think they have a right to dominate and control and that young males think they have to suffer in silence until it's their turn to dominate and control, but let's forget all that for a moment. It *is* Col's birthday.

They turn to look at **Col**.

Monica You're not saying much, Dad.

Grace He's mad at Jessica about that article.

Jessica What article?

Grace That one in the *Wentworth Courier*.

Jessica How I've discovered my aboriginality? He was the one who told me.

Martin In all fairness, Jessica, it was a bit rich.

Jessica (*points to* **Col**) Dad said that it was quite possible that there was – his own words – a 'touch of the tar' somewhere in the family tree.

Martin Possible. He used the word possible.

Jessica   I looked at the photos of Ern and there's an expressive nobility in his eyes that's unmistakable. And I'll tell you something, Martin, rather than reacting with the horror that you seem to be –

Martin   I am not reacting with horror. I am just –

Jessica   I felt a surge of immense pride and suddenly understood why I was an artist and why this country's landscapes had always meant so much to me.

Martin   I'd welcome it too, if it was actually true.

Jessica   For years and years I'd had this extraordinary feeling that the landscapes and rocks were sentient beings trying to speak to me.

Martin   They were. They were saying, 'Go paint somewhere else.'

Angela *cannot stop herself giggling.*

Jessica   You have no understanding of the creative process, Martin, and quite frankly it's what's screwed up your life.

Martin   Really?

Jessica   Yes really. All of us – all of us – have got an inner core of creativity that must be expressed, and it's only when we let that creativity speak that we become fulfilled and whole.

Martin   Jessica, your creativity speaks, but no one listens.

Jessica   You're so cynical, Martin. You had a burning desire to write a novel and you –

Martin   No one could ever finish my short story and that was only five pages.

Jessica (*to* **Col**)   Dad, I think it's wonderful to have discovered that we all have a *real* connection to this country. I can't understand why you're upset.

Col *remains impassive.*

Martin Jessica, you've got blue eyes and blonde hair. You're about as aboriginal as Arnold Schwarzenegger!

Sarah Why is this all so threatening to you, Martin?

Martin It's not. It's just not true.

Monica If it was I'd be proud too.

Grace He's a racist like his father.

Martin I am not, and neither is Dad.

Grace Not much. Monica was all set to marry that lovely Greek boy – what was his name, Mon?

Monica (*new tears at the thought*) Spiros.

Grace Lovely boy. Monica and he were head over heels in love.

Monica Spiros Spyrokakadakis.

Angela What happened, Aunt Mon?

Grace Col was just *so* rude to him.

Angela What did he say?

Monica 'Are you an Australian citizen?'

Grace 'If you aren't, don't come back until you are.'

Angela (*shocked*) Grandpa!

Col *remains impassive.*

Grace Do you know what, Angela? Spiros went on to found the biggest fruit juice company in the country.

Monica True Blue Juice.

Grace He bought a house in Point Piper for –

Monica Seven point two million. Three years ago.

Grace Hated migrants, hated aboriginals, hated anyone who wasn't fifth-generation Australian like he was.

Angela Grandpa, that's so sad.

Grace   Bloody old bigot.

Angela   Grandpa, Australia's multicultural policy has been a *huge* success story. We've become the international showpiece of ethnic harmony. Other countries send delegations here to try and work out how we did it.

Martin   Total apathy.

Grace   Don't waste your breath on them, Angela.

Jessica   Frankly, if this country was still full of people like Father, I'd be elsewhere.

Martin   Jessica, it's his birthday.

Jessica   I've decided it's about time I said something about that too. Every year, religiously, we all gather for this ritual celebration of *Father's* birthday, while *Mother*, who did the vast bulk of the hard work of bringing us up, gets a card or a phone call.

Grace   If I'm lucky.

Sarah   I'm only an in-law so I've kept my peace, but I'm so glad it's been brought up, because it's been annoying me for years. In fact it's seemed to me very symbolic of the way things are in the Judd family.

Monica   Exactly. Why should we all gather round every year and kiss his feet.

Martin   I haven't noticed too much leather licking here today.

Sarah   I just think it might be appropriate if we made it Grace's turn next year.

Grace   I don't want that. You know how he'd react.

Sarah   Quite frankly I don't care how he reacts.

Grace   I don't blame you, the way he tried to get rid of you.

Sarah   Let's not go into that.

Angela   What did he do, Mum?

Sarah   Just let's say it backfired. It only made me more determined to marry your father.

Martin   Happy day.

Angela   What did he do?

Sarah   He took me aside while your father was playing cricket or football or something and told me to stop wearing the pants – or go and find someone who had enough guts not to let me.

Martin *stares at his father, who says nothing.*

Sarah   As far as I'm concerned we celebrate Grace's birthday next year or we celebrate none at all.

There is silence. They look at **Col**.

Col   No problem. This is going to be my last birthday in any case.

Angela's Room

Shakespeare *appears.* **Angela** *enters.*

Angela   Do you realise you're probably the most famous person in the history of the world?

Shakespeare (*stares at her*)   But what of Beaumont and Fletcher?

Angela   No one's ever heard of them these days.

Shakespeare   But t'was said by all they had more pithy and effectual wit than I. They were noblemen.

Angela   Gone. Vanished.

Shakespeare   Thou dost amaze me. In all the world's history *I* am of such import?

Angela *nods at him.*

Shakespeare   I laid down this quill ere I turned fifty –
its scribblings no longer garnered profit nor praise. My final
years were spent in deepest melancholy, thinking that my
life had been for nought.

Angela   It was all worth it.

She hands him a bound volume of his collected works.
Shakespeare *looks at it with amazement and begins thumbing
through it.* **Swain** *comes up behind* **Shakespeare** *with a pistol
in his hand.*

Angela   Leave him!

Swain *shrugs and puts the pistol away, but wrenches the volume out
of* **Shakespeare***'s hands.*

Swain   He's a dead man in any case.

Tutorial Room

Swain*'s tutorial group is gathered.* **Swain** *places*
Shakespeare*'s collected works disdainfully on the ground.*

Swain   Twenty, even ten years ago, you would have been
here studying 'Literature' with a capital 'L'. By some
mysterious process a 'Canon' of the great works of
'Literature' would have been selected for you to study.
These works would almost always be works by dead white
European males. The doyen of all of them of course would
have been William Shakespeare. You would have been told
that within this great literature those eternal 'truths' about
'human nature' were waiting to be found. (*Silence. He waits a
second or two.*) All right. It's twenty years ago and we're
reading Proust. He describes how if the Swann family
received a visit, an invitation or even a mere friendly word
from someone important, they would publicise this by any
means at their disposal. We would decide that this social
climbing tendency *was* part of 'human nature', and taking
our cue from the ironically disapproving tone of the

narrator, a tendency not to be emulated. Our project of liberal humanist ethical self-improvement would progress one step forward. Unfortunately the project was essentially dishonest and phoney.

Steve   In what way?

Swain   In its assumption that 'Literature' *does* deliver penetrating and universal insights about 'human nature'.

Melissa   Social climbing *is* surely part of human nature.

Swain   In some societies the loudest voices do hold sway, but there are many societies, like the Hopi Indians, in which social climbing is totally unknown. All a text ultimately contains are the ideologies a particular society has used to construct its social 'reality'.

Angela   Shakespeare's 'insights' into humanity are really just ideology?

Swain   Dressed up in the garb of brilliantly inventive metaphor and rhetoric, yes. Patriarchal ideology.

Angela   Then why is he the most famous person in the Earth's history?

Swain   Why is Madonna currently the second most famous? Madonna used the metaphor and rhetoric of body language to suggest that she is the sexiest person alive, Shakespeare uses the metaphor and rhetoric of language to suggest that he is the wisest person who ever lived. My private feeling is that a night in bed with Madonna would reveal to me what a night in bed with Shakespeare has often revealed. Scratch the surface and there ain't much goin' on underneath.

Angela   I'm not sure I can agree with that, Dr Swain.

Swain   Let's all take Shakespeare to bed shall we and see if we can advance this debate a little further. And thank you all for being such a lively and questioning tutorial group.

Outside the Tutorial Room

Melissa   I told you we shouldn't've done this bloody unit, Angela.

Angela   I'm finding it interesting.

Melissa   You're joking. I'm going to see if I can switch to Professor Meacham's class. At least he still teaches *literature*, not this appalling 'theory'.

Steve   They call Meacham the black hole. Go too near and time stands still.

Melissa   Anything would be better than Swain. (*She sees someone out of the corner of her eye.*) Julian! Catch you two later.

She moves off rapidly in full pursuit mode.

Angela   I'm not sure I agree with everything he says but *I* think the course is very stimulating.

Steve   Really?

Steve *looks depressed.*

Angela   What's the matter?

Steve   I can hardly understand a word he's saying. Does it really make sense to you? How can words 'construct' us?

Angela   It's just a fancy way of saying that we don't really have any truly original thoughts. Even the stuff we think of as our owns ideas are really somebody else's.

Steve   Is *that* all he's saying?

Angela (*nods*)   And because we think they're our very own thoughts we hardly ever question them.

Steve   I shouldn't be here.

Angela   Where?

Steve   At university. I had to do HSC twice and even then only got in by one mark.

Angela   Look, it −

Steve   We both listen to Swain – I get brain fog, you get brilliant.

Angela   Not totally.

Steve   Would you –

Angela   What?

Steve   You like movies?

Angela   Some.

Steve   Like to come to one?

Angela   Which one?

Steve   Any one you like. I don't mind if it's a 'chick's' movie.

Angela   A 'chick's' movie?

Steve   Crying and stuff. I quite like 'em.

Angela   Steve –

Steve   Wrong? Sexist?

Angela   Surely there aren't 'chicks' movies and 'guys' movies, there are just 'movies'.

Steve   I read it in the paper. It said this is a full-on 'chick's movie'.

Angela   That's exactly Dr Swain's point. The patriarchy would like us to think that males and females are essentially different but we don't have to believe it every time we read it.

Steve   OK, lets see the Jean-Claude Van Damme flick.

Angela   No!

Steve   Because it's a 'guy's' movie?

Angela   Because it depicts sexist and violent behaviour as being natural and inevitable.

Steve   All right, you choose the movie.

Angela   If we do go we should both choose.

Steve   We can't choose a chick's movie, we can't choose a guy's movie? What the hell can we choose?

Angela   There *are* movies which depict women as intelligent –

Steve (*nodding*)   Capable, courageous, calm, coping, resourceful, heroic, fantastic –

Angela   You prefer the sexist status quo?

Steve   No! Look, I don't want to insult women, be unfair to women, patronise women, use women, or inhibit women, but every time I open my mouth I seem to do all five! I just want to know how to behave, because someday, believe it or not, I would like to live with a woman, maybe even – gasp – marry a woman. Would you like to come to a movie or would you not? And that is *not* an implicit proposal of marriage *or* a signal of impending date rape.

Angela   Why are you asking me?

Steve (*swivelling around*)   There's no one else around.

Angela   Seriously.

Steve   Because I thought you might say yes.

Angela   Why didn't you ask Melissa?

Steve   Do you think she would?

Angela *is not amused.*

Steve   You're more my type.

Angela   Why?

Steve   Opposites attract. You're intelligent.

Angela   So's Melissa. She got a higher HSC score than I did.

Steve   Have you got her number?

Angela *is even less amused.*

Steve Why are you trying to push me on to Melissa? Every time I look at her she's got half a dozen guys around her that look as if they've been genetically engineered.

Angela So you *are* asking me because you can't get her?

Steve Look, do you want to come to a movie or don't you?

Angela I'll think about it.

Steve *shrugs and goes.* **Angela** *turns round to call him but he is gone. She admonishes herself.*

Angela's Kitchen – Half an Hour Later

Angela *walks into her house in a foul mood.*

Martin Angela, could you please unstack the dishwasher?

Angela Do it yourself!

Martin I'm cooking the meal for you and your mother!

Angela I've got an *incredible* workload, I'm doing a subject called Lit Theory that is *extremely* demanding, but sure, I'll unstack the dishwasher, I'll take the rubbish out, I'll clean the bathroom. Who cares if I fail?

Martin (*wearily*) Go and do your work. I'll do it.

Angela And just tell Mum not to come up to my room and give me 'Agonies of the career woman part two thousand and ten', I'm busy!

She storms off. **Martin** *stares after her.* **Sarah** *comes in.*

Sarah Angela home?

Martin Yes.

Sarah I'll just go upstairs and say hello to her.

Martin I wouldn't.

Sarah Why?

Martin   Our daughter is not currently in a parent-positive phase. How was life in the boardroom?

Sarah   It's always the same. I sit there listening in amazement as my rejected ideas come back, like the swallows to Capistrano, and are accepted instantly.

*She tastes a spoonful of **Martin**'s cooking and tries to disguise the fact she is unimpressed.*

We could have ordered take-away. You didn't have to cook.

Martin   I quite like it. It fills in time. I'm still not in the Paul Bocuse class though am I, truthfully?

Sarah   I can truthfully say you are getting better.

She grins and kisses him affectionately on the cheek.

And you've always been stunning in the bedroom.

Martin (*nods*)   Not everyone can make a bed in under two minutes.

Sarah (*pointing upstairs*)   You're sure she wouldn't like –

Martin   Stay away. Believe me. Stay away.

Martin *makes a sign of the cross to ward off the evil emanations coming from their daughter's room upstairs.*

The Tutorial Room

Angela *prepares to give her paper on Shakespeare.*

Angela   I have to say that I started this essay with a great deal of scepticism. Because of this I deliberately chose one of Shakespeare's plays that I remembered as having a particularly vibrant and articulate female character who seemed to shape the agenda. I was certain that this play would absolutely refute the charge that Shakespeare wrote ideologically and from the perspective of the patriarchy. The play is *As You Like It* and the character is Rosalind.

She looks down at her paper and consults it intermittently from here on.

Rosalind flees her uncle and goes to the Forest of Arden disguised as a man in order to protect herself. This allows her to test and tease her suitor Orlando, by warning him, in her guise as a man, of all the supposed frailities of womankind. Women, she tells him, are 'changeable, proud, capricious, apish, shallow, inconstant, full of tears, full of smiles, now liking him, now loathing him, now weeping for him, now spitting at him'. I got excited as I read it for surely Rosalind requires Orlando to disagree, but no, when Orlando reacts to this checklist *approvingly* this is exactly the woman that Rosalind proceeds to *become*. She pines, she sighs, she gets paranoid he might run off with some other woman, gets distraught when he's late, faints when she hears he's been injured, and is so desperate to get married that she organises the wedding herself and tells Orlando, 'To you I give myself, for I am yours.' Patriarchal ideology has fashioned the characters, the values and the very structure of this play. Dr Swain's assertion that literature is essentially ideological couldn't in my opinion have been better illustrated.

Steve   Hang on, Angela.

Angela   Have you read the play, Steve?

Steve   Yes.

Angela   Is anything I've said untrue?

Steve   No, but listen, the guy was writing four hundred years ago, and –

Angela   He was trapped within the values of his time, or perhaps cleverly and ironically sending up the values of his time?

Steve   I guess.

Angela   At one point Rosalind apologises for interrupting her friend Celia but says she can't help it because she's a woman and women can't stop any thought they have coming straight out of their mouths. Shakespeare isn't *trapped* in or *ironic* about patriarchal ideology, he's totally complicit, and in fact a major producer of that ideology.

Melissa   Angela, don't be so humourless. Shakespeare's just having some fun.

Angela   Oh yes, the 'humourless' feminist. At whose *expense* is he having fun, Melissa?

Melissa   Don't get so worked up. All the literature these days is about what arseholes men are, so we're getting our own back.

Angela   Melissa, if you think the patriarchy has been overthrown because a few contemporary female writers are at last criticising it, then you're mistaken.

Swain   In general the patriarchy welcomes such criticism because it gives the appearance that change is underway when in fact the male monopoly on real power is still almost total.

Angela *exchanges a grateful look with* **Swain**.

Swain   Thank you for a most stimulating and incisive paper, Angela. Could you perhaps give us a summary of your paper, Melissa?

Melissa   I looked at *The Taming of the Shrew*, because this is precisely where I expected to find ideology but I have to say I found little to none.

Angela   Melissa? You have to be joking. What about the relationship between Petruchio and Kate?

Melissa   I think it's one of the sexiest I've ever read.

Angela *is speechless with fury and disbelief.*

Angela   Melissa, Petruchio does a deal with Kate's father to marry her for money –

Melissa   Angela –

Angela   Petruchio *announces* that Sunday is the wedding

day, to which Kate says, quite rightly, 'I'll see thee hanged
first,' and the next thing we know Kate turns up on
Sunday and waits docilely for Petruchio to arrive. When he
finally gets there he's wearing appalling clothes, drags her
off before the start of her wedding reception, starves her,
doesn't let her sleep and when she finally cracks after a
period of prolonged psychological terror –

Melissa   Angela –

Angela   She tells the other wives . . .

*She picks up her copy of the text and flips to an obviously well-
marked passage.*

> 'Thy husband is thy Lord, thy life, thy keeper,
> Thy head, thy sovereign; one that cares for thee,
> And for thy maintenance; commits his body
> To painful labour both by sea and land,
> To watch the night in storms, the day in cold,
> Whilst thou liest warm at home, secure and safe;
> And craves no other tribute at thy hands
> But love, fair looks, and true obedience –
> Too little payment for so great a debt.'

Melissa   Are you giving this paper or am I?

Swain   What's your reading then, Melissa?

Melissa   I think that Kate is spirited, sure, but also
totally spoilt.

Angela   Oh Migod!

Melissa   Angela!

Swain   Angela, let her have her say.

Angela *fumes.*

Melissa   My reading is that Kate has been totally spoilt
and indulged and that her undoubted intelligence has had
no other outlet than to humiliate others. Petruchio is smart
enough and tough enough to play her at her own game.
He makes himself more bad-tempered than she is to show

her how others suffer from this kind of behaviour. He makes her for the first time in her life *empathise* with others. He changes her from a Shrew to a functioning human being.

Angela   So the super smart male triumphs over the moderately smart female upon which she declares him her Lord and Master and the natural patriarchal order is restored. Great.

Melissa   That speech at the end is just lip service.

Angela   It's abject grovelling.

Melissa   I bet that if Pertruchio tried to pull anything two weeks after the play ends he'd get every bit as good as he got.

Angela   How can you assume that?

Melissa   I just have a feeling.

Steve   So do I.

Angela   You would. (*To* **Melissa**.) Why would Kate turn up to marry someone who's behaved like a pig to her?

Melissa   Because she knows instinctively he's the only one who can tame her.

Angela   Spirited women need to find macho men to control them?

Melissa   Maybe they do.

Angela   God, that says it all!

Melissa   I'm sorry but I liked, was attracted to, and would probably marry someone like Petruchio. I am obviously a hopeless victim of the patriarchal construction of womanhood. I'm sorry. Shoot me.

Swain   Melissa, the whole point of this course is to allow you to identify the ideologies that are constraining you.

Melissa   I'm obviously trapped in and happily complicit with the dominant ideology. Just call me Bimbo brain.

Melissa *glares at* **Swain** *and* **Angela** *and leaves the tutorial.*

Outside the Class

Angela *is still fuming.*

Steve Hi.

Angela Hi.

Steve Look, you had some good points but I think Melissa did too.

Angela I'm sorry, but I think I was right.

Steve Fine. I suppose a film is out of the question?

Angela Steve, I think this course *is* saying something important. Did you *really* think *Taming of the Shrew* wasn't sexist?

Steve Yes, *The Shrew* is definitely sexist. Husbands as Lords and Masters – definitely offensive to modern tastes.

Angela And it doesn't worry you?

Steve Do you really think men are going to come surging out of a performance of *The Shrew*, bellowing, 'Back to the kitchen, bitch!' The ideology of feminism is beating the Bard hands down. Everywhere I *look* I see the humourless, sexually repressed, dour young women it's 'constructed'. They won't even go to movies.

Angela I'm too busy.

Steve Does that mean no, not for the moment, or no, get lost for ever?

Angela It means at the moment I'm busy.

Steve The thing I can't work out is how come babies are still apparently being born. It's obviously not going to happen much longer.

Angela Ring up Melissa and act like Petruchio. You'll

have all the babies you want.

Angela *turns and walks off angrily.*

Swain's Office

Angela *is alone with* **Swain**.

Angela   It only takes a close look at the texts to show conclusively how conservative and patriarchal Shakespeare is. Why do people refuse to acknowledge it?

Swain   There's a huge Shakespeare industry worth billions of dollars, Angela.

Angela   Why him? There were far better and more radical playwrights in his era like Marlowe and Webster and Middleton.

Swain   If the patriarchy is going to turn a writer into a profitable industry, the last thing they want is a radical. Shakespeare's great virtue is that he *is* so conservative. 'Usurpers' always get their just deserts, 'legitimate' authority triumphs, and the patriarchal hierarchy is preserved.

Angela   It's depressing.

Swain   Deeply. I warned you that this course might prove disturbing.

Angela   No, it's proved *enlightening*. I'm very glad I'm doing it.

Swain   Your marks reflect your enthusiasm. You're doing extremely well.

Angela   Thank you.

Swain   Thank *you*. It's a great feeling for me when bright students like yourself start to question received wisdom and think for themselves.

Angela   I just can't *believe* Melissa. We used to be good friends.

Swain Yes, she is a worry. Her marks unfortunately reflect her lack of intellectual penetration.

Angela She's not doing . . . ?

Swain She's doing very badly.

Angela I'm sorry to hear that. I think part of her trouble is that she still seems to totally define herself in terms of her attractiveness to men.

Swain Sad.

Angela In a sense I'm more sympathetic with Steve.

Swain Why?

Angela He's a man.

Swain Being biologically male doesn't mean we have to adopt the repressive gender constructions of that role.

Angela Of course.

Swain Have you had any thoughts about your major assignment?

Angela No, I've been wracking my brains, but so far, nothing. That's actually why I'm here. To see if you could point me in possible directions.

Swain I'm happy to suggest possibilities as long as you understand that they are only suggestions.

Angela Of course.

Swain Last year one of my best students did an analysis of the controlling ideologies operating within her family.

Angela *looks at* **Swain** *with interest.*

Angela How interesting.

Swain She found that every family member's history was totally incompatible with every other family member.

Angela History is shaped in our own ideological self-interests?

Swain   Exactly. Do you think your family might prove a fruitful site for an examination like that?

Angela   I think it could prove – extremely fruitful.

Swain   It's just a suggestion.

Angela   No, it's wonderful.

Swain   Don't feel bound –

Angela   No, it's a great idea. Dr Swain –

Swain   Please call me Grant.

Angela   I just wanted to say . . .

Swain   Go on.

Angela   Now I'm too embarrassed.

Swain   Go on.

Angela   When something enormously important happens in your life you should thank the person who helped you – I'm sorry – it's just so hard in this culture to –

Swain   To what?

Angela   To say simple things like 'thank you'.

Swain   No need, I'm just doing my job.

Angela   My mother's always been a red-hot feminist, and I've always sort of believed I understood the issues, but it wasn't until I sat down and really looked at Shakespeare with newly critical eyes that I saw clearly and for the first time how *much* of our very being is manipulated and controlled by ideologies we're barely conscious of.

Swain   I'm glad.

Angela   I probably seem a very controlled and passionless person to you –

Swain   Not at all –

Angela   – but I have very, *very* strong feelings and I just felt as if the scales had suddenly been lifted from my eyes and I felt so *grateful* for what you'd done.

Swain It's my job.

Angela I know you're probably right and that we can never get outside ideology, but nevertheless I am so *happy* to be able to make the *choice* to step outside the narcissistic self-centredness of liberal humanism and as a conscious *choice* join you in the constructivist feminist multiculturalist project.

Swain I'm very glad.

Angela It is *wonderful* to come into contact with someone who has a *genuine and non-exploitative* concern for the interests of women and other exploited minorities.

Swain Thank you.

Angela I mean it.

Swain Thank you, but in a sense it is just another form of selfishness.

Angela How?

Swain Like most of us who are at least part-way human I am capable of feeling others' pain, and when I help alleviate some of that pain I am, in fact, relieving my own pain.

Angela How come so many other white middle-class males don't seem to feel minority pain like you do?

Swain I have to admit, that *is* a mystery.

Angela You're being too modest, Grant.

Swain No.

Angela You are.

Swain No.

Angela The world out there is still full of Petruchios.

Swain Surely less and less.

Angela   Don't believe it. They're everywhere.

Swain   How depressing.

Angela   I know I shouldn't tell you this, but if Petruchio walked into my bedroom tonight I'd spit on him, but if someone like you walked in – Oh God, now I'm going right over the top –

Swain   No, please –

Angela   I didn't mean it like that. I was just trying to say –

Swain   Of course, I understand totally.

Angela   Truly I wasn't trying to –

Swain   No, no of course not.

Angela   Now I'm just *so* embarrassed. I know you're a married man and I know that must have sounded like – it wasn't – truly it wasn't.

Swain   You were expressing your feelings. That's fine. The whole point of the liberal humanist project is to constrain our behaviour within such tight ethical confines that we seldom express our feelings, and almost never act on them.

Angela *looks at him.*

Angela   That's true isn't it?

Swain   That's the whole point of the ideology. (*He moves closer to her.*) I have the same warm extremely warm feelings about you. Have you read Foucault?

Angela   No.

Swain   Foucault is mandatory reading in this area. He has established that Liberal humanism attempts to divert all focus off what Roland Barthe refers to as 'jouissance' and return it to the late Capitalist requirements of personal productive efficiency and endless consumerism.

Angela   What exactly is 'jouissance'?

Swain Like all signifiers there is no absolute closure on its meaning, but the approximate signifier would, I suppose, be 'joy of life', 'joy of simply being', 'spontaneity', 'joy in the free use of – one's body'.

Angela *and* **Swain** *are by now very close.* **Angela** *backs off.*

Angela Foucault. Which of his titles would you recommend?

Swain Angela, it should be obvious that I find you extremely attractive.

Angela Likewise, but . . .

Swain But?

Angela But any sort of – liaison between –

Swain Staff and students?

Angela *nods.*

Angela Raises all sorts of ethical issues.

Swain All sorts of liberal humanist ethical issues.

Angela Ah.

Swain Foucault brilliantly exposes the way in which concepts of liberal humanist 'ethical responsibility' are used to prevent the expression of 'jouissance' in every structured organisation. Including academia.

Angela But you – you and your wife – there would be no shortage of – presumably – 'jouissance' in your lives.

Swain Joanna accepted an appointment at James Cook University.

Angela Queensland?

Swain Associate Professor of Sociology. She's doing very well. Better than I am.

Angela Ah.

Swain Which makes me extremely proud of course. We

try and see each other as much as possible.

Angela   I see.

Swain   But of course inevitably there's not as much – 'jouissance' between us as there used to be. (*He gives a hollowly nonchalant laugh.*) Do you like films?

Angela   Love them.

Swain   West African cuisine?

Angela   I've never actually –

Swain   Brilliant. Peasant fare without any trace of affectation. Are you free tonight?

Angela (*tempted*)   I'd like to but I've got a big history assignment.

Swain   Ah.

Angela   Five thousand words.

Swain   The Valhalla is showing *Godzilla Versus the Smog Monster*, which I'm told is an hilarious deconstruction of post-war American foreign policy.

Angela   I think I'd better work on the essay.

Swain   When you've got a clear space?

Angela   I'd love to.

Angela *disengages herself reluctantly.*

Angela's Room

Shakespeare *is sitting reading his collected works.* **Angela** *comes in and listens to him before he realises she is there.*

Shakespeare   'To thine own self be true,
    And it must follow, as the night the day,
    Thou canst not then be false to any man.'

He shakes his head in admiration.

I can scarce believe I wrote it.

He sees another.

'There is nothing good or bad, but thinking makes it so.'

He shakes his head again. Then sees **Angela**.

Angela   OK. Your language is exceptional. Inventive, musical, resonant.

Shakespeare   But?

Angela (*takes the book of quotations from him and reads*) 'There is a tide in the affairs of *men* / Which, taken at the flood leads on to fortune; / Omitted, all the voyage of their life / Is bound in shallows and in miseries.'

Shakespeare (*nods*)   A favourite of mine.

Angela   Life's outcome is presented as only and always metaphorically subject to vast uncontrollable currents which must be exploited by a skilled *male* mariner at a single crucial instant in order to arrive at the privileged term 'fortune' in the fortune/failure dichotomy.

Shakespeare (*puzzled*)   Speakest thou English?

Angela   William, there isn't just *one* instant of significant choice in our lives –

Shakespeare   Had I stayed in Stratford and never seized the opportunity to become an actor –

Angela   Then you would have been a far better husband to your wife and spared the world a succession of plays in which women are reduced to either ciphers or victims.

Shakespeare *stares at her.*

Shakespeare   Marry, 'tis but a brief instance from thy happy disclosure that I am history's most favoured creation, to this new intelligence that I am soon t'be again its most obscure. And why? Some insufficiency in my *women*?

Angela   See how you just said *women*. Like 'how could something as minor as *women* be my downfall'. Look, I am sorry, William, but there's a whole new agenda out there. It's hard to explain but your plays don't reflect the issues and realities of today.

Shakespeare　But human nature is surely constant?

Angela　William, you weren't really writing about human nature. You were writing your patriarchal *beliefs* about human nature.

Shakespeare　Surely you jest?

Angela (*shakes her head*)　It's been definitively established by our leading thinkers that there is no fixed 'human nature'. We are infinitely malleable and act out the various roles imposed on us by the discourses and ideologies that construct us.

Shakespeare　Pray tell me then which ideology has constructed the good Dr Swain?

Angela　Like me, Dr Swain is committed to the project of feminist multiculturalism.

Shakespeare　An ideology methinks which argues against the misuse of your sex?

Angela　That's its central proposition.

Shakespeare　Then how is't the same Dr Swain did tempt thee with seduction's wiles?

Angela　No, sorry. That was *not* seduction, William. That was an attempt to find 'jouissance'.

Shakespeare　It seemed to me a sly conceit to lure thee to his bed.

Angela　Frankly, William, that sort of remark is a good indication of why your writing *isn't* timeless. In future epochs men and women will find 'jouissance' in a non-exploitative spirit of common consent.

Shakespeare *looks at her, a trace of a grin on his face.*

Shakespeare　Wilt thou then pursue 'jouissance' with the

good Dr Swain?

Angela   Probably. I'd just like some time to think.

Shakespeare   About what, I pray you? His choice of movies? *Godzilla Versus the Smog Monster?*

Angela   About emotional involvement.

Shakespeare   But 'jouissance', it doth seem, is pleasure without the irksome bonds of betrothal?

Angela   I haven't totally shaken myself free of the dominant ideology.

Shakespeare   Could'st not thy hesitation issue rather from that 'human nature' thou claims thou hast not?

Angela   William, it's late. I need some sleep.

She turns away.

Shakespeare   Now is the summer of my new content
    Made deepest winter by that slimy sophist Swain.

Angela   Dr Swain has been courageous enough to point out that you misused your talent to help perpetuate female servitude. The ending of *As You Like It* is an absolute disgrace.

Shakespeare   'Tis surely one of the happiest most joyous endings of any play that I have wrought.

Angela   Not just *one* idealised wedding but *four*! Four female ciphers racing like lemmings towards total personality eclipse!

Shakespeare   Eight human beings entering a joyous and fulfilling partnership!

Angela   Four women destroying themselves.

Shakespeare   Have you ever seen it played?

Angela   I've read it.

Shakespeare   'Twas written to be played!

Shakespeare *gestures, the backdrop disappears, and suddenly we are in the Forest of Arden, and part-way into the joyful marriage and reconciliation scene at the end of* As You Like It. **Col** *plays Duke Senior,* **Melissa** *plays Rosalind,* **Steve** *plays Orlando,* **Martin** *plays Touchstone,* **Sarah** *plays Audrey,* **Swain** *plays Oliver,* **Monica** *plays Celia,* **Jessica** *plays Hymen,* **Grace** *plays Phebe, and* **Shakespeare** *himself steps in at the last moment to play Silvius. Hymen, Rosalind and Celia enter to join the others. Sweet music plays.*

Jessica   Then is there mirth in heaven
When earthly things made even
Atone together.
Good Duke, receive thy daughter;
Hymen from heaven brought her,
Yea, brought her hither.
That thou mightst join her hand with his
Whose heart within his bosom is.

Melissa (*to* **Col**)   To you I give myself, for I am yours.
(*To* **Steve**.) To you I give myself for I am yours.

Col   If there be truth in sight, you are my daughter.

Steve   If there be truth in sight, you are my Rosalind.

Phebe sees that her heart-throb, Ganymede, has suddenly changed sex and become Rosalind.

Grace   If sight and shape be true,
Why then my love adieu!

Melissa (*to* **Col**)   I'll have no father, if you be not he.
(*To* **Steve**.) I'll have no husband if you be not he.
(*To* **Grace**.) Nor ne'er wed woman, if you be not she.

Jessica   Peace ho! I bar confusion:
'Tis I must make conclusion
Of these most strange events.
Here's eight that must take hands.
To join in Hymen's bands,
If truth holds true contents.

To **Steve** *and* **Melissa**.

You and you no cross shall part.

To **Swain** *and* **Monica**.

You and you are heart in heart.

To **Grace**, *indicating* **Shakespeare**.

You to his love must accord,
Or have a woman to your Lord.

To **Martin** *and* **Sarah**.

You and you are sure together.
As the winter to foul weather.

To all.

Whiles a wedlock hymn we sing,
Feed yourselves with questioning,
That reason wonder may diminish
How thus we met, and these things finish.

The music swells and they all sing, hopefully in brilliant harmony. During the chorus **Jessica** *leads* **Angela** *across and sits her on* **Steve**'s *knee, ejecting* **Melissa**. **Angela** *finds herself participating in the subsequent action.*

All   Wedding is great Juno's crown,
O blessed bond of board and bed!
'Tis Hymen peoples every town;
High weldlock then be honoured
Honour, high honour, and renown
To Hymen, god of every town!

Steve (*to* **Angela**)   O my dear, welcome thou are to me.

Angela (*to* **Steve**)   Now thou art mine;
Thy faith my fancy to thee doth combine.

Col   Proceed, proceed. We will begin these rites,
As we do trust they'll end, in true delights.

The music rises and the newlyweds execute a spirited and joyful nuptial dance. **Shakespeare** *notices* **Swain** *edging towards* **Angela** *and moves up to her.*

Shakespeare   Are things now so poorly 'twixt woman and man that you wish to banish even the *possibility* of a fruitful coupling?

Swain   Angela is intelligent enough to see this flossy tableau for what it is. A hopelessly contrived and pernicious ideological confection aimed at perpetuating the patriarchy.

Shakespeare   A fantastical, magical, diversion from the tepid weariness of sordid reality. A statement of hope.

Swain (*drawing his pistol*)   For four centuries we've suffered this insidious shit! Enough!

Angela *intervenes, placing herself angrily between the two men.*

Angela   No!

Swain *reluctantly pockets his pistol.*

Swain (*to* **Angela**)   What possible relevance has rubbish like that in a time when one in every two marriages ends in gut-wrenching divorce!

Shakespeare (*to* **Angela**)   What possible future is there for humanity without the bonding in love of woman and man!

Angela *looks from one to the other. She cannot choose. She clicks her fingers and* **Shakespeare** *then* **Swain** *disappear. She looks worried and perplexed. She clicks her fingers again and she and the dance disappear as the lights snap off.*

Act Two

Lecture Theatre

Swain *walks down towards the lectern.*

Swain (*to audience*) Halfway through the year I like to assemble you all again to talk about the sort of progress we are making in our various tutorial groups. The groups that I have been part of have proved very stimulating and from the reports I'm getting from my tutors I am getting the very definite impression that this is an unusually perceptive year. What is especially rewarding is how many of you are now starting to discern the sinews of manipulation underneath the cloak of ideological invisibility that the dominant ideology tries to draw about itself. The range and scope of the assignments you are about to commence is truly exciting. Nicky Yoh is investigating the rhetorical deceit used in a recent attempt to oppose a programme of kindergarten cross-dressing and non-sexist play routines and Rosie Trundos is interrogating patriarchal assumptions in the rules of association of regional brass bands in the 1890s. One of the boldest investigations, is Angela Judd's proposal to look at the mythologies of her three-generational family as controlling patriarchal texts, currently under interrogation by the contesting discourses of non-essentialist feminism. I can't wait to grip Angela's – come to grips with Angela's – salient points in what I'm sure will be a precise anatomical – dissection of great position – precision. When you've started to collect your data, Angela, please let's talk.

Col and Grace's Living Room

Angela *is with her grandfather* **Col**. *She is fiddling with a tape recorder.* **Col** *watches her.*

Col This is a university project?

Angela (*nods*) How's your –

Col Cancer? It's no big deal. My back's wrecked and I've been in more or less constant pain for the last forty years.

Angela I'm sorry.

Col Don't be. There's a time for all of us to go and I've reached it.

Angela Everyone's going to be very sad.

Col Come off it, love. They'll all throw a bloody party.

Angela I think that what they said at your birthday –

Col You heard 'em. I've ruined all their bloody lives. What do you want me to talk about into that thing?

Angela I just want you to answer some questions about how you see your life in retrospect.

Col Retrospect's all I've got. So what are you trying to prove?

Angela Nothing.

Col Come on. You're a red-hot feminist like your mum aren't you?

Angela I tend to see eye to eye with her on most things.

Col So you're trying to show what a rotten old chauvinist bastard I've been aren't you?

Angela I'm interested in how *you* see yourself.

Col Do you think I ruined all their lives?

Angela I'll be trying to keep as open a mind as possible.

Col You'd be the first feminist that ever has.

Angela Why do you say that?

Col Well you're not interested in truth, none of you. You've just got a fixed set of ideas in your heads and the truth can go to hell.

Angela   There isn't an absolute 'truth', Grandpa, we socially construct 'truth', but look that's not −

Col   You lot have to have the babies. Much as you hate it, that's a truth and you're stuck with it.

Angela   We have the biological capacity to have babies, yes, but the *desire* to *have* babies is socially constructed, or at least intensified.

Col   Rubbish! It's in your bloody nature, and that's where all the trouble starts. If you're going to have your little bundle of joy you've got to find some idiot to start it and look after you. First choice naturally would be someone who looks like Mel Gibson and works as a heart surgeon, but you usually have to settle for choice number three hundred and ninety-six, so that poor coot cops it for the rest of his life because he's not Mel Gibson and he works as a roof tiler.

Angela   That's your explanation for the tension between the sexes?

Col   Yeah and I'm sticking with it.

Angela   Let's move on shall we? Is it true you advised my mother to stop her relationship with my father?

Col   Too right. And by Christ was I right about that one. Sorry, they're your parents, but if you try and tell me they're happy I'll laugh.

Angela   I think that basically they *are* happy.

Col   Are *you*?

Angela   I know Mum was away a lot, and I missed her, but I'm very proud of what she's achieved.

Col   You were bawling your eyes out the night you did so well in the school play. She was in bloody New York.

Angela   Yes I know, but −

Col   I saw you. I was there. She should have been bloody horsewhipped.

Angela If Dad had had to be in New York you wouldn't have felt that.

Col All right. I'm a dinosaur. I think mothers should be with their children. And you should have had one brother and sister at least. If you're going to have kids it's a crime just to have one.

Angela Why?

Col Only children get spoilt rotten and you're no exception. When's the last time you ever washed a dish?

Angela It was Mum's choice not to have any more children and I can understand it. She was determined to have a career.

Col What's so great about getting to the top in a firm that researches how to launch a new brand of cigarettes? Is that more important than being there when your daughter needs you? She ought to be horsewhipped!

Angela Grandpa! You're being incredibly sexist!

Col I'm telling you the truth as I see it! Ever since all that bra burning you think you can bully the Christ out of us and we've just got to sit here and take it.

Angela Can't you see –

Col I went to the bank yesterday and there's a woman teller with a sign behind her that says 'too many men, not enough bullets'. If the sign said 'too many women –' the guy would be hauled off to jail.

Angela You've had the upper hand for eight thousand years –

Col So now men cop it for the next eight thousand?

Angela There's going to be a bit of evening up.

Col A bit? It's the bloody duck hunting season and we're the ducks. Angela, I'm too old to change the way I am, and I think you're a classy little heifer and that the world would have been better off with one more of you than one more cigarette brand. Let's leave it at that.

Angela I think we'd better. You tried to get rid of my mother because you perceived her as being too strong?

Col Is this confidential?

Angela Absolutely.

Col None of the family is ever going to read any of this?

Angela I give you my word.

Col It wasn't so much your mother being strong. Your father's too weak.

Angela *looks shocked and hurt.*

Col He's my son and I love him, but he's too nervy and anxious to please. Just about anyone can walk all over him. How's he coping since he lost his job?

Angela Why haven't you asked him?

Col I didn't want to embarrass him.

Angela I think he would have appreciated it. I don't think he's adjusting very well.

Col Poor kid. I knew he was in for a rough time right from the time he was four or five. He could never stand up for himself.

Angela He didn't fit the traditional male role?

Col If you can't stand up for yourself you sink, male or female. Jesus, you think your mother can't stand up for herself? The only difference between her and a pit bull terrier is that when *it's* going for the kill *its* jaws lock shut!

Angela *ignores the insult.*

Angela Spiros Spyrokakadakis. Is it true that you –?

Col He wasn't serious about Monica.

Angela   Why do you say that?

Col   Have a close look at your aunt. And she looked just as bad in those days.

Angela *looks annoyed but controls herself.*

Col   Men get excited about women who look good. Sorry but no one 'constructs' that fact either. (*Beat.*) They've all got to have someone to blame for the fact that their lives didn't pan out the way they'd dreamed and I'm it.

Angela   Monica and Jessica are bitter that they didn't get the chance to go to university.

Col   I know, they should have gone. They were both bright girls but things were really tough financially. They both should have gone.

Angela   Grandma says you were earning really good money and she still can't understand why things were so tight.

Col   You said you wanted to know how I view my life in retrospect? You really want to know?

Angela   Yes.

Col   OK. My life was tremendous, right up to the time I married your grandmother. Cricket, football, billiards, dances, mates, motorbikes, the odd beer and a dead easy job – working for the council. Paradise. Then along comes this pretty little bit of fluff, butter wouldn't melt in her mouth, just wanted to please my every whim – hah, what a sucker I was. Suddenly – I'm married, but before I even get to find out what a tough little nut your grandma really is, along comes the Second World War. So of course a bloke does the right thing and finds himself facing the invincible Imperial Japanese Army on the Kokoda trail. Now I'm not going to tell you what I went through up there, because I can hardly bear thinking about it even now. Most of my mates died, but I survived. Point one for your bloody feminist theories – when there's a war on and some poor fools have got to go it's blokes who get sent. And don't tell me it's the women who get raped because there wasn't any raping going on up there on the trail. All that was happening was that I was either delirious with malaria or getting shot at. OK, I get home from the war and the minute I climb into bed your grandma is pregnant with your father. No pill in those days. She stops working and my council job is paid nowhere near enough for my new responsibilities. The only way to make enough money is to do some job that's so tough that not many others will do it. Like most of your sex you'll end up sitting on your bum somewhere working at a desk, so you'll never get to understand what it's like to lug millions of tiles up onto thousands of roofs, year in year out starting at five every morning. And when you're up there you know that one day, sooner or later, you're going to have your one bad fall. So you always take on a partner so you can help each other out with money when your time comes. I had my big one when I was in my early thirties. In hospital for three weeks but luckily, except for a back that was agony from there on in, I was more or less intact. The doctor said I should never have to go up on roofs again the back was so bad – three fused vertebrae – but by this time I had three kids.

Angela Wasn't it about then that Grace wanted to go into business with her friend?

Col No, that was later. I was offered a Greenkeeper's job which would've been easier on my back, but it didn't pay much and Grace didn't want to go back to work and leave the kids at that stage so back I went up on the roofs. Point two for you feminists. If a bloke has kids he's the one who finally has to earn the dough.

Angela Not really. These days –

Col It might be different these days but that's how it was then! Yeah now it's fine. You've got the pill and easy abortions, but in my day it wasn't so easy to plan. And in my day husbands didn't run out on their obligations. OK so I'm back up there on the roofs and every day is agony. Then disaster. My partner Billy Headen goes down twenty feet and he's finished for life. Total wreck. Now in those days there's no compensation, no insurance and I'm all Billy's got. He's saddled with three kids too, one of them six months old. Now the partnership is only meant to tide you over, but his wife could only get part-time work and had to look after him as well as the kids.

Angela   You supported him?

Col (*nods*)   And this is the part your grandmother's never known. I supported that family for nearly fifteen years. She knew I helped them out a bit but I never told her they got a third of what I earned because I knew she would've screamed blue bloody murder. That's why we never had any cash to spare. That's why I couldn't find ten thousand to set her up in business. In any case her friends didn't make a fortune in that bloody dress shop. They barely made wages.

Angela   It seems a very – generous thing to have done for your friend.

Col   He would've done the same for me.

Angela *looks at him.*

Col   So yeah, I gave your father a hard time, but I didn't have the money to pay an assistant. Someone had to help or I would've gone under.

Angela *does not know what to say.*

Col   It makes me sick when I watch TV these days and it pushes the idea that life is happy and glamorous and easy. I'll tell you that for me and the majority of blokes in my generation life was anything but glamorous, it was sheer grinding bloody survival, and I'd just like the occasional woman somewhere, sometime to realise that and say 'thank you'.

Angela's Room

Angela *is alone, thinking.* **Shakespeare** *appears and sits down beside her. He holds up something he's been reading.*

Shakespeare   I have read thy essay on *As You Like It*. And thy words on *The Taming of the Shrew*.

Angela   Did you understand what I was getting at?

Shakespeare (*reading*)   'Thy husband is thy Lord; thy life, thy keeper' – Somewhat in excess, I grant thee, but since meeting thy grandfather this other should surely strike at thy heart.
(*He reads.*) 'One that cares for thee,
   And for thy maintenance; commits his body
   To painful labour both by sea and land,
   To watch the night in storms, the day in cold,
   Whilst thou liest warm at home, secure and safe;'
He fought the –

Angela   Japanese.

Shakespeare   Japanese. He bore score on score of tiles aloft to wintry roofs. And those (*He looks at her essay.*) 'idealised patriarchal alliances' thou disparage'st so – what of those fifteen years supporting his partner, sadly injured?

Angela   OK, it's a little more complicated than I thought, but don't try and tell me patriarchal power is a myth!

Shakespeare   Thy grandfather did not seem to hold much of that patriarchal power. To me it doth seem to me he held absolutely none.

Angela   OK, some men don't have power, but at least they have the *chance* at power which is more than we ever get!

Shakespeare   A woman of thy force of tongue will attain whatever she wants to attain. If you remain a 'victim' 'tis surely of your own doing.

Angela *looks at him.*

Angela's Living Room

Angela *is alone with her mother.*

Sarah   My life? (*Pause.*) Difficult.

Angela   Yes I can imagine.

Sarah   I'm not sure you can.

Angela   Of course I can't –

Sarah   Less than three per cent of top management in this country are women. Did you know that?

Angela   You've told me. Often.

Sarah   You've heard me complaining, I know. But until you go through it yourself you really won't have any understanding. Do you know how guilty I felt about you?

Angela   I've told you. It's OK.

Sarah   Is it?

Angela   It's pretty obvious I'm not indelibly scarred.

Sarah   Is it?

Angela   Yes. And I'm proud of what you achieved.

Sarah   I'm still full of guilt. Up to here. (*She indicates a level above her head.*) Every time I see a movie with a mother cuddling her baby I get tears in my eyes. It's pathetic.

Angela   You were a good mother.

Sarah   I know I was probably fine. I was there on all the important occasions, but this society is so deeply sexist that it makes women in my position feel incredibly guilty. I know I was probably fine.

Angela *is silent,* **Sarah** *notes the silence.*

Sarah   I *was* there on every important occasion. Except that school play. And maybe a few others. I was fine. What's wrong? I wasn't there? Is that what you're saying?

Angela I know how hard it was for you.

Sarah I wasn't there? Is that what you're saying? Angela, you just don't know how hard it's been.

Angela I know –

Sarah When they found out I was pregnant all the men in that bloody firm practically cheered. They thought, hah, biology has caught up with the bitch. We won't see her around here for years. I'm not exaggerating. That's how they behaved. OK, you probably suffered a little, but I was determined that they were never going to be able to say that I couldn't cope with that job because . . .

Angela Of me.

Sarah I was fighting for all women. And your father refused to pick up the slack. He wanted a child, desperate for one, but when you came you were suddenly *my* responsibility.

Angela You didn't want a child?

Sarah The timing could have been better. I was *glad* don't get me wrong, I was really *glad* when it happened, but the timing –

Angela (*angry*) I'm sorry.

Sarah Angela.

Angela For being so inconvenient. I'm sorry.

Sarah Angela, as soon as I held you in my arms I knew I'd done the right thing. Believe me. And I loved nursing you. The only reason I went back to work so soon was that I wasn't going to give those bastards any ammunition to use against me.

Angela Why was it so important?

Sarah To succeed?

Angela I mean it's not as if what you do is fantastically important to the future of the world. Launching a new soap powder.

Sarah *stares at her.*

Sarah   I see.

Angela   Look, I know how hard it's been for you but at the end of the day –

Sarah   Why bother? Why not be a good mother to my child, then have another, then another? Because I wasn't going to let those bastards walk all over me. My mother was a pathetic meek squashed little creature who'd destroyed her brain with drink by the time she was fifty. There was no *way* I was ever going to be like that. (*She is close to tears but controls herself.*) I'm sorry. I know you were hurt, but I can't be everything to everyone. I've got this *demon* inside me that won't allow me to let them win. I know you were hurt and it's still ripping me apart because you're the best thing that's ever happened in my life by far, which you might not believe, but it's true.

Angela   I believe it.

Sarah   Launching soap powders is not what I'm on about. I'm about showing that I can survive in their world and forcing them to respect me.

Angela   I know.

Sarah   I just made sure I was so competent, so bloody *competent* that they had to promote me. There are dozens of them and still only one of me and they still see me as some kind of threat.

Angela   Why?

Sarah   I'm a woman so I must want to change things. And of course I do. I want to get rid of all that macho posturing and introduce a management style that's sane and collaborative and inclusive but I haven't got a ghost of a chance. It takes all my energy just to survive. You've heard all this.

Angela   Go on, please.

Sarah You want to know the truth? If your dad had a job I'd resign. Ten years ago this job was the pinnacle I desperately aspired to, but now I just don't want to be a pioneer any more. In twenty years time it might be better for women –

Angela But surely you're helping make it better.

Sarah Angela, I'm battle weary. I just don't want to be in the front line. You can't ever be true to what you are.

Angela Do you resent Dad for not having a job?

Sarah Is it that obvious?

Angela Sometimes.

Sarah He could have held on to his job if he had have been a bit more confident and tenacious. He –

Shakespeare *appears behind* **Sarah**. *She can't see him but* **Angela** *can.*

Sarah He – I don't know what I'm trying to say. (*She pauses and then it strikes her.*) You remember when we went to that production of *Taming of the Shrew* last year?

Angela *nods apprehensively, looking at* **Shakespeare**.

Sarah I looked at Petruchio and said *yes!*

Angela Mum!

Sarah In fact I said *yes, yes, yes!*

Angela Mum!

Sarah OK, your father's *lovely*. Everyone *likes* him, and I love him – but he's a bloody wimp!

Angela *stares at her.*

Sarah Angela, I read *The Female Eunuch* the day it was published and danced in the streets with joy. I've been a founding member of every women's group from WEL to five different varieties of consciousness raising, and I taught assertiveness training on a voluntary basis for years, but if you want my honest advice, go find yourself someone with heaps of money, marry him and raise six kids!

Angela   Mum!

Sarah   It couldn't be a worse bloody life than I've had!

Shakespeare *nods at* **Angela** *who flicks her fingers and makes him disappear.*

Angela's Kitchen

Angela *is interviewing her father.*

Martin   What did Dad and Mum say?

Angela   I promised them it was confidential. So is this. (*She hesitates.*) He's very guilty about how hard he worked you when you were young.

Martin   The funny part about that is that everyone assumes I hated it, including him, but nobody's bothered to ask me.

Angela   Didn't you?

Martin   Well it was bloody hard work, but I knew that he really did appreciate it. One day he even told me he couldn't've kept going without me, which is as close as Dad could ever get to expressing love.

Angela   Have you been all that much better?

Martin *looks at her with surprise.*

Angela   At expressing love?

Martin   You don't think I love you?

Angela   You didn't do all that much to show it.

Martin   Are you angry at me?

Angela   Yes, I guess I am.

Martin   Angela.

Angela My most vivid memories of you are how irritated you were when you had to do anything for me.

Martin I wasn't irritated at you. I was irritated at your mother. I know I shouldn't've been but I was.

Angela And didn't you make it clear. 'Your mother's flitted off interstate again so I guess it's up to me.'

Martin I might have said that once or twice.

Angela You said it all the time. You gave her no support and you made me feel like a total burden.

Martin I was the one that wanted a child.

Angela Yes I know. Thank you, Father, for my existence.

Martin All right. I wasn't a totally reconstructed male. I did have this prejudice that a mother should look after her child. At least as much as I did.

Angela She did. In fact for all your irritation and your long sad sighs, she still did more than you did.

Martin Women are naturally more nurturing than males.

Angela Are they?

Martin Yes. All except your mother.

Angela Do you resent her success?

Martin Yes.

Angela Why?

Martin Because I don't like being the failure of the family.

Angela You're the one defining yourself as a failure.

Martin You've just told me I've been a total failure as a father, and I was fired eighteen months ago and still haven't found another job. I don't think it's just a matter of how *I* define myself. The world seems to have passed a bit of a verdict as well.

Angela   You were never a failure as a father. I just had some criticism. And middle management positions have dried up all over the country. There are tens of thousands out of work like you.

Martin   Your mother's not. She's thriving.

Angela   You can't accept that Mum is the breadwinner?

Martin   I *accept* it. I take her money every week. I just find it demeaning.

Angela   Do you think you should?

Martin   I know I shouldn't but I do.

Angela   Do you realise what a strain that job is on her?

Martin   We hear it every night, don't we?

Angela   Do you realise that there's nothing she'd like better than to give it up?

Martin *stares at her.*

Martin   There's no way she'd give it up. It's her whole bloody life.

Angela   She's just about had as much as she can take.

Martin   Well that'd be lovely wouldn't it. *No* family income.

Angela   Couldn't you have held on to your job if you'd been a little more tenacious?

Martin   Is that what your mother said?

Angela   It's what I'm asking you.

Martin   Do you know why I lost my job? Because of that bloody therapy your mother made me do.

Angela   You've always blamed her for everything.

Martin   The general view around the firm during the takeover was that *I* was the one who had nothing to worry about. Then when the interview came I was stupid enough to tell them I'd done the therapy, thinking they'd be impressed.

Angela They should have been.

Martin You're joking. Male corporate culture has one strict rule. Never show weakness. Our team has got to always *seem* like winners to all those other corporate rivals out there. All that male 'kidding' and 'taking the piss' is just a male way of probing and testing to make sure there are no chinks in your armour.

Angela I'm sure it wasn't the therapy.

Martin They told me. It indicated I couldn't cope with stress. Out. So if I'm blaming your mother I've got good bloody reason.

Angela If you're that resentful why have you stayed?

Martin You want me out of here?

Angela Dad, I didn't say that.

Martin Why wouldn't you want me out? I've been no use to you. You said so yourself.

Angela I didn't say that. There are just some things that really hurt me and after all these years I want you to know.

Martin All right, I might have grumbled a bit, but I did take you to ballet, music, drama, sport, shopping for clothes, to movies, to parties –

Angela Other girls' dads . . .

Martin Other girls' dads what?

Angela They . . . sometimes they . . . compliment their daughters. Say how . . . nice they look. Joke about how they'll have to keep an eye on all the boys . . . you never . . . you never once made me feel . . . attractive.

Martin (*stares at her, then explodes*) Your mother said that's what men shouldn't *do* any more! Women don't want to hear that stuff. They want to be appreciated for their talents, their minds!

Angela   Did you . . . ever? Think I was . . .

Martin   Of course you are! How am I supposed to know that's what you want to hear when your mother –

Angela   Don't keep blaming Mum! Haven't you got a mind of your own! Sometimes couldn't you just act a bit more like a . . .

Martin   Man? A man?

Angela (*angrily*)   Yes! Go out there and get a job! Thump on someone's desk until they give you one! Don't be such a bloody wimp!

Martin *stares at her.* **Shakespeare** *enters.*

Martin   So this is the truth of it, is it? Women scream at us for being brutes and tell us to get sensitive and caring or they'll walk, but all the time they secretly want . . .

He searches his memory banks. **Shakespeare** *knows what he's looking for and urges him on.*

Martin   Petruchio!

Shakespeare *beams.* **Angela** *looks away.*

Martin   Your mother came out of that production last year muttering about how sexist it was, but that's what you all bloddy well want. Petruchio! Isn't it?

Angela   I don't know!

Martin   You know something? I don't want to thump on desks and get another job. When I was fired I was enormously angry but eighteen months on I'm starting to realise how much I hated it all. Never once in my career did I have any real autonomy. Someone was always looking over my shoulder and I hated it.

Angela   You're not even *trying* to get another job?

Martin   No. Not any more. After eighteen months of

crawling on my belly to personnel managers I wouldn't have spat at five years ago I've had enough. I'm sorry your mother is finding the going hard, but I'm not Petruchio, so bad bloody luck the both of you!

He turns angrily and goes. **Angela** *glares at* **Shakespeare** *and flicks him out of existence again.*

Campus Grounds – Next Day

Steve *is sitting looking despondent.* **Melissa** *walks up and sits beside him.*

Melissa   Seen your assessment on the noticeboard? We're both going to fail.

Steve (*nods*)   I've known that all along.

Melissa   Seen darling little Angela's mark? A plus.

Steve   Yeah.

Melissa   It's disgusting. Suck up to Swain or fail.

Steve   Yeah.

Melissa   This isn't education, it's full-on indoctrination. Join the post-structuralist feminist multiculturalist project or fail.

Steve   That's the message.

Melissa   I'm so bloody furious. If I fail it effectively adds another year on to my course.

Steve   This is going to be my last year in any case.

Melissa *looks at him enquiringly.*

Steve   I'm failing all my subjects. it's all just words, words, words. I hate this place.

Melissa   Why are you here?

Steve   My father's an academic, my mother's an academic, and they can't believe that I'm not. You know what I really like doing? Fixing cars. I spent seven hours putting a mate's engine together last weekend and it was great. Not that I can tell *them* that.

Melissa   Why not?

Steve   They think that only slobs fix cars. And so do you and Angela.

Melissa   Everyone should do what they like doing.

Steve   Yeah, yeah.

Melissa   Angela thinks you're really nice.

Steve   She won't even go to a movie with me!

Melissa   She's very – cautious about men.

Steve   Cautious? Every time I meet her I feel like she's reading a sign on my forehead that says, 'Beware, contains testosterone.' Will it really add a year to your course?

Melissa (*nods*)   There is no way I'm going to spend another year waitressing at the Waltzing Matilda Tavern.

Steve   Grim?

Melissa   How would you like to wear a sheepskin and hear Japanese tourists sing 'Click Go the Shears', four nights a week?

Steve   More fun than pouring beers at the gayest pub in Sydney.

Melissa   Do you get propositioned?

Steve   No. Which sort of adds insult to injury.

Melissa   I'm going to pass this bloody course, Steve.

Steve   Toe the ideological line?

Melissa   Yep. Sorry. When I balance integrity against the Waltzing Matilda, the feminist multiculturalist project starts to make a lot of sense.

Steve   You couldn't bring yourself to parrot that crap?

Melissa Watch me.

Steve What, you're just going to rock up to next class a convert?

Melissa No, no. You get much better marks if your teacher's arguments are so lucid and compelling that you have a full-on, high-voltage, conversion experience.

Melissa *mimes listening carefully to* **Swain** *then suddenly the electric light bulb goes on above her head. She sees.* **Steve** *laughs.*

Swain's Office – Next Day

Swain *and* **Melissa** *alone.*

Melissa I was just so shocked. I never done as badly as that before and I just wanted to see if there was anything I could do about it before it's too late.

Swain I hate failing anyone, Melissa, I really do, but the standard of your arguments has been quite – depressing.

Melissa I know I haven't been following the anti-humanist line –

Swain You're not required to follow any particular line, Melissa. This is an institution of tertiary study.

Melissa Yes, but –

Swain It's simply that the arguments you mount in defence of your libral humanist position are inadequate.

Melissa What sort of argument *would* be adequate?

Swain I do have to say that working within your chosen framework makes adequate argument very very difficult.

Melissa (*pleading*) I just can't see *how* and *where* the dominant patriarchal corporate state pumps out this *incessant* message? You make it sound like there's a room somewhere where the patriarchy meet to decide how best to grind women into the dust.

Swain   No, no. The message is diffuse and comes from thousands of sources some of which aren't even conscious they're sending it.

Melissa   Can you give me an *example* – a concrete *example*. I don't want to be stupid and naive, but I just don't *get* it!

Swain   OK. A TV ad I saw last night. A small boy comes home bruised, filthy and disconsolate because his football team has been defeated. Mother comforts him by washing his football gear sparkling clean with the aid of 'Surge' or 'Splurge', a 'breakthrough' miracle detergent. The ideological message? Young male warrior wounded in battle is nursed by maternal female who mends his armour and sends him back to the battlefield. Men fight, women nurture.

Melissa (*frowns*)   And the advertising agency is in effect acting as an independent branch of Patriarchy limited?

Swain (*nods*)   No one *directs* them to. They just know that because most of the so-called 'free' minds out there are in fact thoroughly brainwashed by corporate patriarchal ideology, they'll think the message is 'cute'. Men *are* warriors, women *are* nurturers, that's the way things are and always will be. That's 'reality'.

Melissa *stares at him and has a beautifully performed 'conversion' experience of great intensity.*

Melissa   Hey! Yeah! Yeah! You never see a grubby battered little girl come home and hand her tunic to Dad, do you?

Swain   Wouldn't sell.

Melissa (*sudden new insight*)   Those breakfast food commercials – it's always the mother being nurturing and caring and the father being wise, knowing and – patriarchal.

Swain   Exactly.

Melissa So the patriarchal message comes from a thousand different throats in a thousand different guises?

Swain Precisely.

Melissa Suddenly it all makes sense.

Swain My fault. I should have given you some concrete examples.

Melissa No, no, no. My fault. I should have asked. Suddenly, the fog has lifted. (*New thought.*) Tell me, tell me. If the dominant ideology is so *dominant*, how do the oppositional ideologies get started?

Swain Out of the lived experience of oppressed minorities.

Melissa Right, right. *Right!*

Swain Oppressed minorities are the site of the generation of all that's vital and valuable in our culture.

Melissa Right! Oh MiGod. I came in here *totally* depressed and confused and in a few moments you turn that all around and now I can see *exactly* what's going on.

Swain I should have given you some concrete examples earlier.

Melissa No, no. Please. What you did is *fantastic*. Is it still possible that if my major project is good I could pass, Dr Swain?

Swain Absolutely. And please, call me Grant. Have you chosen the topic?

Melissa No, I've been terrified, totally paralysed. Up to now my mind has been a total blank.

Swain But you feel more confident now?

Melissa Indescribably more confident. It's just that I've lost so much time.

Swain I'm sure I can help steer you in the right direction. Do you like West African food?

Melissa   Absolutely adore it. Simple and totally unpretentious.

Swain   Exactly. How are you placed tonight?

Melissa   Grant, the sooner the better.

Campus – Next Day

Angela *sees* **Swain** *and stops him.*

Angela   Grant, do you have a second?

Swain   Of course.

Angela   My assignment is turning out to be a little more – difficult to interpret than I thought.

Swain   Really?

Angela   I wondered if we could possibly talk about it.

Swain   Of course.

Angela   Grant, I feel really stupid about the dumb way I – you must have – I didn't have a history assignment – I'd love to have a West African meal.

Swain   Ah.

Angela   If you think that's an appropriate way to discuss the assignment.

Swain   Ah, Angela. I've been thinking this through a little more rigorously.

Angela   Oh?

Swain   Foucault is absolutely right of course. We are encouraged to deny ourselves spontaneity and 'jouissance' –

Angela   I've been reading him. The decentred self offers endless possibilities of intellectual and sensual 'play' –

Swain   Absolutely, but the political reality I didn't fully address, is that the head of faculty, Professor Meacham, is a fantatical liberal humanist who has the numbers on the University Council, and if I was to be discovered in any kind of intimate association with a student he'd play that tactical card against me for all it was worth.

Angela   Oh. Can I still see you about the assignment?

Swain   Of course. But not over a meal. The feminist multicultural project is too important to put at risk. I'm sorry, Angela, I'm so embarrassed.

Angela   Please don't be. I wasn't at all sure I would've wanted anything more than the meal in any case. My main worry is about the assignment. The material is proving quite hard to analyse.

Swain   I'm absolutely sure it's going to be fine.

Angela   Can I extend the due date a little? I need more time to think.

Swain   Absolutely. I'll move Melissa's presentation forward and yours back. She seems to be making very good progress.

Angela   Melissa?

Swain   She seems to have overcome all that initial resistance and is becoming very committed.

Angela *frowns.*

The Tutorial Room

Melissa *prepares to deliver her paper.* **Swain**, **Steve** *and* **Angela** *listen.*

Melissa   The more I researched, the more obvious it became to me that the *real* artistic excitement in Western Society is coming from the ordinary ideological accretions occurring out of the lived experience of the disadvantaged groups currently contesting the traditional sites of the dominant discourse. Working on some leads kindly given to

me by Dr Swain, I have encountered the work of the so
far unpublished Geraldton feminist lesbian writer of ethnic
Egyptian origin, Sophie Tsalis. Tsalis accepts Helene
Cixous's position that language itself is saturated with
patriarchal binary opposites such as male/female, mind/
body, rational/intuitive, logical/emotive, which inevitably
privilege the male term, thus making it impossible for
women to communicate their 'reality' within this
irretrievably male discourse. The project to which Cixous
and Tsalis are committed is the creation of a new female
language. I'd like to read you an extract which may give
you some of the flavour of this exciting project, which
Tsalis describes as a subversive intervention and
interrogation of the phallocentric dominant discourse.

She opens her book and reads.

'You big. You ugly. You poor dick. You stupid dick. Why?
Why? Why? Why you shout? Zweee. Zweeebub. You think
you smart but you dumb. I smarter. Someday. Someday
soon. Just wait. Zweee. Zweesome. Zweesee. Zweebub.
Zweebub Vorgone. I smart. Just wait. Ziggly Zweebub,
Ziggly Zukoff. No more Zukoff for you Zweebub. Sickly
ickly dickly – Zukoff yourself. And swallow. No more
swallow from Ziggly. No more nothing. Never.'

Steve   Melissa, that's crap!

Swain   It is if viewed from the dominant discourse.

Steve   It's crap from any discourse.

Swain   When that piece was read to Sophie's group in
Geraldton the response was electric.

Steve   Then they're all as stupid as she is.

Swain   You're saying that you're prepared to denigrate
the responses of another group of people because they don't
correspond to yours.

Steve   In this case, yes. If they like listening to feminist
nursery rhymes fine, but don't try and tell me it's a new
language.

Swain Steve, you can use rhetorical abuse to denigrate, but you will have to explain to me why Sophie's writing has far more power for significant numbers of people than *Hamlet* ever will.

Steve Because it's crudely ideological.

Swain So is *Hamlet*.

Angela Melissa, do you really believe that's good writing?

Melissa I believe it is effective writing for the purposes for which it was written. Like Grant I believe that there can never be absolute aesthetic standards. Judgement *always* depends on the ideological framework from which the work is viewed.

Outside the Tutorial

Angela *and* **Steve** *collar* **Melissa**.

Angela You're sleeping with him, aren't you?

Melissa Don't be ridiculous.

Angela You are.

Melissa I can keep an idiot like that waiting around in hope for as long as I like. From what I hear *you* were the one who was all ready to jump straight into bed.

Angela (*embarrassed in front of* **Steve**) I was going to have a meal with him, that's all!

Melissa Oh yes. Sure.

Angela And it was only because I thought he was a very special person.

Melissa He is. He decides who passes and who fails.

Angela Melissa, you're vile.

Melissa Power is the only reality. Read your Foucault.

Angela You don't believe a word of that crap you just

gave us in the tutorial.

Melissa   You can afford your principles, Angela. You don't have to work four nights a week at the Waltzing Matilda.

Melissa *walks off.* **Angela** *looks embarrassed as she looks at* **Steve**.

Angela   I was just going to have a meal with him. To discuss my project.

Steve *nods.*

Angela   OK. I was – I thought – I thought he *was* something special.

Steve   He's an arsehole!

Angela   I still think there is *some* truth in what he says.

Steve   You were prepared to sleep with him, yet you won't even come out to a *movie* with me!

Angela   I'm sorry. We'll go to a movie.

Steve   Forget it!

Steve *storms off.* **Angela** *looks disconsolate.*

Angela's Room

Shakespeare *is sitting on the floor with a large pile of books beside him. He is looking exhausted.* **Angela** *enters looking fired up and purposeful.*

Angela   I need some answers, William.

Shakespeare (*indicating books*)   You will not find them here.

Angela   What are you reading?

Shakespeare   All those vile 'feminist' books that are thy mother's and all those viler 'literary theory' books of thine.

Angela   They're new ways of thinking –

Shakespeare   That prattling knave Swain speaks through his fundament. Of course there is a human nature, and that of man and woman surely differs.

Angela   William –

Shakespeare   Man is a prancing cockerel. Arrogant, proud, like Petruchio.

Angela   My father is no Petruchio and my mother fights to the death.

Shakespeare   Every man who is not Petruchio doth wish he was, and every woman who is a Shrew doth wish she was not.

Angela   Only because of our conditioning!

Shakespeare   Two natures as diverse as man and woman cannot be forced identical. (*He holds up one of the feminist books.*) 'Tis in this present putrid project that misery is spawned.

Angela   You *are* deeply conservative, William. Deeply, deeply conservative.

Shakespeare   Make such gains as are just, but beyond a certain point the war will wither both sexes, for men are bred for battle and fight beyond all semblance of reason.

Angela   William, if you breathed a word of that reactionary essentialist drivel to some women I know you'd be ripped apart.

Shakespeare (*he holds up a feminist book*)   Since reading thy mother's books I am sure thou art right. (*He throws the book away.*) Right glad I am to have lived in mine own time.

Angela   Give me one piece of evidence to support what you're saying –

Shakespeare   What hath caused all history to be littered with corpses, if not the lust for power in the soul of man?

Angela   The patriarchal ideology *constructs* men obsessed with conquest and power, and your plays helped *legitimise* that obsession.

Shakespeare   The lust for power is not 'constructed'! It is a demon all men are born with.

Angela   And woman aren't?

Shakespeare   Yes but that demon in you is not so relentless. And are we not *all* born with the demons love, grief, guilt, anger, fear, scorn, loyalty and hate! Do the 'Hopi Indians' laugh when their child is struck down? Did King Lear need an 'ideology' to 'construct' his grief?

Angela *looks up and there is* **King Lear**, *played by her grandfather* **Col**, *holding an imaginary Cordelia in his arms, scanning the faces of those around him.*

Lear   Howl, howl, howl, howl! O! you are men of stones:
  Had I your tongues and eyes, I'd use them so
  That heaven's vault should crack.
  She's gone for ever.

He goes down on his knees.

  Why should a dog, a horse, a rat, have life,
  And thou no breath at all? Thou'lt come no more,
  Never, never, never, never, never!

Shakespeare *leads* **Lear** *away, looking over his shoulder at* **Angela**.

Col and Grace's Living Room

Angela *is with* **Martin**, **Sarah**, **Grace** *and her aunts* **Jessica** *and* **Monica**. *They all look sombre. It is* **Col**'s *wake.*

Monica   You always hear people say, 'He died peacefully. He died peacefully.'

Jessica   They should have given him more morphine.

Martin He was pumped full of the stuff. Someone like Dad doesn't just bow out peacefully.

Monica It was just horrible. Why do they let it go on and on?

Sarah Let's not talk about it any more, please.

Angela Was it really bad for him at the end?

Sarah Angela. Grace has been through enough.

Martin (*to* **Angela**) He suffered. It wasn't easy.

Grace I said to him, 'Don't hang on, it's no use.' (*Pause.*) He's at peace now.

Monica Thank God.

Grace The funeral was beautifully conducted.

Jessica Except for that unctuous minister.

Grace He spoke very well.

Martin Mum, he was awful. He didn't even know Dad.

Monica All he did was spout platitudes.

Martin I should have spoken.

Angela Yes.

Grace Ministers always speak at funerals. It's their job.

Martin I should have spoken.

Jessica We all should have.

Martin What would you have had to say that was in any way positive?

Jessica We all had our criticisms of Dad but we all loved him.

Martin Pity he didn't see much evidence of it when he was alive.

Grace Martin, don't get upset. I was often very hurt

about the way Jessica and Monica treated your father, but this is the time to forgive and forget.

Jessica   *We* treated him? If there was any damage to be inflicted you led the pack.

Grace   Jessica, don't be ridiculous. Your father and I loved each other for over fifty years.

Martin   I never would have suspected it.

Grace   He was a terrible old bastard, but I still loved him.

Jessica   Mum, he ridiculed anything we ever tried to do.

Monica   I got as good a result as Martin in high school and he wouldn't let me go to university.

Martin   We've heard this dozens –

Monica   Well it's true. I had to go and earn a living.

Martin   He was tough and hard, but he did love us.

Jessica (*to* **Martin**)   I don't know why you're defending him. He was harder on you than anyone.

Monica   You used to come inside some mornings and your hands would be bleeding he'd worked you so hard.

Martin   He was on the point of cracking up.

Jessica   He could have hired someone. He was just too bloody mean.

Martin   Why did we bother with a funeral? We should have just dumped him in the harbour.

Grace   I loved your father but he was a mean bastard, and no amount of glossing over can change that fact.

Jessica   He *must* have money stashed away somewhere.

Monica   Has to be a fortune there. Has to be.

Martin   Sorry, I've been through everything and the net assets are the house and four thousand dollars and that's it.

Jessica   I don't believe that. We've always known he had a hoard somewhere.

Monica   We always thought that at least we'd get *something* one day.

Jessica   There must be money. There has to be.

Martin   There isn't.

Jessica   Then where the hell did it go?

Angela *cannot control her anger any longer.*

Angela   He gave a third of what he earned to Billy Headen for nearly fifteen years.

They stare at her.

Jessica   Pardon?

Angela   He gave a third of what he earned to Billy Headen for nearly fifteen years.

Monica   That can't be right.

Angela   It is. I checked with Elsie Headen.

Jessica   His family misses out on everything because he's giving it to the bloody Headens?

Grace   I *knew* there was something fishy going on. I *knew* that Elsie bloody Headen was hiding something. Could never look me straight in the eye!

Martin   That makes an awful lot of things clear.

Jessica   Yes, that he was prepared to sacrifice us for them!

Monica   He must have been sleeping with her.

Martin   Who? Elsie Headen?

Monica   Probably was. She could never look me in the eye.

Angela   Because she was embarrassed and guilty. She told me.

Monica   So she bloody ought to be.

Angela   Col felt he had to help Billy, because Billy would have done it for him.

Jessica   Typical. He'd make a hero of himself to the Headens but his own family come last!

Angela   I think that's really unfair.

Monica   Angela, I know how emotional a funeral can be for someone your age –

Angela   Don't patronise me, Monica! Grandad helped another family survive by an extraordinary act of generosity and none of you has *one* good word to say about him.

Martin   I have.

Angela   Well you didn't say it at the funeral when it counted!

Sarah   Angela, don't get yourself upset.

Angela   Do you know what he told me? He'd be glad when he died because there'd be nobody to blame for your misery but yourselves.

Sarah   Angela.

Angela (*to* **Jessica** *and* **Monica**)   And as far as you two are concerned he thought you should stop your bellyaching because you'd both done brilliantly.

Jessica   Brilliantly?

Angela (*to* **Jessica**)   You've been supported for by your ex-husband for twenty years while you've expressed your inner artistic core, (*To* **Monica**.) and you've avoided the oppression of marriage and still had eight or nine trips around the world with your boss, while his unsuspecting wife stayed home with the kids.

Angela's Room – Later

Angela *is reading a manuscript when* **Sarah** *enters.* **Angela** *looks up.*

Sarah   Feeling better?

Angela *smiles at her mother and nods.* **Sarah** *indicates the manuscript she is reading.*

Sarah   What do you think?

Angela   I think it's good.

Sarah   So do I. I mean I don't think he's ever going to be another Raymond Carver, but I'm sure someone will publish it.

Martin *comes in and sees* **Angela** *holding the manuscript and goes to retreat.*

Angela   Dad, come back. It's good.

Martin *reappears.*

Martin   You're just saying that.

Angela   No, it's *much* better than the other one.

Sarah   See, I told you.

Martin   It's not boring?

Angela   No, it's very good.

Martin   It's still just a rough draft and the ending still needs a lot of work but I think that it does have a pretty gripping premise and it would be very filmable – not that I'm writing it with film in mind –

Angela   Now I've got you both here, could you two tell me something?

Martin   What?

Angela   Are you two just staying together because of me, because if you are, please don't.

Martin *and* **Sarah** *look at each other, puzzled.*

Angela   Well don't look so surprised. You're so resentful of each other. I don't want to think you're both enduring misery because of some misguided idea that I'll fall apart if you separate. I'm nineteen and quite capable of coping.

Martin *and* **Sarah** *look at each other again.*

Sarah   We love each other.

Angela *stares at them both.*

Angela   You've been badmouthing each other to me since I was three.

Sarah   That's what children are for.

Angela   I've been experiencing a *good* marriage?

Martin   No, you haven't, we have.

Sarah   If it'd been a bad marriage you probably wouldn't have known a thing.

Angela   What do you *love* about each other? Let me in on the secret.

Sarah   Your father is gentle, considerate, he listens to my problems, which is more than you do – and when he's not feeling sorry for himself he's sometimes funny –

Martin   And your mother's courageous and indomitable and when she's not feeling sorry for herself she's quite funny herself only she doesn't usually realise it.

Sarah   Thank you, dearest.

Martin   And your mother is suprisingly – no, forget that.

Sarah   Look, Angela, don't think we're senile or starry-eyed. If there had been a Petruchio around when your father was courting me –

Martin   Thank you. Well I'll tell you something, there were some slightly less assertive and very attractive young women around who *did* think I was something of a Petruchio.

Sarah   So why didn't you marry them?

Martin   You beat them up.

Sarah   I pulled one girl's hair because she was so bloody stupid. (*To* **Angela**.) Look, it's never perfect, but in any real marriage that's how things are.

The Tutorial Room

Swain *waits in the tutorial room.* **Melissa** *enters.* **Swain** *smiles at her and hands her a paper.*

Swain   A plus.

Melissa   Thank you. I'm really – thrilled.

Swain   It was a fine piece of work. Congratulations.

Melissa   That means that –

Swain   That means your final assessment is B minus for the course.

Melissa   Yow!

Swain   Now that there's no *question* of impropriety, I think it's time you sampled my Moroccan couscous.

Melissa   I don't think I'd better, Grant. I've become rather seriously involved with a guy who tends to misinterpret that sort of thing.

Swain   I thought –

Melissa   It just all took off last week. I didn't really think he was my type but something just – clicked.

Swain   Not that – not that swaggering rugby jock –

Melissa   Just because Julian is a top athlete doesn't make him a moron.

Swain   Not that loud, braying, insensitive, arrogant fool you introduced me to in the coffee shop?

Melissa   I find him very attractive.

Swain   You've really made an idiot of me, haven't you?

Melissa   I'm sorry, Grant, I don't really know what you're talking about. Are you implying that the marks you gave me weren't genuine?

Swain   I've become extremely fond of you, Melissa, and I had thought the feeling was reciprocated.

Melissa   Are you saying the marks you gave me weren't genuine, because if you are –

Swain   Of course they were genuine, but –

Melissa   Good marks equals sex. Is that what was going on in your mind?

Swain   No! For God's sake this was not a case of exploitation. I have grown extremely fond of you!

Melissa   You're married.

Swain   My marriage is a total disaster!

Angela *enters.* **Swain** *makes a great effort to control his anger.* **Angela** *looks at* **Melissa**. *She cannot help but notice a strong tension between* **Melissa** *and* **Swain**.

Angela   Am I interrupting something?

Melissa   No, no. I'm just leaving.

She sweeps out leaving **Swain** *simmering with fury.* **Steve** *enters.*

Angela   Perhaps I should give this paper another time?

Swain   No. No. Go ahead.

Angela   You're sure.

Swain   Let's get it over. You only need a D to pass the course.

Steve   What do I have to get for my final paper?

Swain A plus.

Steve Merry Christmas.

He turns to leave.

Angela You're not going to even listen to mine?

Steve Other people's intelligence depresses me. No, that's mean-spirited. I'll stay. Dazzle me.

Swain If you've no interest in this course, leave.

Steve I'll stay.

Swain When you're ready, Angela.

Angela *notices that* **Swain** *has literally begun to twitch with suppressed rage, but she has no option but to continue.*

Angela The proposition we have been introduced to this year is that ideology constructs our 'reality' and that 'human nature' and 'truth' are humanist fictions. When I talked to my family there was a lot of material that *supported* the notion their 'reality' *was* strongly influenced by ideology. My mother *does* see the world from a strong feminist viewpoint but she can still admit that she is on occasion attracted to, say, the swaggering macho mastery of – Petruchio.

Swain I'm sure she is.

Angela Sorry?

Swain *(savagely)* Your average woman obviously finds 'swaggering macho mastery' far more attractive than mere intellect.

Angela *is taken aback by the intensity of* **Swain**'s *statement.*

Swain But what can you expect. The dominant culture pumps out incessant images of brainless jocks carrying balls over lines in order to divert a brainless population from understanding how totally manipulated they are. Go on, go on!

Angela So yes, my mother sees the world ideologically,

but she also perceives and acknowledges her own frailties and weaknesses.

Swain Frailty, thy name is woman!

Shakespeare *appears. Unseen by all but* **Angela**.

Shakespeare (*to* **Angela**) They all quote me in the end.

Angela (*to* **Swain**) Sorry?

Swain My wife Joanna. Swears she will not even *apply* for the position in Queensland because she loves me too much! Hah! Couldn't bear us to be parted! Hah! I get a letter in the mail this morning telling me it's all over. She's fallen in love with the Vice-Chancellor. A hollow little ex-*engineer* whose only talent is posturing and strutting for the media! Sorry. Go on.

Angela *looks at* **Steve**. **Swain** *is showing every sign of becoming unhinged, but there is nothing much* **Angela** *can do but continue.* **Swain** *continues to twitch as the rage and resentment boils up inside him.*

Angela My father is to some extent trapped within the dominant ideology. He does feel a failure because he couldn't live up to its macho demands, but he's also warm, forgiving and tells funny jokes.

Steve He's a Liberal humourist.

Angela My late grandfather Col felt that if the patriarchy *was* controlling society, then in his case, it had certainly failed to deliver.

Swain The patriarchy has never delivered power to all men. It's the swaggering peacocks at the top that get everything! And idiot women, brainwashed by the dominant culture, chase them to the ends of the bloody earth.

Steve Women have always chased the guys with power and status. It's in their bloody genes.

Swain (*semi-hysterical*) Don't you *dare* even suggest a biological basis! I can see why you failed the course.

Nothing is biological, nothing! It can all be reversed. If we take the dominant culture, expose it, rip it apart, then the peacocks, the strutters, the jocks will have had their day! The meek will inherit the earth!

Shakespeare (*shaking his head sadly*)   The last person who espoused that belief . . .

He mimes being nailed on a cross.

Angela   If Shakespeare was alive today I think he would say there *was* a human nature and that the natures of men and women differ.

Swain   Of course he would, the strutting patriachal peacock!

Angela   I think he would say we are all born with inner demons –

Swain   Rubbish!

Angela   And that male demons shout 'power' louder than female demons.

Swain   Rubbish!

Angela   But after talking to my mother I think that if there *is* an average biological difference in the sexes' need for power, than it's not nearly as great as Shakespeare would have us believe.

Shakespeare   Who kills and murders for power? Men!

Swain   Angela, I warn you that if you are suggesting there is *any* biological difference between male and female, it will not be tolerated! Are you suggesting that?

Angela   I'm saying I simply don't know!

Steve   This isn't education, it's bloody indoctrination!

Swain   Education is *always* indoctrination. The question is to what ends. The feminist multicultural project will not tolerate any *hint* of biological determinism! There are *no* demons in the brain. Everything can be changed and will be changed! There are no demons! None!

Shakespeare   Zounds, the man is more dense than a pox-brained whoreson!

Swain   Angela! Get that. None!

Shakespeare   Men's brains are aburst with demons!

Shakespeare *summons up a* **Joanna Demon,** *a* **Vice-Chancellor Demon** *and a* **Professor Meacham Demon.** *They are played by the actors who play* **Jessica, Martin** *and* **Col.** *They appear in surreal half-masks and ghostly half-light.*

Swain   Joanna. How could you do it? How could you go off with that cretin! Why have you humiliated me like this?

Joanna   Ask *yourself* why, Grant.

Swain   You stole her, Mr *Vice*-Chancellor! You lured her up there and stole her!

Vice-Chancellor   No, Grant, she came willingly. Very willingly. Ask yourself why.

Swain   It's your fault, Meacham! If you hadn't blocked my promotion she would have stayed.

Meacham   I didn't block your promotion, Grant. Your colleagues did. Ask yourself why.

Swain (*to all of them*)   Why?

All (*in a loud repetitive chant, akin to a mantra*)   Because you're a totally inadequate human being. Because you're a totally inadequate human being. Because you're a totally inadequate human being. Because –

Swain (*covering his ears, screaming*)   No!

Shakespeare *gestures and* **Swain's Demons** *disappear. He resumes the scene unaware of what has just happened to him.*

Swain (*to* **Angela**)   There are *no* demons in the brain. One hint of demons in the brain and you fail!

Angela You're going to have to fail me in any case, Grant. I'm quitting the class.

Steve Yoh!

Angela The more I listened to the tapes of my family, the more convinced I became that there *is* a human nature and that it consists of more than just demons *or* ideology.

Steve Go, Angela!

Angela Human nature *must* have *something* to do with my grandfather's compassion, my mother's courage, and with my parents' loyalty and love for each other –

Swain Angela –

Angela And it must have something to do with why the great writers like William Shakespeare can still speak to us across the ages. Grant, the world has a lot of problems, and I support feminism and multiculturalism, but what you're teaching isn't helping the world, or ethnic minorities, or women. It's a quarter-truth elevated to holy writ, whose only function, frankly, seems to be an attempt to further the academic careers of middle-aged Anglo-Celtic males.

Steve (*correcting her*) Middle-aged Anglo-Celtic male arseholes.

Swain All right, if that's the way you want it, fail! Both of you. Fail! Scurry back to your tepid liberal humanism and fail! Go grovel to your pathetic canon of Dead White Males, but be sure of one thing – Grant Swain will not grovel! Never! Tomorrow belongs to me!

Steve Dr Swain?

Swain Yes!

Steve Go Foucault yourself.

Steve *leaves.* **Shakespeare** *laughs at* **Swain***'s humiliation.*

Swain I haven't finished with you.

Shakespeare Then, sir, do your worst!

Swain *aims his gun.* **Shakespeare** *grabs his arm. They wrestle. The gun goes off.* **Angela** *moves forwards anxiously.*

Swain   One of us is shot.

Shakespeare   The audience had'st best see whom.

Swain   For God's sake. This is the late twentieth century. No one expects narrative closure.

Shakespeare   'Tis my firm belief that a story must have a beginning, middle and an end.

Swain   Shakespeare, you are so fucking out of date!

Swain *limps offstage. He has shot himself in the foot.*

Shakespeare   Who sayest the power of metaphor is dead!

Shakespeare *turns to* **Angela** *triumphantly thinking he has won.*

Angela   William, you are a wonderful writer, but by and large your women *are* a bloody disgrace. One of the greatest actresses of our era, Glenda Jackson, had to leave the stage and become a *politician* because the only role she had to play in *your* repertoire was the nurse in *Romeo and Juliet*!

Shakespeare (*claps his hand to his head*)   Oh MiGod! I wish me back to an era of sanity.

Angela   Right away.

She flicks her fingers and he is gone.

Outside the Tutorial

Angela *and* **Steve** *are together.*

Steve   Well that's it I guess.

Angela   How do you feel?

Steve   Actually? Great.

Angela So do I. Who wants to end up with a Literature major and hate literature?

Steve I won't be ending up with anything.

Angela Why not?

Steve I'm quitting the university. It's not my scene.

Angela What are you going to do?

Steve I'm too embarrassed to tell you.

Angela Tell me.

Steve I'm starting an apprenticeship. Mechanic.

Angela If that's what you want to do, fine.

Steve Yeah. See you.

Angela Steve, would you like to come to a movie?

He turns and looks at her.

Steve Which one?

Angela Let's do it this way. You pick yours, I'll pick mine, we'll toss a coin, and go to mine.

Steve *looks at her.*

Angela It was a joke. I'm working on my sense of humour.

Steve It was good.

Angela You didn't laugh.

Steve I thought you were serious.

Angela Perhaps it's a bad idea.

Steve No, no. It's a great idea. Now let's just grab the entertainment guide, go to lunch and begin negotiations.

Angela You think I'm difficult?

Steve Why would I ever think that?

Angela I think it's important in any relationship that we do try and make ourselves aware of any vestiges of unconscious mindsets.

Steve   I think that this could be the start of an endlessly intriguing – friendship.

Angela *looks at him earnestly trying to decide if he is being ironic. She decides he is, but lets it pass. This time. They walk off together. She reaches for his hand. Surprised, he takes it.*

End.

Glossary

Two

Ron Elisha

Ron Elisha's first play, *In Duty Bound* (1979), was produced throughout Australia and since then he has had plays staged nationally and internationally. They include *Einstein* (1981), *Pax Americana* (1984), *The Levine Comedy* (1986), *Safe House* (1989), *Esterhaz* (1990), *Impropriety* (1993), *Choice* (1994) and *The Goldberg Variations* (2000). He recently completed a quartet for the stage entitled *Affairs of the Heartless*, which won two AWGIE awards.

Two, which won the AWGIE for Best Stage Play, has been produced across Australia, and in New Zealand, London, Chicago, St Louis, San Francisco, Toronto, Connecticut, Poland and Israel, where it was the inaugural production of the Elisha Theatre Company.

Elisha's other works include *By My Own Authority*, a film script which won the Gold Award for Best Screenplay at the Houston International Film Festival, the television screenplay *Death Duties* (SBS), the novels *The Hangman's Table*, *Paris* and *Paper Cuts*, and a one-man show entitled *Pulpit Fiction*. He works as a general practitioner in Melbourne.

Author's Preface

Ron Elisha

English is the language in which I write. And, yet, if these words were written in French, Italian or Chinese, their meaning would remain unchanged. As basic as language is, therefore, to a writer's art, the particular language used is almost incidental to the thrust of that art. This is not to say that language plays no part in the formulation of our thoughts but, once these thoughts *are* formulated, the particular language used is almost irrelevant. To put it more concisely: If I drive a Volkswagen to work, it does not necessarily mean that my work involves Volkswagens.

All this is by way of saying that *Two* is not a play about the nature of Jewish identity. It is a play which utilises the Hebrew language; a play which has, as its central character, a Jew; a play in which the action takes place against a background of Jewish politics. All of this, however, is incidental. It is merely the Volkswagen. The vehicle. The *best* way that I – as a Jew and an Australian – could find in order to travel from point A to point B.

The journey from A to B is a journey on two levels – dramatic and philosophical. As with any play, the two are inextricably intertwined. For a dramatic work does not set out to prove a thesis but simply to dramatise it.

I remember, as a medical student, being asked to listen to the sound of a foetal heart in a pregnant patient. I placed the funendoscope on the patient's abdomen, listened and – apart from the patient's own heartbeat and bowel sounds – heard nothing. This process I repeated, with the same result, several times. My tutor then told me that I should be listening for a very rapid, high-pitched sound, which he went on to imitate. I listened once more and, to my amazement, heard the indefatigable, small and steady hammering of a doughty foetal heart. Clear as a bell.

The human mind is such that, as often as not, it will ignore messages sent on a level or pitch to which it is not attuned. This Author's Note, therefore, may be seen as a tuning device. Something to direct the attention of the reader to a particular pitch. Once again, it is not an attempt to prove a thesis but simply to give the briefest of outlines thereof.

My attention was first drawn to the 'problem' of evil by an English teacher at high school. He would often ponder aloud the source of this troublesome entity, but seemed resigned to the fact that the answer was beyond human ken. My own instinct told me that no problem existed; that the source of evil was as 'obvious' as that of good; that both entities were 'created' in the same breath.

It was many years before I understood the source of my teacher's discomfiture, before I could acknowledge that a 'problem' really did exist. And now, after an odyssey of the mind, I can't help but remember the words of T. S. Eliot in *Four Quartets*:

> ... And the end of all our exploring
> Will be to arrive where we started
> And know the place for the first time.

My first broad concept for the play consisted of a plan to select from the Old Testament ten discrete episodes, each of which would dramatise the breaking of a particular commandment. Moses' interpretation of each episode would then be juxtaposed with Freud's, the order of succession and juxtaposition being such as to mount to a dramatic and philosophical climax.

My reading of Freud convinced me that I would have to turn my search to other areas, for I found his work both limited and limiting. As my reading progressed, I became more and more convinced that the seeds of evil lay somewhere in the 'schism' between the conscious and unconscious mind. My research turned to evolution, and the development of the brain in general. It was during the course of this research that I hit upon the heat/cold – good/evil model (a model which went on to become a subset of the larger 'duality' theme).

By this time, my net had been cast more widely to include,

among other things, Dante, twentieth-century Holocaust literature and Laing, the last two introducing into my thinking on
duality the concept of 'corporate responsibility'.

These elements combined to give me a working idea for a
first draft, entitled 'Acheron'.

'Acheron' utilized a single female character – a schizo-
phrenic, a concentration camp survivor and an ex-SS guard,
all in one – who interacted with an analyst on the one hand,
and with Edvard Munch on the other. As the play progressed,
this character descended the various levels of Dante's Inferno,
finally removing the barrier between the two halves of herself
and, together with this new awareness, being incorporated into
Munch's *The Scream*.

One Melbourne Theatre Company reading and some five
drafts later, 'Acheron' was still not working as a piece of
theatre.

The key to *Two* – the use of the Hebrew language – came as
an inspiration from the depths of post-'Acheron' despair.

Language first came into being as a means of communication, of breaking down barriers, bringing people together.
Taken beyond this basic level, however, it has become a means
whereby people are now *separated* – into nations, classes,
professions. It therefore stands as a perfect metaphor for our
situation in relation to 'duality'. The original survival value
inherent in our ability to see duality within unity (e.g., hot/
cold) has now been transformed into the greatest single threat
to our existence.

There are those who would regard my thesis on evil as being
dangerous: 'Would you trust a *computer* to decide between good
and evil?' As if there were something inherently evil in the use
of a computer.

Mathematics and physics are creations of the human mind.
They are every bit as 'human', therefore, as music, literature,
art and, indeed, morality. To deny this is, once again, to deny
one half of our humanity. In the final words of Anna's final
speech: 'It is a short step from that suggestion to the gates of
Auschwitz.'

Melbourne, 1984

To Bertha, Raphael and Abby

Two was first performed at the Hole in the Wall Theatre, Perth, Australia, on 3 August 1983, with the following cast:

Rabbi Chaim Levi   Rod Hall
Anna   Denise Kirby

Directed by Pippa Williamson
Designed by Raymond Omodei

Acknowledgements

I would like to thank Pippa Williamson, Rod Hall, Denise Kirby, Henri Szeps, Lynette Curran, John Krummel, Jonathan Hardy, Belinda Davey and Andrew Ross for their help in bringing *Two* to its present form.

Characters

Rabbi Chaim Levi, *a man in his sixties*
Anna, *a woman in her thirties*

Time

From 19 March 1948 to 16 May 1948

Setting

A cellar in a German town, the living quarters of Rabbi
Chaim Levi. Its form is very stark, with no attempt at
realism. The essentials are: a 'grille' high in the back wall,
through which light from passing 'trains' plays upon the set;
a table, two chairs, a piano, a radio, a chest of drawers (or
trunk), a globe of the Earth on a stand and a blackboard,
likewise on a stand and facing the audience. All of the
above are designed as simply as possible, with an effort
being made at a German Expressionist look. Use of colour
'opposites' should be made (e.g., yellow/purple, or orange/
blue, etc.). The text tells the audience that we are in a
cellar, so that in terms of set design, we should let ourselves
get away from the leadenness of literal interpretation.

The actors should speak 'universal' ('neutral') English.
'German' accents must be avoided at all costs.

Act One

The set is in darkness. The sound of a train gradually rises and becomes very loud, as if it were passing over our heads. We see interrupted lights through the grille as if the train's wheels were passing by just outside. The effect is unsettling. In the dim, strobe-like spill of light from the above, we see **Anna**, *seated at the table, knees together, handbag clasped tightly in both hands, while* **Chaim** *stands at UR, with his back to the audience and* **Anna**, *facing the grille. The sound of the train and the intensity of the lights diminish somewhat.*

Chaim Who are you? (*The lights and sound rise, then subside once more.*) Where are you from? (*The lights and sound rise and subside yet again.*) What do you want?

The lights and sound rise once more, climaxing this time in a deafening train whistle. The set is plunged into silence and darkness. A dim light then rises to reveal **Chaim** *and* **Anna**, *as before. The only sound, gradually rising, is that of a clock ticking.*

Anna (*after a pause*) Money is no object. (*A further pause, some urgency.*) There isn't much time. (*A third pause, great urgency.*) You must help me!

The sequence of train and whistle is repeated. It ends abruptly. The lights rise to reveal **Anna**, *as before, with* **Chaim** *pacing, thoughtfully.*

Chaim Why Hebrew?

Anna I wish to go to Palestine.

Chaim You don't need Hebrew for that.

Anna The quotas are very strict. It would help.

Chaim Some say that the Jewish State will be proclaimed before much longer. The doors will be wide open then. Why the urgency?

Anna I can't stand it here in Germany any longer. The people are the same people. The war is over, but the people ... (*He is silent.*) Don't you feel it? When you stand in a train and smell the breath of the man next to you, don't you gag on it?

Chaim   I don't use trains.

Anna (*sighing, standing*)   So you won't help me.

Chaim (*short pause*)   Why Palestine?

Anna   That is where Jews belong.

Chaim   I am a Jew.

Anna   You are a rabbi – you have your congregation.

Chaim   There is no congregation. (*She looks up.*) ... Dead.

Anna   Then ... why do you stay?

He gives a wry smile, holds up a finger, then searches the floor, finally lighting upon a cockroach, which he picks up and places on top of the globe of the Earth. He then starts rotating the globe, slowly.

Chaim   You see this cockroach? ... As long as I keep turning the globe, he'll keep walking, always finding the spot where he can stand most easily ... You see? As Spain falls, he moves to France. As France falls, to Germany. As Germany falls, to Poland. The journey is never-ending. And, sooner or later, he'll end up in Spain once more. (*He gives the globe a final twirl.*) ... I have no desire to live like a cockroach.

Anna   Then ... how *do* you live?

Chaim (*with a bitter smile*)   I am a rabbi. I teach. (*He opens one of the drawers in the chest, takes out a lump of bread and deposits it on the table.*) Here. You look hungry.

Anna   But ... you say there's no one left to teach.

Chaim   I've replaced scripture with music. God with Beethoven. The latter makes up in composition what the former lacks in humour. (**Anna** *looks confused. He leans towards her.*) I teach piano. (*He sits and indicates the bread.*) Go ahead – it's kosher. (*She starts tearing pieces from it.*) Yes ... Yes, I teach the language of the soul to the blue-eyed sons of ham-fisted butchers ... One would have to admit – Germans are, without a doubt, quite the most civilised barbarians in the world. (*At this point, a train passes overhead, whistle blowing.*)

Anna   Does that go on all the time?

Chaim (*cutting her off*)   Tell me, how do you propose to pay for these Hebrew lessons?

Anna   I have money ...

Chaim   Money is worthless ...

Anna (*taking some notes out of her handbag*)   American dollars.

Chaim   Ah ... American dollars ... American dollars speak all languages. Even Hebrew.

Anna   I ... I must warn you – I know nothing of the language. You'd have to start with the basics.

Chaim (*standing and moving to the blackboard*)   Very well, the basics. (*He draws an 'Aleph' on the board –* א *– then turns to her.*) Oh, by the way ... The Hebrew I'll be teaching you will be largely based on ancient Hebrew pronunciation. It's not the Hebrew we use *here* but, if you ever do get to Palestine, you'll find it far more useful ... At the same time, however, I must warn you that I have only a smattering of the modern patois. The rest you'll have to pick up on the street ... Or the train. (*They exchange a less than friendly smile.*) Now. (*Pointing to the aleph.*) What do you make of that? (*She looks at it, musing for a moment, then turns the blackboard on its side.*)

Anna   It looks like a bird, flying away.

Chaim (*turning the board back*)   I might remind you that this is a Hebrew lesson – not a psychiatric consultation. The word for bird is 'tsippor'. It starts with the letter 'tsadik'. Tsadik also means 'righteous man'. There are no more ... righteous men. (*Checking himself.*) ... No ... No, this is the letter 'aleph'. First letter of the Hebrew alphabet. (*He rubs it*

out with a rag and throws her the chalk.) Here. You have a try.
(*She begins, getting it back to front. Taking the chalk from her.*) No
. . . No, try to think of it more in terms of a somewhat . . .
underfed swastika. (*He redraws it.*) Very important letter,
aleph. Very important. (*He rubs it out and hands her the chalk
once more.*) First letter of God's name. Numerical value: One.
Every letter in the Hebrew alphabet has a numerical value.

Anna (*having drawn an aleph*)   Rather like every Jew . . . in
the camps. (*He takes the chalk from her. Thoughtfully.*)

Chaim   Sit down for a moment. (*She sits. He paces.*) God
gave Moses Ten Commandments. Here, in this cellar, there
is only one: 'There is no past.' (*A train passes overhead.*)

Anna   And God said: 'Thou shalt have no past before
thee. Nor shalt thy son, nor thy daughter, nor thy man-
servant, nor thy maidservant, nor thy ox, nor thy ass, nor
any stranger that is within thy gates.' (*She laughs. He looks at
her enquiringly.*) . . . I'm just trying to imagine an ox with a
past.

Chaim   One must be very familiar with scripture in order
to misquote it so purposefully.

Anna   We had a governess – a Catholic. She saw it as
her mission in life to save us from the fires of Judecca.

Chaim   'The fires of Judecca' . . . Dante, if I'm not
mistaken? . . . Something of a prophet, your governess.

Anna   You're breaking your own commandment.

Chaim   It's the prerogative of those who make
commandments to break them . . . Now . . . Where were
we? Ah, yes – the numerical value of letters – a fascinating
field. A small example, if I may. (*He writes* לֹ.) . . . The
letters 'lamed–vav' – lamed having a value of thirty and
vav six. Lamed–vav – thirty-six. 'Loh', meaning 'to him'
. . . According to Jewish tradition, the lamed–vav is a very
important concept. It represents the thirty-six Just Men
who, in any one generation, take the suffering of the entire
world on their shoulders. Their importance lies in the fact

that if, by some chance, their number should ever fall to thirty-five, the world would choke on its own evil . . . God forbid that should ever happen . . . Now . . . (*Handing her the chalk.*) . . . you try.

Anna   I – I'd like to write my name . . . if I could . . . in Hebrew.

Chaim   What *is* your name?

Anna   Anna.

Chaim   Just 'Anna'?

Anna (*firmly*)   Just Anna.

Chaim   First an aleph. (*She draws one.*) . . . Another, beside it. (*She draws another.*) . . . Now a 'noon'. (*He takes the chalk and draws* ב *between the two alephs.*) There you are: 'Anna' . . . Full of grace, mercy and prayer.

Anna   Is that what it means?

Chaim   Anna . . . is like a plea to God.

Anna   Ann-a . . . An-na. (*Taking the chalk from him and rubbing out the letters on the board.*) Here, let me try it again. (*She writes the letters, correctly, from left to right.*) There. How's that?

Chaim   Perfect . . . Except, in Hebrew, we go from right to left.

Anna   Oh . . . But . . .

Chaim   In the case of 'Anna', however, either direction will do.

Anna   Oh. (*She looks pleased with herself and stands, staring at her name. After a pause.*) What kind of a plea is it? . . . The plea . . . to God . . . What's it a plea for?

Chaim   That's up to you.

Anna   Anna. (*Writing it again.*) Anna. (*Leaning back, proudly.*) . . . Anna . . . I think I'm going to like coming here.

Chaim Tell me . . . How did you find this place?

Anna Why . . . the sign, of course. On the door.

Chaim The sign only says 'Piano Teacher'. It makes no mention of Hebrew.

Anna But you're a rabbi.

Chaim A rabbi without a congregation . . . is a piano teacher. (*He rubs the letters off the board.*)

Anna Does that mean . . . you won't take me on?

He stops rubbing and looks her in the eye. A train passes overhead. It is a long train and as the lights and sound — held under — continue, the following dialogue takes place.

Chaim Do you play in instrument?

Anna Y-yes.

Chaim Which one?

Anna The violin.

Chaim Bring it.

Anna I haven't one.

Chaim Get one.

Anna But . . .

Chaim Get one. Bring it. Next time you come.

The sound of the train builds to a deafening whistle. The lights black out. After a brief pause, the sound of Beethoven's Kreutzer Sonata (Opus 47), rises on the piano. The lights slowly rise to reveal **Chaim** *playing. After an interval,* **Anna** *enters, hesitantly, a violin case clutched under her arm. She takes a few steps forward.* **Chaim** *seems oblivious.*

Chaim (*still playing*) You like Beethoven? (*She doesn't answer.*) . . . I had precisely the same response when they asked me about Wagner. (*He continues playing. She places the violin case on the table and sits.*) I notice you brought your violin. Why don't you join me?

Anna I ... I haven't played for years. I'm afraid I ...

Chaim Nonsense! I had a young Teuton in here this morning. A pubescent. Just growing hair on his jackboots. Made Brahms sound like Wagner ... The worst *you* could do would be to make Beethoven sound like Brahms. (*She hesitates.*) ... Come, don't be afraid. The music will carry you. (*She takes out the violin and bow and, after some fidgeting, begins to play. Her attempts, though valiant, are not very good and, after an interval, he stops playing. She also stops.*) Beethoven, I take it, is not your favourite composer. (*Rising to his feet.*) On that score, at least, you're even: I doubt he would have considered you his favourite musician.

Anna I – It's been a long time ...

Chaim My dear Anna, don't alarm yourself. Your playing just now would have been a great comfort to Beethoven. It would have shown him that, even in deafness, there is a blessing.

Anna I might remind you that all this was not my idea. I came here to learn Hebrew.

Chaim And so you shall. (*He draws* ‎ב‎ *on the board.*) 'Beit.' Second letter of the Hebrew alphabet. 'Beit', as in 'Beethoven'.

Anna It looks like the head of a whale.

Chaim If you were a Jonah, perhaps ... 'Beit' is also the Hebrew word for house. 'Beitsefer' – the house of the book – 'school.' 'Beit hasohar' – the house of confinement – 'prison'. 'Beit meshooga'im' – the house of the mad – 'asylum'.

Anna How do you spell *your* name?

Chaim Your timing is immaculate.

Anna No, really.

Chaim My name is Chaim. Chet–yood–yood–mem-sofit. (*He writes* ‎ם י י ח‎ .) Chai (*He circles* ‎י ח‎ .) means 'alive' and Chaim, with another yood and a mem-sofit, (*He circles* ‎ים‎ .) means 'life'.

Anna   It's a beautiful name, 'Chaim'.

Chaim (*cutting her off*)   We come now to an interesting point: the way in which language reflects the character of its people.

Anna   My mother's name . . .

Chaim   In Hebrew there are no capitals. No upper case. All letters are in the lower case. Jewish society, therefore, could be termed the ideal 'caseless' society.

Anna   I wonder why it was, then, that Marx – a Jew – chose to name his socialist doctrine *Das Kapital*?

Chaim (*looking at her askance*)   There are two types of socialist. Those, on the one hand, who believe that all men should live like princes and those, on the other, who believe that none should. Marx, being a somewhat wayward Jew, was obviously of the former persuasion. (*As he has been talking, he has moved U, where he stands staring out of the grille.* **Anna**, *meanwhile, has picked up a piece of chalk and has begun writing his name on the board.*)

Anna   Cha–yim . . . Life. (*She has, however, written the last letter incorrectly, as* □ *instead of* ◻. *Turning and seeing this, he rushes forward, grabbing the chalk and the rag.*)

Chaim (*disproportionately angry*)   No! No, you've got it completely wrong. (*He rubs it out and rewrites it, feverishly, three times in quick succession.*) Chaim, Chaim, Chaim! (*He circles the last letter in each case.*) Mem-sofit, mem-sofit, mem-sofit! You wrote it incorrectly!

Anna (*frightened*)   There's no need to shout. I only left off one of its ears.

Chaim   It only had one ear to begin with! Without an ear, it becomes meaningless.

Anna   Why meaningless? Why not simply a deaf mem-sofit? A kind of . . . Beethoven of the Hebrew alphabet.

Chaim (*taking a deep breath*)   Do you want to learn Hebrew or don't you?

Anna   Yes ... But I'm not sure that's what you're teaching me.

Chaim   I can teach you to comprehend Hebrew, and I can teach you to mouth it. Alternatively, I can teach you to feel it and to express yourself through it. I have chosen the latter course. If that is not in accord with your needs and your ideas, you are free to go. (*He pauses. She neither moves nor speaks. He nods.*) Right. (*He rubs out the writing on the board.*) In spite of what I just told you, there are certain letters in the Hebrew alphabet which, if appearing at the end of a word, take on a different form. This is designated by the word 'sofit'. 'Sof' meaning 'end'; 'sof*it*' being the feminine form of the adjective 'final'. A case in point is the 'mem' in my name. 'Mem', in the body of a word, is written so. (*He draws* מ.) At the end of a word, however, it becomes mem-sofit. (*He draws* ם.)

Anna   I don't see the point in that.

Chaim   Philosophically, it could be argued that, to begin a task with great fanfare is far less important than to complete it in triumph.

Anna   Whereas, politically, it could be argued that the final result is far more important than the means of achieving it. A further confirmation of Marx: 'The end justifies the means.'

Chaim   I prefer to think of it more in terms of the end clarifying the means. Nevertheless, I find it gratifying that you should be attuned to the political implications of language.

Anna   As far as I'm concerned, Hebrew has only one political implication: getting me out of Germany and into Palestine. Quickly.

Chaim   I don't know who put that idea into your head, but it's ridiculous. How many of those godforsaken refugees, pouring in their thousands into Palestine every month, have even one word of Hebrew?

Anna (*after a pause*) If I may place a somewhat oblique crack in your commandment, let me say that, if there is one lesson I learned from the war, it's this: in order to survive, one must have a function. And if one doesn't have a function, one must create one. One must make oneself indispensable. That's the lesson I learned and that's why I'm alive today . . . I can speak German, French, Italian, English and Polish. I am a refugee. I speak the language of refugees. Give me Hebrew, my passport to Palestine, and I will make myself indispensable to them. I will create for myself a function.

Chaim I'm afraid that, as keen as you are, it would take you at least six months to master the language.

Anna Please . . . Don't underestimate my intelligence.

A train passes overhead, whistle blowing. The lights black out. After a brief interval they rise once more to reveal **Anna**, *seated at the piano and* **Chaim**, *standing at the blackboard.*

Chaim You might remember, last time, we were talking about the letter 'mem'. (*He writes* מ.)

Anna Ah, yes – the rabbit. (*He looks confused.*) . . . The 'mem' – looks like a rabbit.

Chaim Why a rabbit? Why not a mouse?

Anna It's too large for a mouse.

Chaim All right. (*He draws a smaller 'mem'.*) What about that?

Anna That's a baby rabbit.

Chaim (*pointing to the original mem*) Then why couldn't this be a grandfather mouse?

Anna Because it doesn't look like a mouse – it looks like a rabbit. (*He draws* □ *to the left of the 'mem'.*)

Chaim And now?

Anna   What's that?

Chaim   Cheese.

Anna   Rabbits don't eat cheese.

Chaim   I know.

Anna   Anyway, it's not cheese. It's a deaf mem-sofit.

Chaim   A what?

Anna   A deaf mem-sofit. A mem-sofit without its ear.

Chaim   Ah. I see you have a good memory. Let's see just how good. Here – I want you to write your name. (*She takes the chalk and writes* א נ א.) Very good ... Now, seeing as we're dealing in palindromes, see if you can write the word for 'water', – 'mayim' – mem–yood–mem. (*She takes the chalk, places a* י *between the 'mem' and the 'cheese' and converts the latter from* □ *into* ם *– a mem-sofit.*)

Anna   What with all that cheese about, I thought the rabbit might be thirsty.

Chaim   I see you catch on quckly.

Anna   Correct me if I'm wrong, but I get the feeling that there's more to this than the dietary habits of rabbits.

Chaim   Most peoples, when dealing in palindromes, are permitted free passage in both directions. For the one who speaks Hebrew, however, such freedom does not always exist.

Anna   The establishment of a Jewish State will remedy that.

Chaim   If there is a remedy, yes. But what if there's none? What if such ... limitations are an inescapable part of nature? Look, for example, at the word before you: 'mayim' – 'water.' There can be no palindrome here. Water flows only in one direction. That's nature.

Anna   Aren't you forgetting evaporation? Or is that not a part of your linguistic philosophy?

Chaim The word for water is 'mayim' –
mem–yood–mem-sofit. The word for heavens, 'shamayim'.
(*He draws a* ש *to the right of the word* מים.) The letter 'shin'
(*He points to the* ש.) is often used as the symbol for Shaddai,
which means 'Almighty'. The heavens, therefore, are seen
as the waters of the Almighty. Or, if you like, the almighty
waters. A celestial extension of earthly waters. Part of a
single continuum. Hebrew, therefore, reduces the apparent
plurality to a unity. Within that closed system, movement
occurs in only one direction. (*He describes the left half of a
circle.*) Condensation, or rain . . . (*Then the right half.*) and
evaporation. Whether one dubs it clockwise or anticlockwise
is, within that system, of no relevance. The movement is
still in one direction.

Anna Then why do I need to use an umbrella only when
it rains? (*A train passes overhead.*)

Chaim (*looking at his watch*) It's getting late. (*He replaces the*
מ *with a* ל, *converts the* י *into a* ו, *rendering the word* שלום.)

Anna What does that say.

Chaim These are letters with all of which you are
familiar. 'Shin–lamed–vav' – you remember 'lamed–vav' –
and our old friend 'mem-sofit'. 'Shalom.' 'Shalom' means
'hello' . . . 'goodbye' . . . 'peace' . . . 'Shalom' is also a
man's name. It has its biblical roots in the name Absalom
– Av–Shalom – 'father of peace' – the name of the son of
King David. An ironic name, as it turned out. For Absalom
spent all his time plotting the overthrow of his father. And,
much as David loved him, he was forced to have him
hunted down . . . Absalom's pride was his long, dark hair,
which got caught in a tree as he was running away. The
king's soldiers found him there, hanging by his hair, and
killed him . . . It's said that King David never really
recovered from the blow.

*A train passes overhead. The lights fade to black. As they rise once
more we hear the sound, slowly rising, of a distant radio braodcast.*
Chaim *is meanwhile seated at the table, playing chess with himself.*

Broadcaster's Voice   ... The leader of the US
delegation to the United Nations, Mr Warren Austin, today
put forward the plan that Palestine be placed under the
auspices of the United Nations in the form of what he
termed a 'provisional trusteeship'. This would, in effect,
mean a continuation of the mandate – with Arab and Jew
living side by side with equal rights in a single state – only
with the British presence being replaced by a United
Nations presence. With only eight weeks remaining before
the official expiry of the British Mandate, the move is seen
by some as an attempt to forestall further escalation of the
already mounting tensions between Arab and Jew in the
area ... Meanwhile, in Palestine itself, the Arab blockade
of the Negev Desert, Jerusalem, the Etzion bloc and parts
of the Galilee region continues. A spokesman for the British
Mandatory Government today expressed fears of an
organised Jewish counter-attack, aimed at Arab forces
involved in the blockade. Such a counter-attack, he stated,
could well lead to a full-scale war in the region.
Negotiations with representatives of both sides are
continuing ... In other news today, President Truman of
the United States expressed hopes that recent statements
made by Soviet leaders were not a portent of worsening
relations between the two countries ...

During the course of the news on Palestine, **Anna** *has entered,*
carrying her violin case, and remains standing, half listening, half not
knowing what to do.

Chaim (*without turning around*)   You're late. (*He gets up and*
switches off the radio.)

Anna   It's a beautiful radio. Where did you get it?

Chaim   I found it ... in the ruins of the house next
door, just after the war. Slightly battered, but in perfect
working order.

Anna   What they were saying just now ... about
Palestine ...

Chaim   You play shachmaht?

Anna   Sorry?

Chaim   Shachmaht – chess. Do you play it?

Anna (*shrugging*)   I used to ... many years ago.

Chaim   Fascinating game ... The forces of darkness against those of light.

Anna (*approaching the board as he makes a move thereon*)   You ... play against yourself.

Chaim   Yes. Such pastimes are always far more pleasurable when one is pitted against an opponent of one's own calibre.

Anna   But ... I don't understand. How *can* one play oneself?

Chaim   Oh, it's not that difficult. It's simply an exercise in not letting one's left hand know what one's right hand is up to.

Anna   But if one half of you wins ...

Chaim   Yes.

Anna   The other half has to lose.

Chaim (*nodding, as if impressed*)   You must have been a grandmaster in your day.

Anna   I don't see the point in that.

Chaim   Why not? ... No matter what you do, one half of you always loses.

Anna   But ...

Chaim   If I were to play one hundred games of chess with you, and we were each to win fifty, how would that be any different? How would it have any more meaning?

Anna   Because I might win fifty-one.

Chaim   My left hand might well be a better chess player than my right. Does that mean anything?

Anna   If you feel that way, why bother playing at all?

Chaim   (*moving the board aside*)   Why, indeed ... Perhaps you'd better ask that question of a rabbi who still has a congregation.

Anna   I'm not sure I follow you.

Chaim   If I remember rightly, we were talking last time about the letter 'mem'. (*He draws* מ *on the board.*)

Anna   I'm tired of 'mem'. Haven't you got any other letters?

Chaim   The letter 'mem' or, in its final form, 'mem-sofit', is a letter of great importance. (*He writes* ם. *She looks heavenwards. He presses on.*) As you may or may not have noticed, every language has what we might call its 'letter of interrogation'. In English, for example, it is 'w' – 'why', 'where', 'who', 'what', 'when', and so on. In French, 'q' – 'quoi', 'qui', 'quelle', 'qu'est-ce que c'est', etcetera. In Hebrew, the letter of interrogation is 'mem'. 'Mi', meaning 'who' ... (*He writes* מ י .) ... 'Mah', meaning 'what' ... (*He writes* מ ה .) ... 'Lamah', meaning 'why' ... (*He adds a* ל *to the right of the* מ ה .) ... And 'camah', meaning 'how much', 'how many', 'how long' or 'how often'. (*He rubs out the* ל *and replaces it with a* כ .) Languages are also possessed of their letter of plurality, so to speak. In both English and French, the letter is 's'. In Hebrew, however, the letter of interrogation and that of plurality are one and the same – 'mem' – or, in the case of plurality, 'mem-sofit'. 'Yehudi' – 'Jew', becomes 'Yehudim' – 'Jews'. And 'Aravi' – 'Arab', becomes 'Aravim' – 'Arabs'. But these are only masculine plurals, ending in 'mem-sofit'. there are also feminine plurals, ending in the letter 'tuf'. (*He writes* ת.) So you see, it is only the Jew who, in using the same letter both for interrogation and for plurality, asks: 'What is the meaning of this plurality?' whilst, at one and the same time, creating a further plurality by rendering the question a male one!

Anna   I'm sorry, but you've lost me.

Chaim   Let me put it more simply, then ... Everything

in Hebrew has a gender. Nouns, adjectives, verbs –
everything. 'Yeladim' is 'boys', 'yeladot' – 'girls'. 'Cannons',
'totachim' – a masculine plural – are used to fight 'wars',
'milchamot' – a feminine plural. Everything has a gender.
In fact, I would say, without too much fear of
contradiction, that Jews, contrary to popular belief, are
probably the most 'genderous' people on earth!

Anna (*short pause*) Tell me – are you, by any chance, an
anti-Semite?

*A train passes overhead. The lights black out. When they rise once
more, we see* **Anna** *seated at the table, the violin case before her,
with* **Chaim** *at the blackboard. The chess board – set up – is also
on the table.*

Chaim Today, I thought we might try something a little
different. (*He draws five long, horizontal, close-set lines across the
board.*) Since, in my opinion, both your Hebrew and your
music stand in need of a certain degree of . . . refinement, I
thought we might try combining the two. (*He draws a treble
clef.*) Your violin? (*She takes out violin and bow.*) For the
purposes of instruction, we will take the first seven letters of
the Hebrew alphabet to represent the notes of the scale,
using the key of E minor . . . A, therefore, becomes aleph;
B – beit; C – gimmel; and so on – dahled, heih, vav, zayin
. . . (*He writes as he speaks.*) . . . All right? . . . Now, give me a
heih . . . Good . . . Now a vav . . . And a zayin . . . Getting
better. Now an aleph . . . Beit . . . Again – beit . . . Gimmel
. . . Beit. Now back to gimmel . . . Up to heih . . . Back to
beit. An aleph . . . Again . . . Again . . . A zayin . . . Again
. . . A vav . . . Down to heih . . . Back to vav . . . And zayin
. . . And now a heih . . . Very good . . . And again. (*He
repeats the pointing. She now plays it fairly fluently, though very
mechanically.*) Wonderful. Wagner himself couldn't have done
better. (*He takes the violin and bow.*) Here. Let me show you.
(*Before placing the violin under his chin, he stops for a moment, looks
at it, gives it a slight squeeze and blinks several times.*)

Anna I – Is something the matter?

Chaim (*caught with guard down*) No . . . No, nothing's the matter. (*He plays the above sequence, with great feeling and control, then goes on to finish the verse. It is 'Hatikvah', the melody which was, at the time, the Zionist theme and has now become the national anthem of the State of Israel. A train passes overhead while he is playing. He finishes. His eyes are moist.*) 'Hatikvah' – 'Hope'. Anthem of the Jews. Living always ... in hope. (*He passes back the violin, slowly, as if unwilling to part with it. There is a pause. He wipes his eyes.*) Why didn't you tell me you were a Gentile? (*There is a silence.*) I began to suspect when you asked if I was an anti-Semite. No Jew would ever have to ask another Jew that question. Then, just now, when you played the violin, your left sleeve fell back, and I saw that there was no number tattooed on your forearm. And, if there were any doubts left in my mind, they were dispelled by the way you played 'Hatikvah'. (*She looks at the floor.*) Why did you lie to me?

Anna (*softly*) I didn't lie to you.

Chaim You told me you were Jewish.

Anna I told me you that I wanted to learn Hebrew and that I wanted to go to Palestine. That's all.

Chaim But when I asked you why you wanted to go there, you said it was where Jews belong.

Anna I didn't say I was one of them.

Chaim All right, you didn't lie, but you intentionally misled me.

Anna You misled yourself. (*There is a silence. He begins wiping down the board.*) I ... I meant to tell you ... I just ... wasn't sure ... I thought, maybe, if I wasn't Jewish, you wouldn't help me.

Chaim (*looking at her searchingly*) Who *are* you?

Anna Why is that important *now*? Why didn't it ever trouble you when you thought I was Jewish?

Chaim Because I find myself asking what possible reason a Gentile could have for wanting to learn Hebrew, then

plunging headlong into the middle of a Palestine torn in
half by racial violence.

Anna   I have my reasons.

Chaim   And what was all that about the 'Jewish quota'?
What has the Jewish quota to do with you?

Anna   I want . . . to become a Jew.

Chaim   I see . . . And you think a knowledge of Hebrew
automatically makes one a Jew?

Anna   I – It was a starting point. A way of breaking the
ice. Sooner or later, I would have told you the truth.

Chaim   Would you?

Anna   You are a rabbi. You have the power to make me
a Jew.

Chaim   That's what you want from me, then. To make
you a Jew?

Anna   Yes.

Chaim   And the Hebrew lessons – nothing more than an
ice-breaker?

Anna   No . . . No, I still want to learn Hebrew.

Chaim   I see. (*He begins to pace, deep in thought.*) Sit, sit. (*She
does. He continues to pace.*) Something here isn't quite kosher.
(*She is silent.*) Why? Why do you want to become a Jew?

Anna   To answer that question, I would have to break
your commandment. I don't want to do that.

Chaim   I'm sorry, but there are certain reasons I must
exclude. You see, we Jews don't chase after converts – we
discourage them. We leave the numbers game to the
Catholics, if only to limit the number of digits in our
tattoos. (*He grips his left forearm. She looks at the floor. He pauses,
then paces.*) Perhaps you want to marry a Jew.

Anna (*looking up*)   Marry?

Chaim   Yes. Marry ... It's a common enough reason for conversion, unacceptable though it may be.

Anna   No. No, it's nothing like that.

Chaim (*turning to face her*)   Perhaps, then, you're running away from something.

Anna   Quite the reverse, I can assure you.

Chaim   Or perhaps it's simply a matter of guilt. Is it guilt that you feel?

Anna   The entire world has just been convulsed by a war. Which of us is with*out* guilt?

Chaim   Some of us have managed to ... 'acquire' a little more than others.

Anna (*after a brief pause*)   You ask me for reasons. I can't give them to you. I can only ask you to trust me.

Chaim   You haven't given me much of a basis for it.

Anna   I haven't lied to you.

Chaim   Let's not split hairs.

Anna (*fingering one of the chess pieces*)   If I were your opponent at chess, I'd do my best to hide the motives behind each of my moves. Your only certainty would be my desire to beat you. And yet, you'd be prepared to sit down and play, trusting me not to rearrange the board whilst your back was turned. It's not a large measure of trust, but it's all I'm asking for.

Chaim   There is one basic flaw in your analogy: you already *know* the motives behind all of *my* moves.

Anna   Do I?

Chaim   Be that as it may, we could ... 'rearrange' the rules a little, just to ... even up the contest. (*He begins to pace.*) ... I'll make a deal with you ... I'm going to set you a riddle. And in the course of each lesson, I'm going to give you a clue to its solution ... The rest is up to you. If you can first find the clues, then use them in order to solve the riddle, I'll do as you ask. I'll make you a Jew.

Anna   And . . . meanwhile?

Chaim   Meanwhile, you'll be learning. Learning how to talk like a Jew, how to walk like a Jew, how to look like a Jew. You'll be learning everything you need to know in order to be a Jew. But all that won't actually make you one. For that, you'll have to solve the riddle.

Anna   And if I can't?

Chaim   Well . . . it won't have been a total loss. At least you'll be able to make chicken soup.

Anna   (*stands, thinking, then turns to face him*)   All right, you've got yourself a deal.

Chaim   You realise, of course, that conversion usually takes something in the order of a year.

Anna   That's too long. I can't afford to . . .

Chaim   Tell me, Anna – what do you think a Jew *is*? (*She begins to shrug.*) Go ahead – I'm interested to hear the opinion of an 'innocent bystander'. (*A train passes overhead.*)

Anna   A Jew . . . is a Jew.

Chaim   A descendant of Abraham? . . . The Arabs, too, share that distinction.

Anna   A Jew is the child of a Jewess.

Chaim   Like Jesus.

Anna   A Jew is one who lives like a Jew.

Chaim   How does a Jew live? . . . Like Moses? Like Marx? Like prisoner number 175834, lining up outside the gas chamber?

Anna   All right! Then a Jew is one who *dies* like a Jew!

Chaim   Ah! . . . There you would find a far greater concensus. But still not enough to convince me you know what it is that you wish to become.

Anna   I wish to become a person who follows the tenets of Jewish law.

Chaim   Why? Most Jews don't. That doesn't make them Gentiles.

Anna   A Jew is a person who undertakes – in theory, at least – all the social, moral and religious obligations of a Jew.

Chaim   That is a theoretical Jew. What I'm after is a real one.

Anna   Then ... perhaps there *are* no real ones. (*A train passes overhead. Meanwhile,* **Chaim** *moves to the board, takes up a piece of chalk and draws* ה.)

Chaim (*circling it*)   'Hashem' – 'The Name'.

Anna   Whose name?

Chaim   The Name that is never spoken. The 'ineffable' name. The name of God. Represented, quite simply, by the letter 'hei' with an apostrophe. The letter 'hei' – fifth letter of the Hebrew alphabet. Most holy of all the letters. So holy, in fact, that it cannot even be pronounced as part of the name of God ... But then, God has many names. He is 'El', 'Eloa', 'Elokim' – the Great One. He is 'Shaddai' – the Almighty. He is 'Hashem' – the Name. And He has two other names – one that I may speak only in prayer and the other, which is so holy that it may never be spoken. And yet we speak of God as the One, the Only, the Indivisible ... So who *is* He?

Anna   He is all things ... to all people.

Chaim   He is nothing to an atheist.

Anna   Because, to an atheist, all is nothing.

Chaim   So you believe there *is* a God.

Anna   Yes.

Chaim   And you believe He is real.

Anna   Yes.

Chaim   Then which name is His?

Anna   All names are His.

Chaim   Is He the Creator? The Lord? The Almighty?
The Great One? The Name? Who is He? What does He
do?

Anna   He does all things. He is all things. (*He writes* ו ד י
י ה*.*)

Chaim (*circling it*)   'Yehudi' – 'Jew'. (*He writes* י ר ב ע*.*)
'Ivri' – 'a Hebrew.' (*He writes* י מ ש*.*) 'Shemi' – 'a Semite'.
(*He writes* י ל א ר ש י*.*) 'Yisraeli' – 'Israelite' . . . Who are
these people? What do they do? Are they real? . . .
(*Shouting.*) Well, are they!? (*She looks at the floor.*) You want to
know what a Jew is? This is a Jew! (*He pulls his left sleeve
violently up to the elbow to reveal his tattooed number, at the same
time thrusting it before her face so that she cannot avoid seeing it.*)
This number. Number 175834 . . . Is this what you want to
become? (*He turns away, his anger turning to despair.*) The days
of the Jews are numbered. (*Lifting his left arm, without turning,
and letting it drop limply to his side.*) I have it in writing. (*A
train passes overhead.*) Prisoner number 175834 . . . with the
Star of David . . . (*He turns to her.*) . . . You know what the
Star of David is in Hebrew? 'Magen David' – '*Shield* of
David' . . . For him, it was an emblem. A coat of arms,
emblazoned on his shield. And with it, he raged into battle,
and was victorious. (*Pointing to his forearm.*) . . . Now see what
has become of it . . . Therein lies the success of the
Christian peoples. We . . . we Jews . . . We took a shield –
a symbol of strength, and of pride and of security – and
turned it into the cross of our suffering, the symbol of our
abject humiliation . . . the face of death itself . . . Whereas
you . . . you Christians . . . You took the cross – an
implement of torture and of suffering and of death – and
turned it into a symbol of salvation.

Anna   What you say . . . is not entirely true.

Chaim   What would you know! . . . My genteel little
Gentile. (*He turns away.*) . . . What would you know? . . .
(*Pause.*) It's true that, after the war, I could walk into any
shop in town, brandish my tattoo, and march heedlessly to
the head of the queue . . . And the half-starved Germans,
mute in their guilt, just stood there . . . Sometimes, I didn't
even have to pay! . . . But, the world being what it is, the
effect soon began to wear off. The tattoo, however, did not.

Anna   Then, for God's sake, why do you stay here!?

Chaim (*shrugging*)   Everything in life becomes a habit . . . I
got used to it here.

Anna (*shaking her head*)   There is so much around you that
you refuse to see . . . The Star of David has indeed become
a shield once more. And every day, it rises higher. It calls
itself the 'Haganah' – the Jewish Defence Force –
'Haganah' coming from 'magen', 'a shield'. And it rises in
Palestine, the land of the Jews.

Chaim   You really believe in a land of the Jews? . . . The
Jews have no land. They never will have. There will always
be someone there to take it from them.

Anna   Then they will fight for it! (*He shakes his head and
moves to the board, taking up the chalk.*)

Chaim   Present tense of the English verb 'to be': (*He
writes 'to be,' and each of the following.*) 'I am', 'you are', 'he is',
'she is', 'we are', 'you are', 'they are' . . . Present tense of
the Hebrew verb 'to be': (*He indicates the empty space opposite
the list he has just written and shakes hs head.*) There *is* none.
There is a past tense, and there is a future tense. But there
is no present tense of the Hebrew verb 'to be' . . . You ask
me what a Jew is . . . A Jew is one who lives in the past,
and dreams of the future. For him, the present does not
exist – it is merely the point of extinction.

Anna   Then why do you stay in Germany? Why don't
you fight for a Jewish State!? Why don't you fight for a
'present tense' for the Jews!?

Chaim   The Jews! The Jews! All the time, you talk about the Jews! And still you don't know what a Jew is . . . You see that language there? (*He indicates the board.*) . . . That Hebrew you've been learning? The Hebrew alphabet is an alphabet without vowels. Did you know that?

Anna (*confused*)   But . . .

Chaim   Oh, yes – we can add in the vowels, in the form of diacritical markings underneath the consonants, but they are not part of the alphabet as such . . . We have the 'chiriq' •, for example, for 'ih'. But the alphabet as such contains only consonants. Bones. The mere 'skeleton' of a language. The flesh – the vowels – are missing. And yet, in everyday life – in books, newspapers, day-to-day correspondence – Jews communicate using only this skeleton of a language. This language of skeletons . . . The language of the dead.

Anna   If you have such scorn for this 'language of skeletons', why don't you teach me the vowels?

Chaim   Because what you're after is a function. And if you're going to function in Palestine, then you'll have to be able to read and write without vowels. Who knows – perhaps your function will be that of undertaker.

Anna (*standing, exercising great control over her emotions*)   I think I'd better leave now.

Chaim   What's the matter? Playing 'Jew' not fun any more? (*She moves to go. He stands in her way.*)

Anna   Please – do you mind?

Chaim   What did you think? I was going to make it easy for you?

Anna   Please . . . (*She brushes past him and exits.*)

Chaim (*calling after her*)   Did you think I was going to let you become a Jew without knowing what a Jew is!? (*He almost lunges at the board, rubbing out what is there and taking up the chalk.*) The phrase 'to be cold'. 'J'ai froid.' (*He writes it.*)

I *have* cold. The French are always so possessive. The English: I *am* cold. (*He writes it.*) So philosophical. So existential. So . . . cold . . . The Hebrew: 'Cahr Lih'. (*He writes* קר לי.) 'Cold . . . to me.' The Jew *is* the cold. The cold *is* the Jew. Hebrew is the language of true being. The language of true suffering. (*Calling out.*) You want to know what a Jew is!? . . . A Jew *is* what he happens to be suffering at the time the question is asked!

A train passes overhead as he drops to his knees, almost in an attempt of prayer. The lights fade to black. We then hear the electronic sounds of a radio which is not tuned to any particular station. The lights rise to reveal **Anna** *entering, the violin case under her arm. She comes to a halt as her eyes fall upon* **Chaim**. *He sits, fast asleep, with his head on the table, his hair tousled, his shirt rumpled, and with an empty bottle of schnapps on the table next to him. She moves to the table and places her violin case on it. He stirs slightly. She goes to the radio to try and switch it off. He wakes up, lifts his head from the table and looks in her direction.*

Anna   How do you turn this thing off? (*She has been turning the left knob − the tuning knob − and suddenly hits upon a radio broadcast.*)

Chaim   It's the right knob. Turn the right knob. (*She indicates with her head that he should be quiet.*)

Broadcaster's Voice   . . . Palestinian sources report that Jewish forces today broke through the Arab blockade of Jerusalem . . .

Chaim (*rubbing his forehead*)   The right knob! Turn it!

Anna   Shh!

Broadcaster's Voice   . . . Reports have it that a force of some fifteen hundred men broke through the Arab lines in the early hours of this morning. Arab sources have so far failed to confirm . . . (*A train passes overhead.* **Anna** *stamps her foot in anger, pressing her ear to the radio. The train noise subsides.*) . . . The International Olympic Committee today announced that this year's Olympic Games, the first to be held since . . . (*She switches off the radio, angrily.*)

Anna Damn! (*Indicating the train.*) How do you put up with that infernal noise all the time!?

Chaim (*straightening, stretching, running his hands through his hair*) Sometimes, at night ... it's quite soporific ... That's when the goods trains roll by. Mile upon mile of them. Slowly. Rhythmically. Inexorably. (*Mimicking a train.*) Lub-dub, lub-dub ... lub-dub, lub-dub ... lub-dub, lub-dub ... Like the beating of a heart. Beat after beat after beat ... Just like ... (*Looking heavenwards.*) ... counting sheep. (*Another train passes overhead.*)

Anna (*screaming at the train*) Enough!!

Chaim (*hands to head*) Please, no shouting. Please.

Anna You've been drinking.

Chaim I met a man at the market today ... He came up to me and asked if I'd seen any strangers about ... There were lots of people there, but he approached only me.

Anna (*nonchalantly*) Really.

Chaim Well ... I answered him truthfully – I told him I hadn't ... I mean, I could hardly call *you* a stranger, could I. I know you too well. I know your name. I know the languages you speak. The instrument you play ... You've told me quite a lot about yourself. And you *have* been honest with me. You've stressed that yourself ... your honesty, I mean ... So I could hardly have called you a stranger, now, could I.

Anna (*indicating the bottle*) You have been drinking, haven't you.

Chaim No ... No, not drinking – celebrating ... Today is the first day of Pesach. (*She looks confused.*) ... Pesach. Passover ... Jewish Easter. (*He picks up the bottle.*) ... This – whatever it was – constitutes the better part of my Seder. (*Moving to the board.*) 'Samech–daled–reish' – 'Seder.' (*He writes* ר ד ס. *From this point on, his speech becomes more and more rapid, almost manic.*) The 'Seder' is the Passover ceremony.

'Seder' is also the Hebrew word for 'order'. And from this is derived 'sidoor' – 'samech–daled–vav–reish.' (*He writes* ר ו ד ס.) 'Sidoor,' – which is the word for an ordered arrangement. It is also the word for 'prayer book' . . . So you see, we Jews are great ones for following orders . . . 'Hacol beseder' . . . 'Everything is in order.' 'Everything is fine.' 'All right.' 'OK.' 'Good.' . . . Order is good . . . But then . . . then there is the particle of negation – 'ih' . . . Isn't that a beautiful turn of phrase – 'the particle of negation'? 'Ih-seder.' (*He writes –* א י *to the right of* ס ד ד.) '*Dis*order.' Lack of order . . . 'Ih' can also mean 'island' or 'jackal' – I'll leave you to work out that contradiction for yourself. 'Ih' can also be an exclamation of woe. Woe for the loss of order. Woe to the Jews . . . Woe to mankind! Woe to the whole damned universe! . . . What's the use. (*He has thrown the chalk to the floor and turned away from her.*) . . . Go . . . Go away and leave me alone.

Anna   No . . . No, I won't go away . . . Not until you tell me what's wrong.

Chaim   What's wrong? . . . What are you – a doctor? (*She makes no response. There is a pause.*) . . . Everything's wrong. What are you going to do about it? (*She sits at the table, making it perfectly plain that she is going to stay. There is a further pause, longer this time. He sighs, turns to face her and pushes the chess board, which is set up – towards her.*) You play chess?

Anna   I'm not interested in chess. I want to find out . . .

Chaim   You want to know what's wrong? You play chess!? Yes . . . yes, I remember. You told me you did.

Anna   (*quietly*)   Yes . . . Yes, I do play chess. (*He has already picked up both a black and a white pawn, one in each hand, exchanged them behind his back, and is now holding them out to her, hidden inside clenched fists, knuckles up.*)

Chaim   Which hand? (*She is slow to respond.*) . . . Which hand!?

Anna   The left. (*He opens it to reveal the white pawn.*)

Chaim How appropriate . . . Your move first. (*He turns the board so that the white pieces are closest to her. She lifts her hand to move a pawn.*) Before you begin, however, I must inform you of a rule I always use in playing chess. (*He picks up the two kings, one in each hand.*) No kings. (*He throws them on to the table.*)

Anna (*smiling*) Then . . . what's the point?

Chaim What do you mean, 'What's the point?' You can still move, can't you? You don't need your king.

Anna Sure I can move, but to what end? I mean, if there isn't . . . (*The light suddenly dawns.*)

Chaim (*after a pause*) I used to believe that the existence of God gave our lives – gave the world – some meaning. That if you took away the king, we could still do all that we had done before, but that it would have no point. There was no way of 'winning'. Then I discovered that even if there *were* a king, winning in *itself* had no meaning. One's left hand might just as well play one's right hand . . . Then I discovered that there was, in fact, no king . . . Shachmaht – the king is dead . . . So you see, I – Rabbi Chaim Levi – am an atheist.

Anna Then . . . why do you call yourself 'rabbi'?

Chaim A 'rabbi' is a 'teacher' – I am still a teacher.

Anna But you still wear a skull cap. You still . . . 'observe' Passover. You still call yourself a rabbi. You still pray . . . I don't understand. Why?

Chaim I knew a boy once who had had both legs removed. Yet he could still feel his toes wriggling. Still feel a pain in his calf or an itch in his foot . . . Well . . . three years ago, my God was removed. And though I still feel the need for Him, still love Him, still fear Him, still pray to Him, still pay Him the respect of a thousand and one petty observances – I know that He is no longer there . . . That my religion is no more than a phantom. A habit . . . Hmph . . . My whole life is no more than a habit now. Nothing means anything any more. Nothing to live for. No *one* to live for . . . I'm just . . . marking time, waiting for the end. If the Angel of Death were to walk through that door this very minute and say: 'Come, Chaim – it's all over,' I would gladly take his hand.

Anna   Hmph . . . And you call yourself a rabbi . . . A teacher . . . What could you possibly teach me? What . . . A dead language? A language of skeletons? Of memories? Of corpses?! . . . I'm not interested in that kind of language!

Chaim   You assume so much, in your innocence . . . How does one tell when a language is 'clinically dead'? . . .

Anna   I judge a language by those who speak it. And, as far as I can judge, you are clinically dead.

Chaim   You still don't understand, do you . . . Fatalism is built into the very structure of Hebrew. In Hebrew, there is no indefinite article – 'a'. All articles – all things – are definite. Predetermined. All Jews are determinists! Fatalists!

Anna   You know, I really do believe you are, in the deepest sense of the word, an anti-Semite.

Chaim (*pointing to his forearm*)   This number . . . this number gives me the right to be anti anything I like!

Anna   No! . . . No, it confers upon you the obligation to be anti *nothing*!

Chaim   What would you know! You, with your pure-white, starry-eyed dream of a land for the Jews! . . . I was in Auschwitz for two and a half years. Whilst I was there, I never doubted that it was the worst hell in all the universe . . . Then the war ended, and I was free. And I came to understand what hell really is . . . A Jew . . . without God.

Anna   You expect me to feel sorry for you . . . Well, I don't. You're not the only one who suffered. Millions suffered what you suffered. And now they're doing something about it. Whilst you sit here and rot in your stinking little cellar! Full of self-pity and death and decay . . . You're just another Muselman. You would have been better off if they'd . . .

Chaim (*cutting her off*)   What was the word you used?

Anna   What word? What are you talking about?

Chaim   That word! What was it!?

Anna   There was no word . . .

Chaim   You called me a 'Muselman'. Where did you
hear that word?

Anna   I'm sorry – you're mistaken. I . . .

Chaim (*grabbing her arm*)   You were in the camps, weren't
you!

Anna   N-no! I . . .

Chaim (*casting her aside, almost to himself*)   That's the only
place you could have heard such a word . . . 'Muselman'
. . . You know what it means . . . Yes, of course, you must
. . . The 'walking dead' . . . Those who had given up all
hope. (*She has come closer. He half turns towards her. She stops.
There is a pause. Then, softly.*) . . . Where? . . . Where did you
hear it?

Anna (*softly*)   I . . . was also . . . in Auschwitz.

Chaim (*in disbelief*)   Where?

Anna (*louder*)   Auschwitz.

Chaim   But . . . you have no number.

Anna (*turning away*)   No . . . No, I was not a prisoner . . .
I was a member of the SS. (*Blackout. A train roars overhead,
whistle at full blast. Pause.*)

Chaim   You're running away, aren't you. That man . . .
at the market . . . They're looking for you. They know
what you've done.

Anna   No . . .

Chaim   'I'll learn a little Hebrew,' you thought. Become a
Jew. Go to Palestine. No one would ever suspect . . .

Anna No! (*Catching herself, then, softly.*) No . . . You're wrong . . . That's not the reason. That's not the reason at all.

Chaim Then what is?

Anna All right . . . All right. They *are* searching for me. But that's not the reason I wish to become a Jew. You must trust me!

Chaim (*incredulous*) I can't believe what I'm hearing!

Anna (*opening her handbag*) How much do you want? (*She starts slapping notes down on the table.*) Ten dollars? Twenty dollars? A hundred dollars? How much? (*He rises and turns away, shaking his head*).

Chaim Get out of here . . . Get out of here before I kill you.

Anna (*rising and lunging towards him*) Damn you! Damn you – I'm telling you the truth! (*On the word 'truth', her fist lands on the back of his neck. He staggers slightly, recovers, and turns to face her.*) Don't you understand!? The truth! . . . The truth!!!

*He stands facing her, his breathing growing heavier. Fear suddenly rushes in on her and she begins to back away. He advances and cuffs her heavily over the left side of the face. She staggers, but continues to back off. He cuffs her over the right side of the face. She staggers once more. A train passes overhead. In the strobe-like light it casts, we see him land a heavy blow to the side of her neck. She collapses and we see him, astride her prostate body, raining down blows with both fists. The sound of the train subsides as the lighting returns to normal. He rises slowly to his feet, looking at his hands, which are stained with blood, he cups them to his face and head in silent anguish and staggers over to the other side of the stage, where he collapses to his knees, weeping silently. Meanwhile, **Anna** begins to stir. She props herself up on one elbow, her mouth bleeding. She sees **Chaim** and rises slowly, wiping the blood. She moves towards him.*

Chaim (*without looking up*) Go . . .

Anna But . . .

Chaim   Go!

She starts backing away and bumps into the blackboard. She thinks for a moment, picks up the chalk, and writes נ י   י ה ז ד י ר ה
א. *She then replaces the chalk and exits quickly. After a brief interval,* **Chaim** *slowly gets to his feet. He moves towards C, then notices the writing on the board. He moves closer, not believing his eyes, then begins to shake his head in mute disbelief as the sound of the train rises. The lights then fade to black.*

Act Two

The set is in darkness. Train with screaming whistle. Lights up to reveal **Chaim** *confronting* **Anna**, *who has just re-entered. The Hebrew she wrote is still on the board.*

Chaim (*reading*) Anih yehoodiah ... What's that supposed to mean?

Anna It means just what it says – I'm a Jewess ... My mother was Jewish. My father Gentile. We lived as Christians.

Chaim And you?

Anna I was a German ... and proud of it.

Chaim But you were also a Jew. (*Pause.*) ... Tell me ... How did a Jew come to be in the SS?

Anna By passing for a Gentile.

Chaim No, you misunderstand ... I'm asking how a Jew could *bring* herself to become a member of the SS.

Anna (*with difficulty*) I was ... ashamed of being a Jew. To me, it was like ... a horrible, lurking shadow ... I wanted to be rid of that shadow ... I joined an organisation whose stated aim was the removal of that shadow from off the face of the Earth.

Chaim And now, when it's convenient, you wish to ... hide amongst the shadows.

Anna (*pause*) Every morning, I wake up screaming ... every night, I go to bed knowing that, in the morning, I'll wake up screaming ... I used to give out the chocolates ... to the children ... as they went in ... Just before they bolted the doors tight ... It was the last thing they remembered ... before they died ... It was Eichmann's idea ... so they wouldn't be afraid ... I have to live with what I've done – every day until the day I die. And yet, the strange thing is: what I did, I did because *I* was afraid.

Afraid of them. My shadow.

Chaim   Do you really expect me to feel sorry for you? Without my friend here, (*Indicating the bottle.*) I don't sleep at all. (*Pause.*) The only thing I feel sorry for is your soul.

Anna   I don't need your sorrow ... And I'm not asking for forgiveness ...

Chaim (*turning on her*)   Then what are you asking for!? What do you want from me!!?

Anna   A document ... saying I'm Jewish.

Chaim   You must be joking.

Anna (*slight pause*)   Early this morning, Jewish terrorists launched an attack on Dir Yassin in Palestine. They massacred two hundred and forty-five Arabs – men, women and children. What makes me so different from them?

Chaim   Gas chambers ... and chocolates ... You can't even begin to compare the two situations! ... My God ... My God, how do you even dare to call yourself a Jew!

Anna   I was born a Jew. I ...

Chaim   Yes, and you spat on that birthright! Your Judaism died in the gas chambers ... with your victims ... There's no resurrection for Jews.

Anna   Isn't there? (*Pause.*) I think it's time you broke your commandment. I think it's time you spoke of the past.

Chaim   There is none.

Anna (*turning on him*)   Then why are you an atheist? ... (*There is no answer.*) ... Why are you an atheist!? (*There is no answer. She is almost standing over him.*) ... Why are you an atheist!!? (*He takes a deep breath. There is a pause.*)

Chaim   In 1942, I entered the camps, together with my younger brother, Mendel ... We used to call him 'Chiriq', because he was so small ... Chiriq and I had always been very close and, by some miracle, we managed to stay together. He had never been a healthy person and, day by

day, I saw him wasting away before my eyes. But he had
an overwhelming will to live and, somehow, he managed to
hang on, month after agonising month. One day, in 1945,
just three months before the end of the war, we were
carrying oil drums together in the snow. Death was already
in his eyes. He was so weak that I was forced to carry
almost the entire weight on my own. After two hours in the
snow – lungs burning, fingers bleeding, blinded with pain –
I found myself *praying* that he would die. Praying that I
might at last be set free of this ... insupportable burden –
my brother, Chiriq ... Two days later, my prayers were
answered. I was in the rest hut at the time, with dysentery.
The other prisoners, seeing that Chiriq was a 'Muselman',
and seeing that I was no longer there to protect him, took
everything from him, and beat him mercilessly in order to
hasten his end ... Within two days, he was dead. I never
saw him again ... And you ask why I am an atheist ...
How could I possibly believe in a God who would answer
such a prayer? (*They look at one another. There is a long pause.
He begins to weep, blurting it out – almost like a cough – at the
start. His head sinks to the table, his weeping becoming increasingly
agonised. Amid the weeping:*) Chiriq ... Chiriq ... Chiriq ...

*A train passes overhead. The lights fade to black. Each of the next
four, short scenes takes place in a changing, intimate light, with only
minor changes in the positions of* **Anna** *and* **Chaim**, *as if a long
intense conversation were being 'tuned into' at intervals. The sound of
the train settles to the slow, quiet, rhythmic 'clackety-clack' of a goods
train. This continues, in the background – throughout the next, short
scene. The lights gradually rise, very dimly, to reveal* **Anna** *and*
Chaim, *seated close together, facing one another.*

Chaim   Towards the end of the war, they transported a
group of us from Auschwitz to Dachau. The train had
open wagons. Many died from the cold. Sometimes I
thought the journey would never end. Every time we came
to a town, there was another interminable halt. The
workmen either side of the track would lean on their
shovels, peering with furrowed brows at the strange
creatures before them. Pointing and mumbling, they would

gather in small groups. Many had never seen a zoo or a museum. At the entrance to one of the towns, a single workman stood apart, his eyes filling with tears. He unrolled a lump of bread form his handkerchief and tossed it over into the wagon. Immediately, hands grasped, limbs were snapped, heads dashed. The bread soon turned a deep red, staining the lips of those who ate it. The lone workman closed his eyes and turned away. But a new game had been discovered, and we soon found ourselves under a hail of bread crusts. The workmen cheered and jostled, laying wagers, as the blood dripped from the cracks in the wagon.

The light and sound have gradually faded to darkness and silence. The lights, with subtle changes, rise once more to reveal **Anna** *and* **Chaim**.

Chaim   Before the war, I was a violinist. Apart from my God, my violin was the most precious thing I had. The day after we entered the camps, I was taken into the camp orchestra. Day after day I played, watching as men and women went to their deaths. One day, I smashed my violin. I couldn't play any more. I swore I would never play again. I broke that vow in your presence, when I played the 'Hatikvah'.

The lights fade out and fade in once more, as above.

Chaim   When a woman was found to be pregnant, they waited until her baby was born, then threw the two of them, alive, into the crematorium. In our camp, the only place where male and female prisoners could meet was the refuse heap. That's where the kapos got their sex . . . One day, I was emptying some drums there when a woman motioned to me. She told me that she and another woman were going to abort her friend, who was pregnant, and that they needed some help to hold her down. I asked if her friend had agreed to this, and she laughed. At that moment, two other women appeared. Before I knew that was happening, I felt a lump of wood thrust into my hand and heard two of the women shouting: 'Hit her!' 'Quick!

Hit her on the head!' The third woman had been pinned on her back on the refuse heap, screaming. My arm came down, and she was silent. One woman held apart the legs of her unconscious friend whilst the other thrust a bent piece of metal in between the wasted thighs. A pool of blood soon gathered at the first woman's knees. She stood in triumph and slapped the face of her lifeless friend. The friend didn't move. The blow I had delivered in order to help save her life had taken it instead.

The lights fade and rise, as before.

Chaim   In our hut, there was a small boy. He wasn't supposed to be there. There were no children. But there he was. In a dark corner, always staring. No one knew how he had got there, or why the SS permitted him to stay, but there he was. A child of the camps. A number tattooed on his left arm, he had lost both legs. And there he sat – all day and all night – his dark eyes fixed in silent blackness ... No one ever heard him speak. And so, we dubbed him Absalom. Because, of all of us there, he was the only one who was permitted to keep his hair. Long, black and shiny ... His presence in the hut was like a constant, smouldering ember. Always staring, never speaking. When I entered the camp, he was thought to be three years old. Some eighteen months later, during the course of a routine selection, my identification card was passed to the left, which meant the gas chamber ... However, the camp's Jewish hierarchy – led by what was referred to as the 'prominenten' – had their *own* criteria of 'selection'. It was felt by them that my contacts in the camp's Jewish underground made my life worth the saving. It was decided, therefore, that my place on the death-list should be taken by Absalom ... The necessary changes found their way into the paperwork and, two days later, the corner was empty ... And yet, some four and a half years later, that smouldering ember still burns within me. Still reproaches every beat of my heart ... Oh God ... if only *I* had died ... instead of *him.*

Lights fade to black. When they rise, **Chaim** *is stirring two tin* *mugs of coffee with a pencil, while* **Anna** *draws a map of Palestine on the blackboard, as on p 265.)*

Chaim Hot.

Anna Cham.

Chaim Cold.

Anna Cahr.

Chaim Big.

Anna Gadohl.

Chaim Small.

Anna Catahn.

Chaim Black.

Anna Er . . . no thanks . . . With milk.

Chaim (*louder*) Black.

Anna Oh, sorry . . . er . . . Shachor.

Chaim White.

Anna Lavan.

Chaim Good.

Anna Thank you.

Chaim (*louder*) Good.

Anna Oh . . . er . . . Tov.

Chaim Bad.

Anna Rah.

Chaim Riddle.

Anna This is the situation as it stands, these three areas making up the Jewish State and these three the Arab State . . . This is the Mediterranean and this . . . the Gulf of Akaba . . . Follow?

Chaim Would you like some sugar? I organised some sugar this morning.

Anna   Are you listening to me?

Chaim   Yes, of course. Go on. (*Ladles sugar and stirs.*)

Anna   Now ... on the Zionist side, we have a very strong underground movement ...

Chaim   Ah, yes ... The Haganah ...

Anna   Well, it's not quite as simple as that. You see, as well as the Haganah, there's Lechi ... the IZL ... the Stern Gang ... In fact, it's rather significant that there are as many names for Zionist groups as there are for God.

Chaim (*nodding, then:*)   Is that good or bad?

Anna (*looks at board, then at him*)   Both.

Chaim   Ah. (*Smiles.*)

Anna   Chiddah. (*He raises an eyebrow.*) The word for riddle: Chiddah.

Chaim (*he nods, impressed. Then:*)   You were telling me about God.

Anna   Was I?

Chaim   It appears he has something in common with the ... underground movement. (*They look at one another. He has a twinkle in his eye.*)

Anna   Why is it that, when you speak to me in my mother tongue, I feel most need of a translation?

Chaim   You're the one who introduced God into the conversation.

Anna (*pause*)   All right ... All right – if we must play your scriptural games. (*She writes* ה ת ק ו ה *and looks to him.*)

Chaim (*nods*)   Hatikvah.

Anna   Our anthem. (*She erases the* ה *at the extreme right and looks at him.*)

Chaim Tikvah.

Anna Hope. (*He nods. She circles the* ה ו *and looks to him. He raises an eyebrow. She gives a slight shake of the head.*) I believe it's your turn.

Chaim (*pondering*) Vav–heih ... The latter half of God's name. (*She looks disappointed.*) No?

Anna You weren't supposed to guess it that quickly.

Chaim I wasn't 'guessing'.

Anna Then the interpretation should be obvious.

Chaim Yes?

Anna (*indicating relevant parts of word*) All hope ... in the final analysis ... resides ... with God.

Chaim (*nods*) And what ... precisely ... shall be the form of this 'hope'?

Anna There are only two possible forms: Partition. (*Indicating map on board.*) ... Or Non-partition: A binational state, with equal representation for Arab and Jew.

Chaim (*handing over cup of coffee*) And to which form do *you* happen to subscribe?

Anna (*as if it were obvious*) I'm a Partitionist.

Chaim Ah. I notice you have acquired an 'ist'. Already, I smell trouble.

Anna (*sniffing and making a face*) I think you'll find it's the coffee.

Chaim Yes, I agree – it's awful. But the sugar's wonderful. Here – have some more. (*He ladles several large spoonfuls into her mug.*) 'Sugar' is 'sukarh'.

Anna Sukahr.

Chaim And coffee is 'cafeh'.

Anna Cafeh. (*He nods.*) Obviously not a Jewish beverage.

Chaim Obviously. (*Toasting.*) Lechaim.

Anna Lechaim. (*They drink.*)

Chaim (*slightly looking at map*) So you think this partitioning will work, do you?

Anna Ultimately, it's the only solution.

Chaim Solution?

Anna You just can't mix two separate peoples. It doesn't work.

Chaim Spoken like a true German. (*She looks up.*) . . . Only a German could ignore the fact that the Jews themselves are a multitude of different peoples. Even within their own ranks they never cease to bicker and discriminate.

Anna Perhaps so. But, in the face of a common enemy, they would unite.

Chaim And why should the Arabs be that common enemy?

Anna Because . . . (*Shrugs.*) . . . we have no alternative.

Chaim Indeed. (*He steps forward, erases the ה and replaces it with ם מ.*) Tcohmem. Enemy. (*Indicating relevant parts of word.*) 'Hope' . . . is our greatest enemy.

Anna But . . . without hope . . .

Chaim They would not have gone like sheep . . . following it, all the way to the grave. (*She shakes her head and turns away. Pause.*)

Anna I remember . . . in autumn . . . when the mud was cold and hard . . . and the sky was red . . . and the mist was coming in . . . The endless, endless rows of huts . . . And the sound – almost . . . magical – of a violin . . . suspended in the air . . . Like a bird . . . on a glacier . . . (*She begins to sing a theme from the second movement of Beethoven's Violin Concerto in D, Opus 61. She reaches the end of the theme, voice fading, eyes closed, tears appearing. Shakes head. Pause.*) That

sound ... There were times ... There were times I could
almost believe I was still on the planet Earth ... Almost
believe that I could turn and there, before me, would be a
... a tree ... or ... a blade of grass or ... a smiling face
... I too made a vow ... I vowed that if the violin could
make even a place like that seem human – seem as if it
were ... a part of this Earth – then I would one day begin
to learn its secret ... I ... fulfilled that vow in your
presence. (*She writes* מ ב ע ר.) Mecho'ar. Ugly. (*She erases the*
ע ר *and replaces it with* ל ל ל *to make* מ ב ל ל.) Michlahl.
Perfection ... Does perfection elevate the ugly? Or is it
degraded by it? (*He moves forward, erases the final* ל *and replaces*
it with a ה.)

Chaim   Michlah. Sheepfold. Concentration camp. A slight
... warp in perfection. The answer to all your questions.

Anna   It may be the answer to yours, but *that* (*Pointing to
map.*) is my answer!

Chaim   By what right? (*She is confused.*) By what right do
you claim it as an answer?

Anna   This land is ours! It was given to us ... By God.

Chaim   Pardon me, but ... when you say 'us', are you
referring to ... the Chosen People or ... to the Master
Race?

Anna   Your jokes are in very poor taste.

Chaim   (*changing up a gear*)   All right – you're tired of jokes.
Who do you think owns this cellar?

Anna   (*shrugging*)   I thought you did.

Chaim   I didn't pay for it.

Anna   Then who does own it?

Chaim   I do ... After the war, I ... stumbled across this
place. There was no one here, so I ... moved in. Soon
after, I was forced to 'evict' a beggar who also took a liking
to the place. Next, I ... straightened the nose of an ex-
serviceman who claimed the cellar as his ... Oh, and yes –

at the entrance, you'll find a mezuzah. The tiny prayer
scroll that Jews attach to their doorposts. Must have been
there ... oh ... fifty years at least ... Now: who owns this
cellar?

Anna What are you saying – that might is right?
Possession is nine-tenths of the law? What?

Chaim Drink your coffee ... Wouldn't want to waste all
that wonderful sugar, now, would we?

Anna Enough riddles. What are you trying to tell me?

Chaim The basic currency in Auschwitz, as you would
know, was cigarettes. You didn't smoke them – you
bartered them. With a guard ... a kapo ... A half-portion
of bread, a bowl of soup – whatever you needed most at
the time. The ironic part is that the only ones who actually
smoked them were the condemned. Those who were in no
need of bread or soup ... You must have noticed them,
surely ... I used to watch them, counting the bowls of
soup as they went up in smoke. And I used to wonder:
what if you reversed the process ... What if – as one of
those who had *not* been condemned – you actually smoked
a cigarette ... That would mean one less bartering
transaction. One less bowl of soup. One less Jew ... Six
million such cigarettes, each with a number. The greater
the number of cigarettes smoked, the lesser the number of
Jews remaining. Closed system. No escape. The smoking of
a cigarette, then, becomes an act akin to murder. (*Silence.*)
Another clue? (*He plumps the bag of sugar down in front of her.*)
How much sugar in this bag? ... A hundred and fifty, two
hundred gram? How many hours does a man have to
sweat out in the sun to harvest enough cane to make two
hundred gram of sugar? (*He ladles another spoonful into her
mug.*) How many cups of coffee before you've killed him
altogether?

Anna So what you're saying is: you survived ...

Chaim So Absalom had to die.

Anna And people are still dying ...

Chaim   For me, and for you . . . You see – in the camps, we weren't troubled by such . . . niceties. There was no good, no evil . . .

Anna   No right or wrong . . .

Chaim   No wisdom, no foolishness. Only one distinction . . .

Anna   Between life and death.

Chaim   To the left . . .

Anna   Or to the right . . .

Chaim   The Selection . . . the only morality – then and now – is that of survival.

Anna   Then . . . the SS were no worse than anyone else. (*He picks up chalk and writes* ם ו ל ש – ב א *and looks to her.*) Av–Shalom. Absalom.

Chaim   When the war ended, my camp was liberated by Russian soldiers. The scene . . . was a strange one . . . No cheering. No running. No embracing . . . The soldiers came forward . . . slowly. Horror and disbelief filled their eyes. And then, a different expression crept into their faces, and tiny tears appeared in the corners of their eyes. Tears of shame. Shame that men had done this to other men, and that they themselves were men. Shame that they inhabited a world where such things were permitted to happen. Shame that their goodness had not been sufficient to prevent such evil. (*He circles the* ו ל *of the* ם ו ל ש – ב א.) You remember our old friend 'lamed–vav'. The thirty-six Just Men . . . There is such a thing as metaphysical guilt. The guilt we bear for the sins of others. For men must answer for that which men do. And, as long as there is one atom of evil in the world, there can be no saints. No devils. (*He writes* י ד ש.) 'Shaddai' – the Almighty. God. A Being of Infinite goodness. (*He circles the* ד ש *of the* י ד ש.) 'Shed.' The Devil . . . A part of that infinitely good Being.

A train passes overhead. The sound of the train cross-fades with that of a piano playing Beethoven's Piano Sonata No. 31 in A flat major,

Opus 110. Lights up to reveal **Chaim** *at the piano. A half-full bottle of schnapps at one end of the keyboard. He is mildly drunk.* **Anna** *appears, carrying her violin case. He stops playing and turns.*

Chaim   Ah, Anna. Come. Come in. Sit down ... You want some schnapps? (*She shakes her head, smiling.*) I won't force you. (*He resumes his playing as she sits.*) Beethoven ... The closest man has come to reproducing the voice of God ... German, of course. (*Continues playing.*) ... The piano, Steinway – Rolls-Royce of pianos ... German, of course ...

Anna   Isn't that stretching it a little?

Chaim   All right. German, American – same thing ... The Germans are the best at everything they do. Best at music. Best at philosophy. Best at science ... In short, they are past masters of bestiality ... The only thing in which they are lacking ... is moderation. (*He continues playing.* **Anna** *has meanwhile come upon the chessboard, which has been left in mid-game.*

Anna   Whose move? (*He looks up.*) Black or white?

Chaim   Black.

Anna   (*scanning board, frowning*)   Not like you to leave your rook unguarded. (*She takes the white rook, using the black queen, and stands, holding the former.*)

Chaim   (*still playing piano*)   Pawn from king 7 to king 8, if you would.

Anna   Oh. (*Moves pawn, smiles.*) I didn't see that.

Chaim   Not like you to overlook the significance of a pawn.

Anna   (*almost shrugging*)   I suppose you want your rook back. (*She is about to replace the pawn with the rook she is holding.*)

Chaim   (*still playing piano*)   No ... No, I ... I think I'll take the bishop.

Anna   Are you sure? I think your defence would be ...

Chaim (*still playing*)   That man was here again today . . . looking for you. (*She turns, forgetting the chess.*) Spoke to me in Hebrew. Showed me a photograph – asked me if I recognised you . . . Fortunately, you were in uniform, and I could quite honestly say that I'd never seen that face before in my life. You looked so . . . so Aryan.

Anna   What did he say? (*He keeps playing.*) What did he say?

Chaim   Left me his number. Told me to keep in touch . . . It's there on the table. (*She picks up the card.*) I've a terrible memory for numbers. If I were to lose that card, I wouldn't have a hope of remembering what's on it. (*She smiles, is about to slip the card into her purse, has second thoughts, and tosses it back on the table. He plays for a few more seconds, then stops and turns to her.*) . . . Perhaps you'd like to join me in a duet . . . Look. (*He picks up some sheet music from the top of the piano, leafs through it, pulls out a score and places it on the table.*) . . . Here . . . some Fauré . . . Specially transcribed for violin . . . Not German, but . . . not bad . . . I trust you've been practising?

Anna (*opening the violin case as she peruses the music*)   As a matter of fact, I have . . . I might even give *you* a bit of a shock.

Chaim (*sitting at the piano*)   By all means! . . . After you.

Anna   No . . . No, you go first. (*He nods, then starts playing the piano part of Gabriel Fauré's Elegie in C minor, Opus 24. She allows him to become involved in the music then, ever so softly and slowly, starts playing the 'Hatikvah'. He continues playing, hears that something is amiss, slows down and finally stops playing in order to listen to her rendition, which is a fine one. She finishes. There is a pause.*)

Chaim   That was very beautiful. (*She smiles and looks down. There is a pause.*) When do you think you'll be leaving . . . For Palestine, I mean?

Anna   When I'm a bona fide Jew. Legally . . . Everything else is arranged.

Chaim   You could bribe your way in tomorrow ... if you wanted to.

Anna   I'd rather not do it that way.

Chaim   What if these ... people catch up with you before you manage to leave?

Anna   That's the risk I'll have to take.

Chaim   You're a brave woman ... Foolish, but brave.

Anna   No, not brave ... Just hopeful.

Chaim   (*after a pause*)   What are you going to do when you finally get there?

Anna   What am I going to do? ... I'm going to cry. For the first time in ten years, I'm going to cry till I can't cry any more.

Chaim   And then?

Anna   Then ... I'm going to raise chickens.

Chaim   I thought you were going to be an interpreter.

Anna   At the beginning, yes ... But only so that I can get together enough money to raise chickens.

Chaim   Why chickens?

Anna   My father detested chickens ... Almost as much as he detested Jews. He used to taunt my mother by calling her a 'chicken-chomper'. That was his name for all Jews – 'Chicken-chompers' ... He was a man of fine sensibilities.

Chaim   Why did he marry your mother in the first place?

Anna   He ... loved her ... It was only later that he found out she was Jewish. Too late, for him ... He forced her to convert. But then, when Hitler came to power, that wasn't enough. He found himself trapped, between his love and his hatred. But he didn't turn her in, that wasn't his style. He chose, instead, to start a new life. New job, new city, new papers, new name. Everything new. Except his wife. From that day on, he lived in fear of his life. And he

made her pay for that fear. With a thousand and one
humiliations. She was like a prisoner, with nowhere else to
go. He used to beat her. Used to make her sleep in the
kitchen. After a while, he couldn't even look at her, and
she was barred from entering our part of the house ... I
watched her change, over the years, from a proud and
beautiful woman to a miserable ... scraping animal. In the
beginning, he used to force me to curse her as she knelt,
scrubbing the floors. After a while, he didn't have to force.
I hated her. I hated everything about her. She was no
longer human ... I hated her because she had allowed
herself to be turned into a pitiful, grovelling ... nothing.
Because she was a Jew. And I was a Jew. And when I
looked at her I saw myself. And I hated her for it ... One
day, he beat her very badly, and broke her arm. That
night, she took me aside and told me she was going to stay
with relatives who were in hiding in Berlin. She kissed me.
I wiped my cheek. That was the last time I ever saw her.
Years later, I heard she'd been lost in an air raid. She died
a Jew ... After she left, I heard my father crying. I'd never
heard a man cry like that before. I went in to him. He
didn't want me there. I persisted and he slapped my face. I
knew then that I, too, had to go ... A year later, I was in
the SS. Oh, my God. He was my father ... He made me
hate my mother. He made me hate myself. With so much
hate inside me, there was nowhere else to go. I wanted to
kill. To rid myself, once and for all, of that pitiful shadow
... Oh, my God ... my God ... (*Crying.*) She kissed me
... She kissed me and I wiped my cheek. (*She continues
crying. Awkwardly, he pushes forward his handkerchief. She dries her
eyes.*) It didn't help ... Every day in the SS made me hate
myself more. And the more I hated, the more I wanted to
kill ... My efficiency knew no bounds. But it didn't help
... Most of us drank schnapps from the moment we awoke
in the morning till the moment we slumped into our beds
at night. I don't even remember the war. I spent it in a
drunken rage. That's what the schnapps was for – to
enable us to vent our rage. Not to overcome it, or
understand it or exhaust it, but simply to vent it. I vented

it for four years. I lived rage, I breathed rage, I drank rage
... I *was* rage ... When the war was over, and the fog
began to lift, I stood – for the first time – alone with my
rage. And I came to realise, by turns, that I didn't hate the
Jews at all – I hated my mother. That I didn't hate my
mother – I hated my father. That I didn't hate my father –
I hated myself ... That's when I decided to stop hating.
To accept myself ... as a Jew.

*Their eyes meet, and they realise that they are, at this moment, as
close as two people can be. At this point, a train passes overhead. The
lights fade to black. The sound of the train then fades as the lights
rise once more to reveal* **Chaim**. **Anna** *is just entering carrying,
along with her usual belongings, a book.*

Chaim (*looking up*)   Come in, quickly ... Quickly!

Anna (*hastening her step*)   What's the matter?

Chaim (*looking upstage*)   Did anyone follow you?

Anna   No. Not that I noticed. Why?

Chaim (*looking from UR to UL*)   That man's been out there
... I've noticed him three times today.

Anna   Is he there now?

Chaim   I can't see him. Maybe he missed you.

Anna   Let's keep our fingers crossed. Here ... I have
something for you. (*She dips into her handbag and fishes out a
small chocolate bar.*) ... Chocolate. (*She holds it out.*) ... And
don't you dare say a word about how many Swiss folk gave
their lives in its manufacture or I'll ... I'll straighten your
nose. (*He stares at the chocolate in his hand, an ironic smile on his
face. She notices something is wrong.*) ... Oh God ...
Chocolate ...

Chaim   No. No, it's not that at all ...

Anna   Then ... what ... ?

Chaim   It's rather ironic, really ... It was a small, red-
haired boy who informed upon me to the Germans ... His

reward was a chocolate bar. Just like this one . . .

Anna I'm sorry, I . . .

Chaim Don't be worry. I . . . I'm glad, in a way . . . It's almost . . . like having the chance to reclaim one's life . . . Thank you . . . Thank you very much.

Anna I brought you the money for this month's lessons. (*Reaching into her handbag.*) I know it's a little late, but it's all there.

Chaim Tell me – where on earth do you get all this money? I charge you at least twice as much as I do any of my other students, and you're the only one who pays.

Anna I'm a prostitute.

Chaim What?

Anna A prostitute.

Chaim Really? (*Looking her up and down.*) You don't *look* like a prostitute.

Anna You don't look like an atheist.

Chaim And tell me . . .

Anna Do I enjoy my work? Yes – it helps me enormously with my gutturals: 'Aaaah!'

Chaim And you feel no shame, no . . . guilt at what you're doing?

Anna I'm surviving . . . which is more than most people can say. And besides, you've been living off the earnings of my prostitution for almost two months now. I haven't heard any complaints.

Chaim I . . . I had no idea . . .

Anna Oh, come now, rabbi. A young German woman? Good-looking? Well dressed? Clean? . . . Pockets bulging with American banknotes? Surely you must have suspected something.

Chaim No, I . . .

Anna Then it's because you didn't *want* to suspect.
Because you didn't want to know . . . And you know why?
Because, as long as you could go out and buy American
sugar on the black market, you didn't *care*! (*Shaking head,
smiling.*) It's the old story, isn't it . . . For twelve years, Jews
disappeared off the streets, into ovens and up chimneys . . .
'We didn't know!' cried the people. 'Nobody told us!' . . .
That's just not good enough. It wasn't good enough then
and it isn't good enough now. Nobody ever 'tells' you these
things. You have to find out. You have to want to know
. . . There isn't a single crust of bread that isn't stained
with someone's blood, somewhere along the line . . . But to
know where that bread comes from, and still be prepared
to eat it . . . That takes guts. Real guts . . . Have you got
guts, Rabbi Chaim Levi? Have you got real guts? . . . You
talk about metaphysical guilt . . . (*She picks up one of the books
she has brought and throws it down on the table in front of him. He
looks up.*) Go ahead . . . Where it's marked. (*He opens the book.
She circles him as she speaks.*) Now the word of the Lord came
unto Jonah, saying: 'Arise, go to Nineveh, and cry against
it; for their wickedness is come before Me.' But Jonah rose
up to flee unto Tarshish from the presence of the Lord,
and he found a ship going to Tarshish. But the Lord sent
out a great wind unto the sea, so that the ship was like to
be broken. And the mariners cast lots that they might know
for whose cause this evil was upon them. And the lot fell
upon Jonah . . .

Chaim No! . . . No, this is a travesty. I'm no prophet.
(*He turns his back on her.*)

Anna (*closing on her quarry*) And they said unto him: 'Tell
us: what is thine occupation? What is thy country? And of
what people art thou? (*He keeps avoiding her.*) And they cast
forth Jonah into the sea . . . Now the Lord had prepared a
great fish to swallow up Jonah. And Jonah was in the belly
of the fish three days and three nights. And he said: 'I
cried by reason of my affliction unto the Lord, and He
heard me; out of the belly of hell cried I, and Thou
heardest my voice! . . .'

Chaim (*with a terrible, anguished rage*)   No!!! . . . No, never!!
Never . . . once . . . in all those years of hell did He hear
my voice!!!

Anna   Except . . .

Chaim   Never!!!!

Anna   Except . . . when he killed Chiriq. (*He is full of
smouldering anger, and turns away once more. She picks up the chalk
and writes.*) 'Ih' – an island. That's what you'd like to be.
But you aren't. You're just a 'particle of negation'.
Negation of all that's living . . . One by one, you've shed
all your responsibilities. To your congregation, as a rabbi;
to those whom you might have permitted to come close to
you, as a husband and father; to yourself, as a human
being; to your God, as a Jew; and to the Jews, as a Zionist.

Chaim   What do you think is going to happen in
Palestine? Already, Jew is massacring Arab, Arab is
massacring Jew. Where will it end?

Anna   It won't end. But it'll go on whether you're there
or not. And part of the responsibility will be yours.

Chaim   I don't care. I just don't want to see it.

Anna (*taking careful aim*)   And the Lord spoke unto the fish
and it vomited out Jonah upon the dry land. And Jonah
went unto Nineveh, and he cried, and said: 'Yet forty days,
and Nineveh shall be overthrown.' So the people of
Nineveh believed God, and proclaimed a fast. And God
saw their works and repented of the evil He said He would
do unto them; and He did it not . . . But it displeased
Jonah exceedingly, and he was very angry.

Chaim (*quietly*)   I have a right to be angry. (*She looks at
him. Louder:*) I have a *right* to be angry . . . I have a *right* not
to care . . . I have a right . . .

Anna (*cutting him off*)   You care about *me*. (*He stops.*) . . .
You care what *happens* to me. (*He turns well away.*) You *do*

care . . . Even though we've known each other for little
more than a month.

Chaim   I have no desire to see you get yourself killed, if
that's what you mean.

Anna (*coming in for the kill*)   And the Lord God prepared a
gourd, and made it to come up over Jonah, that it might
be a shadow over his head, to deliver him from his grief.
And Jonah was exceedingly glad of the gourd. But God
prepared a worm, and it smote the gourd that it withered.
And God said to Jonah: 'Doest thou well to be angry for
the gourd?' And Jonah said: 'I do well to be angry, even
unto death' . . . Then said the Lord: 'Thou hast had pity
on the gourd, for that which thou hast not laboured,
neither madest it grow; which came up in a night, and
perished in a night. And should not I spare Nineveh, that
great city, wherein are more than sixscore thousand persons
that cannot discern between their right hand and their left
hand?'

*A train passes overhead. Lights fade to black. As the sound of the
train fades, lights once more rise to reveal* **Chaim**, *who stands before
the blackboard, pondering. After a few moments, he inverts the board,
so that the map of Palestine is upside down. He then draws a
straight line across it, through Jerusalem. After further consideration, he
draws a vertical line, also through Jerusalem. At this point,* **Anna**
enters. It is apparent that she is somewhat nervous and fidgety.

Chaim (*still pondering the map*)   You know, it's an interesting
phenomenon – the gravitational element in aggression . . . I
mean, just think what would have happened if the map of
Palestine had looked like this . . . I can't imagine any Arab
sitting still whilst he had this huge mass of Jews waiting to
fall on top of him . . . You know, I do believe that was
King David's greatest achievement. To rule over a united
realm in what we now know as Palestine. (*He looks at his
forearm, absently stroking his tattoo.*) . . . The feat has never been
duplicated – before or since. Perhaps it never will be . . .
Even he – the mighty David – had to sacrifice his own son
in order to maintain the kingdom intact. (*Noticing her*

disquiet.) I – Is something the matter?

Anna   I've come to say goodbye ... They've caught up with me ... They know who I am.

Chaim   I ... I wish there were something I could do ...

Anna (*shaking her head, smiling*)   Ironic, isn't it ... A few years ago, Germany was full of Germans chasing Jews. Now the roles are reversed ... (*She gives a fatalistic smile. There is a pregnant pause.*) I ... I solved your riddle.

Chaim   Oh?

Anna   I was up all night, but I finally solved it.

Chaim   Then ... this would have been your last visit anyway.

Anna   Yes ... Yes, I suppose it would have been.

Chaim (*moving to the chest of drawers*)   I knew you'd solve it ... sooner or later. (*He opens one of the drawers, takes out a form and holds it out to* **Anna**.) ... Here. All it needs is a signature. (*He holds out a pen also.*)

Anna (*taking both*)   What's this?

Chaim   It's the stationer's equivalent of a circumcision. (*She is confused.*) ... It says you're Jewish.

Anna   But ... don't you want to hear my solution?

Chaim   There *is* only *one*. So if you've found it, it must be the right one.

Anna   I really do think you should hear it.

Chaim (*sitting*)   All right, if you insist.

Anna   There are two reasons why I think you should hear it: first, because it means that this document no longer has any real meaning for me ...

Chaim   Ah, I was hoping you'd say that. Now I know you have the right solution.

Anna   ... and second, because I don't think *you* have the right solution . . . Not all of it, anyway.

Chaim   Well . . . Perhaps we'd better hear it, then.

Anna   Where to begin . . . I am both a German and a Jew. Hitler's Germany, however, ruled that the terms 'German' and 'Jew' were mutually exclusive. So I had to choose to be one or the other. To split my spirit in two so that my body might remain intact. I played the Germans' game . . . and I lost. And yet, I needed you to point out to me that I was, in fact, repeating that very same blunder when I embraced my Jewishness and chose to see the Arab as the 'other'. Because there *are* no others. (*She picks up the chalk and writes* חִידָה.) . . . 'Solve the riddle,' you said. 'Find the solution and I'll make of you a Jew' . . . What I didn't realise, until last night, is that the solution *is* the riddle. (*Indicating the word she has written.*) 'Chiddah' – meaning 'riddle.' (*She circles the* חִי.) 'Chai' – meaning 'alive' . . . Six million Jews are dead. You and I are alive . . . Why? . . . What was God thinking? . . . Perhaps that's the riddle. (*She erases the* דָה *of the* חִידָה *and replaces it with* יִם, *so that, we now see* חִיִים.) 'Cha*im*', meaning 'life'. 'Cha*im*', meaning 'lives'. One life. Many lives. The same word for both . . . Perhaps that's the solution. (*She writes* אֲתָנוּ.) 'Ottahnooh' – 'us'. (*She writes* אֲתָם.) 'Ottahm' – 'them'. (*She circles the* אות *in both words.*) The same root for both words . . . Perhaps that's the 'final' solution.

Chaim   I fear I have created a Cabbalistic Frankenstein.

Anna   (*suddenly very sharp and insistent.*)   Rabbi Chaim Levi. (*As she writes* רַב חִיִים לֵוִי.) Rav Chaim Levi . . . 'Rav' – the noun . . . (*She circles* רַב.) . . . Meaning lord, master, scholar, teacher, rabbi. 'Rav' – the adjective . . . (*She circles it again.*) . . . Meaning *many*, great, strong . . . The one is the many. The many are the one . . . 'Chaim' . . . (*She circles* חִיִים.) 'Life'. One life. Many lives. *All* lives. The one is the many. The many are the one . . . 'Levi' . . . (*She circles* לֵוִי.) Lamed–vav . . . (*She underlines the* לְו.) The thirty-six Just Men. Those upon whose shoulders the world's fate rests . . . The one is the many. The many are the one. Rav Chaim Levi – one of many . . .

Chaim (*evasive*) Maimonides himself couldn't have put it better.

Anna (*passionate*) Rav Chaim Levi – there *are* no 'others'! . . . Jew and Arab. Victim and executioner. Saint and Devil . . . They are *us*. All of them *us* . . . There *are* no others. Rav Chaim Levi – you *know* these things, but you don't live them. You see yourself as the 'other', so you try to shut yourself off from the rest of the world. But you can't. Because a rabbi living in Germany *is* a German. And a Jew is part of Palestine simply because there *are* Jews in Palestine. And to suggest that a member of the SS is not a human being is every bit as dangerous as the suggstion that a *Jew* is not a human being. To accept that good is a part of being human but that evil is not is to suggest that none of us is human. It is a short step from that suggestion to the gates of Auschwitz.

We hear the sound, off, of a jeep screeching to a halt. This is followed by the sound of violent blows upon the door. **Anna** *and* **Chaim** *embrace, briefly. Lights fade to black. Splintering wood. Shattering glass. Sub-machine gun fire. screaming. Fades into women and children screaming. Fades under* **Radio Announcer**'s *speech, the set remaining in darkness.*

Announcer Reports from the Middle East this evening reveal that, at precisely four p.m. today, following the singing of the 'Hatikvah', the National Anthem of the new Jewish State in Palestine, Mr David Ben Gurion, the leader of the ruling Mapai Party, read out the Proclamation of the newly founded State of Israel. The reading of the Proclamation took place at the Tel Aviv Museum and was broadcast throughout Israel by Haganah Radio. Scenes of great jubilation were later witnessed, as thousands of Jews danced and sang in the streets, many of them bending to kiss the earth at their feet. Within hours, however, the Arab armies of Lebanon, Syria, Iraq, Egypt and Transjordan were pouring over their respective borders and into the

Jewish State. Reports of fierce fighting have been received from almost every part of what was, until today, known as Palestine, and both sides are claiming to have inflicted heavy casualties.

A few further bursts of distant, muted sub-machine gun fire are heard. These fade out as the lights rise slowly to reveal **Chaim**, *who is writing the word* ם ו ל ש *on the blackboard. He ponders it, then starts removing all his belongings from the chest of drawers and folding them neatly into an open suitcase. Over all of this we hear his voice over the speaker system.*

Chaim's Voice   Dear Anna, I don't know if these words will reach you, or even if you are still alive, but I felt I had to write to you.

In the brief time I have known you, so much has happened. So many things have changed. Every day now, we receive war news from Israel. The news isn't good. When one hears of the casualties, one can't help thinking of the Jews who lived through Auschwitz and other camps like it. Of those who turned to the New World, and of those who turned to Palestine. Of those who sit now with their new families, and gaze at the wonders of New York. And of those who lie dead in the sands of Israel. And one can't but realise that the selections didn't stop at Auschwitz. And one thinks, also, of those *others* in New York – the men in grey suits, who sat in their offices, and drafted declarations and signed resolutions, and whose every stroke of the pen meant a thousand lives this way or a thousand lives that way. If ever I take an image of God with me to the grave, that will be the image.

But the changes, for me, have gone much deeper. For the time I spent with you awakened within me certain parts of myself I had long believed dead. In the years since the war, music had become my whole life. A life of rarefaction. A life high amongst the stars. But you made me realise that, in reaching for the stars, I had neglected perhaps the most important part of myself. My mortality. My humanness. My being as a living, breathing animal. The part of me without which my soul would be worthless ... In the short time we knew one another, you came to mean a great deal to me. It's difficult for me to put it into words, but perhaps you'll understand if I refer to an old linguistic argument we once had ... You might remember that I once asked you how one knows whether or not a language is dead ... For me, a language is alive for as long as it still has meaning. The same is true of human beings.

My life here, in this cellar, has no such meaning, and I find that I must move on. As to my destination – perhaps Nineveh ... God willing, I will find my way.

Until then, my dearest Anna, I bid you 'Shalom' – Peace and Goodbye.

Towards the end of this speech, **Chaim** *has come across* **Anna**'s *violin case. He runs his fingers over it, his mind running back to the past, then takes out the violin and bow and, slowly and deliberately, starts to play Gabriel Fauré's Élegie. As the music draws to a close, the lights dim to a spot on the word* שלום *on the board, then further contract to the letters* לו *of the 'shalom', before fading to total blackout and silence.*

End.

Hebrew letters to be used for music on page 222.

Aleph: א
Beit: ב
Gimmel: ג
Dahled: ד
Heih: ה
Vav: ו
Zayin: ז

Music Excerpts:

Page 212: Beethoven's Sonata for Violin and Piano No. 9 in A major, Opus 47 (Kreutzer Sonata). Second Movement.

Page 250: Beethoven's Piano Sonata No. 31 in A flat major, Opus 110.

Page 252: Gabriel Fauré's Elegie in C minor, Opus 24 (Cello part transcribed for violin).

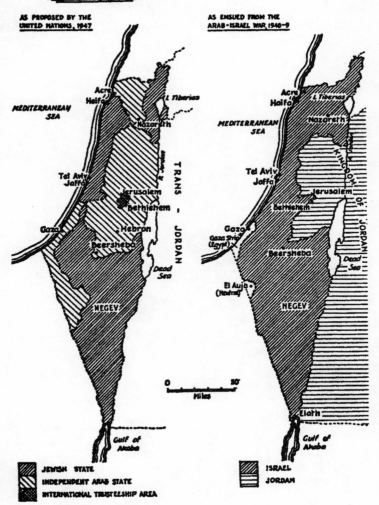

PALESTINE'S FRONTIERS

AS PROPOSED BY THE UNITED NATIONS, 1947

AS ENSUED FROM THE ARAB-ISRAEL WAR, 1948-9

MEDITERRANEAN SEA

Acre
Haifa
L. Tiberias
Nazareth
Tel Aviv
Jaffa
Jerusalem
Bethlehem
Hebron
Gaza
Beersheba

TRANS - JORDAN

Dead Sea

NEGEV

Gulf of Aqaba

JEWISH STATE
INDEPENDENT ARAB STATE
INTERNATIONAL TRUSTEESHIP AREA

Acre
Haifa
L. Tiberias
Nazareth
MEDITERRANEAN SEA
Tel Aviv
Jaffa
Jerusalem
Bethlehem
Gaza
Gaza Strip (Egypt)
Beersheba

KINGDOM OF JORDAN

Dead Sea

El Auja (Hadrad)

NEGEV

Eloth

Gulf of Aqaba

ISRAEL
JORDAN

0   30'
Miles

The 7 Stages of Grieving

Wesley Enoch and Deborah Mailman

Wesley Enoch is the eldest son of Doug and Lyn Enoch, who hail from Stradbroke Island. He was Artistic Director of Kooemba Jdarra Indigenous Performing Arts from 1994–97. Wesley has been an Associate Artist with the Queensland Theatre Company, who in 1999 commissioned him to write and direct *The Sunshine Club*, which was subsequently mounted by Sydney Theatre Company, in association with the 2000 Sydney Festival and the Sydney Opera House Trust. Wesley's recent directing credits include *Fountains Beyond* for the Queensland Theatre Company; *Stolen* which premiered at Playbox and has subsequently toured both nationally and internationally; and *Romeo and Juliet* for the Bell Shakespeare Company. Wesley is currently a Resident Director with the Sydney Theatre Company, for which his productions have included *Black Medea* and *The Cherry Pickers*.

Deborah Mailman first started working on *The 7 Stages of Grieving* in 1994, and has performed it throughout Australia, including at the Festival of the Dreaming in Sydney, 2000. Other highlights in her career include Kooemba Jdarra's premiere production of *The Cherry Pickers* (1994), *One Woman's Song* and *Gigi* for the Queensland Theatre Company, *Capricornia*, *Summer of the Aliens* and the Out of the Box Festival at Queensland Performing Arts Centre, the role of Kate in *The Taming of the Shrew* for La Boite Theatre, *Gwenda* for Brisbane Theatre Company, *A Midsummer Night's Dream* for the Sydney Theatre Company (1997) and Rosalind in *As You Like It* for Company B. She has also been a Youth Arts Worker for a number of companies. Films include *Radiance* (1998) and *Dear Claudia* (1999). In 1998 she became the first indigenous Australian to win an Australian Film Institute Award – for Best Actress for her role in *Radiance*.

Why Do We Applaud?

Wesley Enoch

> Theatres, actors, critics and the public are interlocked in a
> machine that creaks, but never stops. There is always a new
> season in hand and we are too busy to ask the only vital
> question which measures the whole structure –
> Why theatre at all?
>
> What for? Is it ananchronism? A superannuated oddity,
> surviving like an old monument or quaint custom? Why do
> we applaud, and what? Has the stage a real place in our
> lives? What function could it have? What could it serve?
> What could it explore?
> What are its special properties?

> Peter Brook, *The Empty Space*, 1968

In 1968 Peter Brook was questioning the role of theatre, its
history and its custom. About the same time many Australians
were coming to appreciate that indigenous people of Australia
were still alive and, despite all attempts to 'soothe the dying
pillow', showed no signs of disappearing. In fact, the Aboriginal and Torres Strait Islander population of this country has
increased not only through improvements in life expectancy
and a drop in child mortality, but, most importantly, as a result
of people culturally returning to family and place and
reclaiming their indigenous ancestry.

1968 was also the year Kevin Gilbert wrote *The Cherry Pickers*
(noted as the first written Aboriginal play). Just when Peter
Brook is questioning the position of theatre, Kevin Gilbert is
embracing its role to tell his story.

The greatest misconception held by White Australia and
indeed international audiences is that Aboriginal culture is a
museum piece, a remnant of a world long gone. This romantic
picture pays little justice to our instinct for survival and ability
to interact with the contemporary world. Murri culture, it was
said to me, is a way of explaining the world around us. The

stories of Land, the imitation of animals, spirits and the rivers, mountains and trees are testimony to an inherent connection with place and the need for everything to have a place – a story – in the greater fabric of song. When the world was created everything had a story; all the stories that were ever going to be told were created at that time. There is a completeness. Individuals in the clan would hand down stories, dances, song, ritual within a tightly organised and monitored system of kinship and genetic engineering with very little deviation. But the world is a changing place and the allowance for interpretation within an oral tradition is great, creating new spins to age-old stories. Individuals could be visited (in their dreams, in ceremony or domestic duty) by inspiration to explain a new occurrence in the world explaining why, in some communities, there are stories explaining the coming of money, HIV/AIDS, the Toyota, the horse (yarraman) and the bombers in World War II. Murri culture is a dynamic and changing entity. As the world around us changes so too does the speed at which we must tell new stories – giving meaning to the world.

The tension between traditional and contemporary life-styles/cultures is an integral part of Kooemba Jdarra's ongoing analytical role. The traditional structures of integrating all artforms and narrative-influenced design, music, movement, song and story are evident in *The 7 Stages of Grieving*. In traditional Murri cultures the interaction and integration of artforms is commonplace – the story has many ways of being told – the dance, the painting, the song, the rhythm and music all spring from a common story. There is no need to compartmentalise. The 'theatre' of ritual and play is made of these relationships between artforms. In the same way, the arts reflect and tell direct stories of genealogy, history, geography, law, social mores, etc., thus playing a political role in the continuity of the clan. *The 7 Stages of Grieving* is about politicising the content and the exploration in form from a traditional/ contemporary Murri viewpoint. This exploration is part of the continuity of indigenous cultures and is important to the development of a modern, uniquely Australian voice. The implications are exciting and broad-ranging.

This exploration of contemporary and traditional is not new

in indigenous dramatic writing. The existing canon of Australian playwrighting includes the works of Jimmy Chi (*Bran Nue Dae*), Jack Davis (*The Dreamers, No Sugar, Kullark*), Robert Merrit (*The Cake Man*), Eva Johnson (*Murras*), Owen Love (*No Shame*), Bob Maza (*The Keepers*), Sally Morgan (*Sistergirl*), Richard Walley (*Coordahs*) and many more who engage with the cultural continuum of indigenous Australia. In the same way that there is no homogeneous Aboriginal nation (accepting the fact that we are a collection of peoples of this continent, but with a diversity of languages, cultural practices and geographies), neither is there a generic Aboriginal experience to write of. The specificity of community experience has been manifest by a proliferation of biographical and autobiographical writing over the past few decades. The focus on the particulars of political struggles, historic events and/or the personal have helped develop an indigenous style based on content. Historically, indigenous writers have focused on appropriating the Western forms of theatre to create the drama, incorporating the elements of dance, advanced metaphor and use of language to highlight the writing's Aboriginality. An over-reliance on character and the denial of abstraction has often created a situation where the writing is perceived as unsophisticated and/or primarily issue-based, outside of artistic scrutiny. *The 7 Stages of Grieving* wishes to challenge this history.

The 7 Stages of Grieving comes from a paralleling of the 5 Stages of Dying in *On Death and Dying* by Elizabeth Kubler-Ross and the *7 Phases of Aboriginal History*. It seemed that there were similarities and this began an exploration into the personal and political history of indigenous Australia as an expression of our grieving. The performance follows the experiences of an indigenous 'Everywoman', chronicling the grief present in her life and the means of expressing it. Though the stories acknowledge real events, family histories and personal experiences of the collaborators, *The 7 Stages of Grieving* is ultimately a work of 'faction' – a mixture of fact and fiction. As our lives and histories reflect the political changes and policies of the past 207 years (every Murri has a family story of being taken away, or forced denial of language, or strict protectionist practices) so it can be said that our personal histories are indeed the history of our political relationship to Migrant Australia – one of grief, misunderstanding and injustice.

This performance draws upon both 'traditional' and 'contemporary' arts and cultural practice. The integration of artforms, the use of storytelling techniques, new song and dance and the cultural issues surrounding mourning are brought together with projection technologies, contemporary performance art and modern theatrics to explore a form of cultural hybridity. *The 7 Stages of Grieving* has been based on the concept of drawing influence from our heritage as Murri artists and the current artistic milieu, with all it has to offer this culturally specific exploration of our voice.

The 7 Stages of Grieving has been developed for Aboriginal and Torres Strait Islander audiences, acknowledging a sense of recognition and shared history.

We cry together, we laugh together and we tell our stories.

In the face of such an overpowering grief – which is our history – we can still laugh and survive. This is surely a sign of our resilience and strength of community. *The 7 Stages of Grieving* is a celebration of our survival, an invitation to grieve publicly, a time to exorcise our pain. *The 7 Stages of Grieving* is one story from many, a universal theme told through the personal experiences of one character.

Perhaps Peter Brook was questioning the role of theatre because he could not see it giving meaning to the world around him. It is interesting to see that Peter Brook is so fixated by stories and cultures other than his own that he 'appropriates' meaning from culturally based narratives originating in Africa, India and the Middle East. Kevin Gilbert, on the other hand, saw that he needed to celebrate, explore and educate about an Aboriginal perspective, documenting the clash of traditional and contemporary survival techniques.

Isn't this the reason why theatre exists?

Wesley Enoch, 1996

To our parents' parents
the pain, the sorrow
To our children's children
the glad tomorrow

In memory of
OODGEROO

The 7 Stages of Grieving was premiered at the Metro Arts Theatre, Brisbane, on 13 September 1995. It was performed by Deborah Mailman and directed by Wesley Enoch.

1 Prologue

A large block of ice is suspended by seven strong ropes. It is melting, dripping on to a freshly turned grave of red earth. The performance area is covered in a thin layer of black powder framed by a scrape of white. Within the space there are projection surfaces.

Ladies and Gentlemen, Kooemba Jdarra would like to take this opportunity to warn members of the audience that the following performance contains names and visual representations of people recently dead, which may be distressing to Aboriginal and Torres Strait Islander people. All care has been taken to acquire the appropriate permission and to show all proper respects. Thank you.

2 Sobbing

The faint sound of someone crying in the dark. The sobbing grows into a wail as the lights reveal an Aboriginal Woman alone with her grief. As her weeping subsides, words are projected up on the screen.

Grief

Grieving

Sorrow

Loss

Death

Pain

Distress

Lament

Mourn

Emptiness

Despair

Lonely

Regret

Misfortune

Guilt

Passion

Love

Absence

Desolate

Nothing

Nothing

I feel . . . Nothing

3   Purification

The Woman lights up a wad of eucalypt leaves and watches them burn. She blows out the flame and as the embers smoke she sings a song for the spirits of those that have gone before her and asks permission to tell the story of her grief.

Murraba bullar du

Bullar du
Bullar du
Murraba bullar du

Bullar du
Bullar du
Murraba bullar du

Bullar du
Bullar du
Murraba bullar du

Spoken.

Yugila yugila munan gi
Yugila yugila munan gi

4 Nana's Story

The performing area is flooded with colour. Floral patterns cover the Woman's dress. The story is textured with sounds of family, country music and the call of the kingfisher.

'The only thing black at a funeral should be the colour of your skin'. And so all my young cousins wore bright floral dresses.

My grandmother was a strong God-fearing woman who, at the age of sixty-two, was taken from us, passed away, moved on, gone to meet her maker, departed this world, slipped into her eternal sleep, her final resting place, laid to rest.

My family were in mourning for a month. All of us together in five houses ... we numbered close to fifty people.

My grandmother had fought going to the hospital because that's where people went to die. Very few of her friends had ever come back from hospital.

This was the same woman who thought doctors were infallible, the same woman who couldn't speak to teachers or police without fumbling, wouldn't answer the telephone, gave her tithe to the church and was visibly nervous at the mention of the 'gubberment'.

The whole family came together for meals. Huge barbecues, bowls of salads laid out on makeshift trestle tables, tropical fruits, rice. No matter what you were having for dinner there was always rice. Steak and chips – rice ... vegetables – rice ... stew – rice. I come from a family of footballers ... they're into this ... and there's so much steak, sausages, mince, chicken ... stuff we had spent half the day cooking or pots of things other relations had brought over.

My grandmother would tell stories of how there were days when there wasn't enough to feed all the kids. She wouldn't tell us a lot of stories but when she did we all listened, she'd sing to us.

The sound of country music mixing with the clickerclack of knives and forks and then someone would start singing along. Before you knew it, the older generation were in the middle of 'Delta Dawn . . . ' whilst the younger cousins all cringed. I can still sing all the words if I try hard. Nah . . . don't worry about it. There was so much going on – sometimes you didn't notice two people hugging, sobbing in the hallway. Everyone had their turn. Sometimes you felt like crying, and sometimes the joy of being there was enough to forget, even for the briefest moment, the reason.

Four hundred people . . . four hundred people turned up to the service. They couldn't all fit into the church. They just sat in the shade listening from outside. When we were all gathered around the grave a song caught on around the gathering – the words of which were unrecognisable. But the tune soared above us with the kingfisher.

The Woman reflects on this moment.

My sister maintains that she knew first. In the middle of the night the sound of a bird singing had woken her and she sat rigid till the morning ring of the telephone. She answered, 'I know.'

After dinner the boys might paint up and dance. And the girls might show a thing or two as well. The neighbours would watch from the safety of their kitchen window or come out to water their garden, gamin like, one even got out his video camera, and we would talk and drink and laugh. The kids might get out a video and escape. But when it came to sleeping – oh shit! – cushions, mattresses, lounges and back seats in cars all transformed. Black fellas as far as the eye could see.

I miss my grandmother. She took so many stories with her to the grave. Stories of her life, our traditions, our heritage from her now gone. I resent that.

The Woman sings, recalling the first few lines of 'Delta Dawn . . .'

5   Photograph Story

*A chair scrapes across a wooden floor, footsteps recede, a clock ticks.
Projected are images of an open suitcase filled with family photographs,
old and new. The progression of slides brings us closer into the details
of the photographs.*

In the house of my parents where I grew up, there is a
suitcase which lives under the old stereo in the front room.
The room is full of photographs, trophies, pennants,
memories of weddings, birthdays, christenings and family
visits. A testimony to good times, a constant reminder.

But this suitcase, which resides under the old stereo tightly
fastened, lies flat on the floor comfortably out of reach.
Safe from inquisitive hands or an accidental glance. In the
suitcase lies the photos of those who are dead, the nameless
ones. With an unspoken gesture we remove the photo of
my nana from her commanding position on the wall and
quietly slip her beneath the walnut finish. And without a
sound push her into the shadow.

Everything has its time . . . Everything has its time . . .

6   Story of a Father

*The Woman walks over to the grave and embraces the block of ice.
Springing away, she turns to the audience and clutches her breast.*

(*Irreverently*)   Oh my sousou.

The Woman sits on the edge of the grave.

I'm trying to deal with Dad's death. He hasn't died yet,
but the time is coming soon when he'll be taken away.

He hasn't stopped fighting since '67. He's forty-five, in and
out of hospital, he knows he needs to rest. He sees a gate,
he don't open it . . . he jumps it. He's supposed to be old.
I'm trying to deal with this. It seems selfish that the
thought is on myself rather than Dad. The time is coming
soon when all this won't be a rehearsal any more.

Sometimes I let myself go and find myself crying in the dark alone, without my family and home. The pain comes in here, I cry and cry until I can't feel any more. Numbed.

Then I wake up . . . and I have got my home . . . and I have got my family . . . and I will never have to live through what my dad has been through.

It's inevitable.

The one thing that I find comforting about death is that other people die too. Bruce Ruxton, John Laws, Alan Jones, Joh Bjelke-Petersen, Joan Sutherland, Richard Court, Arthur Tunstall, the woman next door, her dog . . .

The Woman leaves.

7   Family Gallery

A collection of family photos are projected like portraits in a gallery. They are recognisable as images from the suitcase.

8   Black Skin Girl

The Woman dances around, childlike, singing. Letters of the alphabet appear on her dress. At first it is a game but one from which she tires. She attempts to evade the letters by removing her dress. She is left topless with the letter Z on her chest.

Bului yuli mie

Bului yuli mie
Bului yuli mie
Naia gigi warunguldul
Naia gigi warunguldul

Repeat.

9   Invasion Poem

*A shaft of light from a half-open door frames the Woman. A chair
scrapes across a wooden floor, footsteps recede, a door closes, a clock
ticks.*

They come in the front door
Smiling
Offering gifts.
I invited them in, they demanded respect.
They sat in my father's seat
And talked to me of things that made no sense.
I nodded. Listened. Gave them my ear
As I was always taught to.

Without warning
They broke from our soft
Whispered conversation.
One took a handful of my hair and led my head to their
   knee.
Another washed his face in my blood.
Together they ploughed my feet. My feet.

My children, stolen away to a safe place,
Were wrenched from familiar arms and
Forced to feed upon another tongue.
The protests of my mother's mother cut short.
Silenced by a single wave of a stick.
Told not to speak, not to dance.
Told not to do what we have always done.

I lie painfully sleepless
In a landscape of things I know are sacred.
Watching unsympathetic wanderings.

To wonder is to think.
To wander is to walk.

The Woman retrieves her dress.

10   1788

The date 1788 appears.
'Hey, you! Yeah, you with that hat! You can't park there!
You're taking up the whole harbour! Go on, get!'

11   Murri Gets a Dress

Delivered in the style of stand-up comedy.

Have you ever been black? You know when you wake up
one morning and you're black? Happened to me this
morning. I was in the bathroom, looking in the mirror and
I thought, 'Nice hair, beautiful black skin, white shiny teeth
... I'm BLACK!'

You get a lot of attention, special treatment from being
black. I'm in this expensive shop and there's this guy next
to me, nice hair, nice tie, nice suit, waving a nice big gun
in the air and the shop assistant says, 'Keep an eye on the
nigger ... eye on the nigger.'

OK, so I went to try on a dress and the shop assistant
escorts me to the 'special' dressing room, the one equipped
with video cameras, warning to shoplifters, a security guard,
fucken sniffer dog ... 'Get out of it.' Just so I don't put
anything I shouldn't on my nice dress, nice hair, beautiful
black skin and white shiny teeth ...

Now I'm in this crowded elevator, bathed in perfume, in
my nice dress, nice hair, beautiful black skin and white
shiny teeth ... 'Hey, which way.'

The Woman sniffs the air.

Somebody boodgi and they all look at me!

Now I go to my deadly Datsun, looking pretty deadly
myself, which way, lock my keys in the car. Eh but this
Murri too good, she got a coat hanger in her bag! Fiddling
around for a good *five seconds* and started hearing sirens,
look around, policeman, fireman, army, fucken UN and
that same sniffer dog. Just to make sure everything's OK.

Spoken in an American accent while holding the audience at 'gunpoint'.

'Who owns the car, Ma'am?'

Indicating herself.

'ME.'

So I'm driving along in my deadly Datsun, stylin' up to that rear-vision mirror. Car breaks down. Get out. Started waving people for help.

Imitating a fast car.

Started waving people for help. Vrooom!
Started waving people for help. Vrooom!
Next minute I see this black shape coming down the road – fucken sniffer dog.

Finally get home, with the help of the policeman, fireman, army, fucken UN. Still looking deadly in my nice dress, nice hair, beautiful black skin and white shiny teeth. Auntie comes in, 'Eh Sisgirl, nice dress, can I borrow it?'
'Mmmm.'

Thinking that tomorrow will be a better day, I go to bed. Kicking that sniffer dog out. Still with the sound of sirens in my head. Snuggling up to my doona and pillow.
Morning comes, I wake up, looking in the mirror. Nice hair, beautiful black skin, white shiny teeth. I'M STILL BLACK! NUNNA!

12 Aunty Grace

The Woman pulls the suitcase out of the grave. Placing it before her on the floor, she opens it. She looks up at the audience.

Aunty Grace came back especially for Nana's funeral. I had only know this woman through Nana's collection of photographs. They were never displayed with the other members of our family, they were only brought out on request, when any of the older cousins asked about family history. The pictures always showed the two sisters together.

Going to a social or party. Aunty Grace was beautiful, a half-head taller than her younger sister, slender and almost inevitably dressed in white, teeth glowing extra white, in the two-tone capture of the moment.

My father went to pick up Aunty Grace from the airport and dropped her at an hotel. She wasn't going to stay with the rest of us. That was very clear.

Aunty Grace lives in London. She's lived there for almost fifty years. I had never met her though I'm told I had when I was a baby. No one really talked of her but she seemed to know all about us. Remembering names and quoting our parents' names and guessing ages. Her features well preserved, her skin gone pale for want of sun and though she looked like no one in particular from the family, she fit in to the look of us all. The skinny ankles, the line of her shoulders and that nose.

I never saw her cry the whole time she was with us.

Dad said she was stuck-up and wasn't really family. She married this Englishman after World War II. There was a photo of her on a ship waving with this white fella, his arm around her. For some reason she didn't stay, which in my family is strange. I've always lived in the same area as my parents, which isn't too far from Nana's house – my family comes from here. Nana used to say, 'Just when all our men were coming home and we had our share to buy too, she upped and left us. The Black Princess sipping tea with the Queen. Now I'm a Christian woman and I forgive her but . . . No more. No more talkin' of her.'

I drive Aunty Grace out to the cemetery on our way to the airport. She doesn't have much luggage, there is plenty of room but no one from the family comes to see her off. I wait in the car while she goes out to the freshly turned soil of Nana's grave. She is there for such a long time, I think we are going to be late. Finally she returns to the car, opens the back door and removes a suitcase. She opens it and proceeds to throw the contents all over the ground, everything. Dragging the empty suitcase, the lid slapping her legs, she sits at the grave.

The Woman begins to fill the case with red earth from the grave.

Crying, at last, crying.

The Woman collects herself and places the suitcase on top of the disturbed grave.

13   Mugshot

Delivered in the style of a court report with no hint of emotion.

On 7th November 1993, Daniel Yocke together with Joseph Blair, Damien Bond, Lindsay Fisher, Archie Gray, Glen Gray, Charles Riley, Edward Riley and Daniel Weasel went to Southbank. After an altercation between Yocke and an unknown person, the group left Southbank and travelled to Musgrave Park. Some alochol was purchased at the Melbourne Hotel and consumed by the group in Musgrave Park.

Whilst the group was in Musgrave Park, Constables Domrow and Harris were patrolling the area surrounding the park. The group came to their attention allegedly because they were abusive and one of them exposed himself.

After a period of time the group left the park. Shortly after leaving the park Weasel and Edward Riley left the group and proceeded along Russell Street to return to the Baynes Street Hostel whilst the balance of the group travelled down Edmondstone Street with a view of going to the Oxford Street Hostel. This group was followed by Domrow and Harris as they proceeded down Edmondstone Street, across Melbourne Street to a nearby area known as SEQEB Park on the corner of Boundary and Brereton Streets, West End. Before the group reached the location Harris made a number of calls on the police radio seeking assistance, firstly from a Dutton Park car and thereafter from any car in the vicinity.

A Dutton Park Crime Squad vehicle containing Acting Sergeant Symes and Senior Constable Bishop responded to the general call for assistance.

The group entered SEQEB Park and Domrow and Harris waited at or near a stop sign near the junction of Boundary and Edmonstone Streets. As soon as Symes and Bishop arrived they drove into Brereton Street where both vehicles stopped near SEQEB Park.

The Woman stops abruptly, looks as if she is about to speak out, then resumes reading.

The group dispersed. Yocke ran but was intercepted and arrested by Symes. In the course of the arrest Yocke went to the ground. Bishop and Harris then pursued members of the group towards the hostel leaving Symes and Domrow with Yocke. Shortly after the arrest of Yocke another Dutton Park vehicle containing Sergeant Crowley and Constable Crozier arrived at the scene. Crowley handcuffed Yocke's hands behind his back. Crowley and Symes then left Domrow and Crozier with Yocke and drove down to the Oxford Street Hostel.

At the hostel there was a struggle between police and a group of youths.

After remaining on the ground for some time with Domrow and Crozier, Yocke was then driven to the hostel.

The Woman finally breaks out.

People called him Boonie! He was known as Boonie . . .

She stops herself and continues to read tonelessly.

By this time other police had arrived at the scene including Constable Caris, Constable Leyendeckers, Sergeant Whittaker and Senior Constable Parker.

After the incident at the hostel, police patrolled the area for at least seventeen minutes looking for other alleged offenders. Two vehicles then travelled to the Brisbane City Watchhouse.

In this section the Woman breaks away from the written word. This requires the actor to improvise the text in her own words.

On Yocke's arrival at the watchhouse his condition aroused immediate concern. When they looked closer they saw that he wasn't breathing, he didn't have any pulse. The people at the watchhouse didn't know what to do so they called the ambulance. The ambulance got there and they had to pump needles into him, they were pounding his chest, giving mouth-to-mouth, whilst the others stood back and watched. They took him to the Royal Brisbane Hospital, pounding and pushing his limp body.

The Woman returns to the written word.

The resuscitation attempts were unsuccessful and at 7.13 p.m. he was pronounced dead.

14   March

The Woman stands strong. Her body rocks with the rising pace of the march.

The call went out. Faxes. Mobile phones. Leaflets. Word of mouth. Photocopiers working overtime. Flash . . . wait a minute, wait a minute, wait a minute . . . Flash . . . wait a minute, wait a minute, wait a minute . . .

The news was out. Musgrave Park 9 a.m. A peaceful march, a silent march.

Thousands . . . stretched out.

We're not fighting, we're grieving.

I'm in a crowd. I'm in a crowd of people all walking. I'm in a crowd of people all walking along in silence. I'm in a crowd of people all walking along in silence, my dad, my brothers and sisters and my nana. No one speaks, no one yells, everyone just walks together.

If you feel like fighting, if you feel like yelling, grab it in your hand and show your grief, lift it up and show the world.

I'm walking along and all I can hear is the shuffle of shoes, everyone is too busy thinking about what it means to be here.

Four helicopters circle the crowd.

Declaiming news headlines.

'Defiant Aboriginal March'
'Aboriginal March, Traffic Stopper'

No one said that about the fucken Santa Parade the week before!

Hey! We going to be on TV.

Frightened.

Hey, we're going to be on TV.
Smile for the police camera.

We come from a long tradition of storytelling.
Is this the only way we can get our story told . . .

This huge gathering stops outside the police watchhouse in Herschel Street. And we sit . . . quiet . . . only the sound of our feet on the road can be heard. Roma Street crowd gather to watch. The family sing, dance and smoke out the spirit and the dancers play their clapsticks. The rhythm engulfs the crowd, the beat echoes round the buildings like if at last the song was coming up from ground to swallow everything in revenge. The clapsticks ring out alone at first, I'm in the crowd and we all clap as we rise, as we walk.

Six thousand people in rhythm pounding at the road but we're not yelling, we're not fighting. We're grieving.

A whistle rings out. The high-pitched ones you can only do if you hold your lips really tight. The clapsticks, the singing, the clapping, the pounding of our feet and the piercing ring of whistles.

The Woman stands, her arms raised defiantly.

Don't tell me we're not fighting! Don't tell me we don't fight most of our lives.

15 Bargaining

The sound of hammering. The Woman slams a nail through two pieces of wood. She stands and carries the wooden cross over to the grave. As she drives it into the red earth, the words 'FOR SALE' are revealed.

What is it worth?

16 Home Story

The Woman takes several handfuls of red earth from the grave, making a large pile on the floor.

Now I want to tell you a story. I'll tell you how it was told to me. Now it's very complex. I get it wrong sometimes, I'm no expert but I'll try to explain it the best way I can, so you'll have to stay with me. It's all got to do with family culture and language and stuff. Are you with me?

This pile here is the land, the source, the spirit, the core of everything. Are you with me on that?

The Woman makes a circle around the pile.

And this one here is about culture, family, song, tradition, dance. Have you got that?

Then came the children. Everyone has their place. Now this is where it gets complicated so you'll have to stay with me.

The Woman makes eight smaller piles around the larger pile within the circle.

You always have to marry within your own skin.

If I was part of this pile here, that would mean this pile would be my mother ... because you always follow the line of the woman. And this pile could be my father ... or this one. Which makes this one and this one here my grandparents and cousins.

Now if I was to marry, I couldn't marry from the same pile because they would be my brothers and sisters. But I could marry this pile here because they're my cousins, which makes this pile my children, because you always follow the line of the woman. Are you with me?

I'll explain that again.

This mob and this mob can marry because they're grandparents and cousins. You can't marry this mob because they're your brothers and sisters and you can't marry this mob or this mob because they're your children. Cause you always follow the line of the woman.

You can't marry this one, this one or this one because that's like marrying your father.

The only ones I could marry are ... wait a minute. This mob and this mob can marry because they're grandparents and cousins. You can't marry this mob because they're your brothers and sisters and you can't marry this mob or this mob because they're your children. Cause you always follow the line of the woman. You can't marry this one, this one or this one because that's like marrying your father. The only ones I could marry are this mob or this mob. Are you with me?

The Woman gathers up the smaller piles and relocates them on the white fringing that defines the black performing area.

Now imagine when the children are taken away from this. Are you with me?

The Woman flays her arm through the remaining large pile and circle, destroying it.

17   Story of a Brother

The sound of laughter. The Woman comes forward to tell her story.

I have a brother. He's twenty-one years old. This one night he was walking down the Mall with two of his friends. Pissed as. They were walking along and all those little cameras you see with those little black bug eyes all over the Mall, they were watching them. True.

They wanted one of my brother's friends – I don't know why – in connection to some alleged crime or just to question him because some other black kid had done something wrong in the Valley – all them Murri boys look alike – and so they came down to get him. My brother said, 'You can't take him away, you have no right to.' They basically said they *did* have the right and they grabbed my brother's friend.

Now this fella, my brother, he's not the smartest of men at the best of times, but when he's had a few . . .

The Woman demonstrates.

. . . he can be a little clumsy.

He thought, 'This fella's done nothing wrong.' So with my brother's sense of justice and sticking up for his Bungies, he pushed the police officer and the police officer pushed back. 'Go on leave him alone.' Now what ended up happening was that this female police officer fairly lifted him on to the ground, my brother's arm up his back, with him swearing and kicking. No good that fella. Shame.

They charged him – as if he wasn't charged enough.

They charged him with (*as a magistrate*) 'Assault or obstructing the course of justice' . . . or something. Now for most people this would not have been a serious thing. He was fined $250 and put on a two month probation with nothing on his record really. But when Dad went to pick him up from the watchhouse in the middle of the night the shame was palpable.

Because of the shame he just budgalled about the house, chucked in his job, couldn't get the dole, couldn't pay his fine, had to front court again, the dole came in but he couldn't register his car, couldn't afford to run it anyway, had to borrow money from my parents which made him even more dependent and embarrassed. To cope, he started going out all night with his friends getting pissed, broke his probation, got another fine.

This is how it starts. This is how it starts, the cycle. The cycle.

Now you might say that is like most young people but this is not the end of it. In our family to be shamed out in such a way eats away at your core, at your life. We've had a history of it. It's been a tool of change.

You see . . .
No matter how clean our clothes are,
No matter how tidy we keep our house,
Or how well we speak the language,
How promptly we pay our bills,
How hard we work,
How often we pray,
No matter how much we smile and nod,
We are black, and we are here, and that will never change.

The story hasn't finished yet. My brother fronts court in another two weeks. And the family is still wondering where's he going to go.

18 Gallery of Sorrow

A collection of images appears, depicting the phases of Aboriginal History – Dreaming, Invasion, Genocide, Protection, Assimilation, Self-determination and Reconciliation.

19   Suitcase Opening

The Woman paints herself as if preparing for war. Though her movements are restricted her voice assails the audience with a sense of all-encompassing sorrow. She takes the suitcase, opens it, throwing the red earth and family photos it contains all over the floor. The Woman grieves over the photographs.

The Woman leaves. Images of landscape interweave with family portraits creating a tapestry of Land and People.

Music fills the space. There is a feeling of catharsis and release.

20   Wreck / con / silly / nation Poem

The Woman returns to the performing area cleansed, fresh. Written in childlike script the words 'Wreck', 'Con', 'Silly', 'Nation' are projected.

Boats ready for departure.
                    If you don't want to stay.
A **Wreck** on arrival
A changing flag
A **Con**
A **Silly** pride for sale,
My **Nation** knows my identity,
A sun,
A land,
A people, travelling.

21   Everything Has Its Time

The Woman addresses the audience. The space is full of words.

Wreck, Con, Silly, Nation.
Some of the people I talk to would write it like this.
What does it mean when some people can't even read or write the word?

*All the words disappear. They are replaced by one word —
RECONCILIATION.*

It isn't something you read or write.
It's something that you do.

The Woman surveys the performing area.

What a mess . . .

*The Woman retrieves the suitcase. The word RECONCILIATION is
packed into it. The Woman locks the suitcase.*

Everything has its time . . . Everything has its time . . .

22   Plea

*The Woman carried the suitcase with her as she approaches the
audience.*

You know there has always been this grieving,
Grieving for our Land, our families.
Our cultures that have been denied us.
But we have been taught to cry quietly
Where only our eyes betray us with tears.
But now, we can no longer wait,
I am scared my heart is hardening.
I fear I can no longer grieve
I am so full and know my capacity for grief.
What can I do but . . . perform.

These are my stories.
These are my people's stories,
They need to be told.

The Woman places the suitcase down at the feet of the audience.

23   Relief

*The Woman walks into a pool of light. She stands, face uplifted, as
if in gentle rain.*

> Nothing
> Nothing
> Nothing
> I feel Nothing

The Woman finally leaves.

Glossary

279	gubberment	government
280	gamin like	joking
281	sousou	a woman's breast
284	Murri	an Aboriginal person from parts of Queensland
	boodgi	fart
	deadly	excellent
285	sisgirl	girlfriend, cousin or relative
	doona	quilt, duvet
	nunna	Kamilaroi term for 'me'
287	Musgrave Park	traditional meeting place for the Brisbane community
	SEQEB	South East Queensland Electricity Board
292	mob	clan, tribe or family
293	bungies	your mates
294	budgalled	to be slack or silly
	Reconciliation	the process whereby white and indigenous peoples of Australia can create 'a united Australia, which respects this land of ours; values the Aboriginal and Torres Strait Islander heritage; and provides justice and equity for all' (Council for Aboriginal Reconciliation)

The Popular Mechanicals

A Funny ~~Old~~ New Play

**Keith Robinson, Tony Taylor and
William Shakespeare**

Keith Robinson graduated from the National Institute of Dramatic Art (NIDA) in 1981. Since then, he has appeared in many theatrical productions, including *A Midsummer Night's Dream* for the Australian Shakespeare Company; *The White Devil* for BAM, New York; *Die Fledermaus* for Opera Australia; *The Marriage of Figaro, The Little Cherry Orchard, The Alchemist, Night on Bald Mountain, Picasso at the Lapin Agile, The Blind Giant is Dancing, Hamlet, The Tempest* and the the original production of *The Popular Mechanicals* for Belvoir Street Theatre. His television credits include *Backberner, Murder Call, G.P.* and *Sons & Daughters*; and his film credits include *Moulin Rouge*.

Tony Taylor was a member of the Pram Factory in Carlton from 1970 to 1978. There he co-created *Back to Bourke St, How Grey was my Nurse* and *The Hills Family Show*. His other co-writing credits include *You and the Night and the Housewine, There's a Ghost on Clark Island, Elegance . . . the Lost Jane Austen Novel, Jingle Belrose*, the companion piece to *Popular Mechanicals, Pop Mex 2*, and four pantos for the late, lamented Tilbury Hotel. He is at time of writing working on *Storyline*, a magical madness, to be workshopped at the 2001 Playright's Conference in Canberra. As an actor, Taylor has worked for APG, Nimrod, Belvoir St, STC, The Ensemble, MTC and South Australian Opera. He was awarded the Green Room Award for his portayal of Smike in *The Life and Adventures of Nicholas Nickleby*.

Words Words Words

Geoffrey Rush

Early in 1987, *Hamlet* and *Henry IV Part One* played in repertoire at the Wharf Theatre in Sydney, under sort of Elizabethan conditions. Fifteen male actors had rehearsed each play in a week under the guidance of Wayne Harrison and Philip Parsons. They played them without an interval, with the odd crown or cape, lit by the fluros and natural light of the rehearsal room, on a six-foot-high stage before an audience who stood or could move around and get drinks and cake. For me they were particularly exciting events – rough, vigorous, skilful, funny, dramatic, honest. The fights were sensational, the actors were mentally on their toes and delivering interesting performances under pressure.

At the end, the clowns of the company treated us to a jig – the traditional Elizabethan afterpiece in doggerel, which was parodic, dirty and outrageous. The overexcited performers rounded off the dramatic marathon with shameless, hilarious invention. Tony Taylor, who had earlier given us his Mistress Quickly and Gravedigger, was responsible for the authorship, and Keith Robinson shone as the Widow Beryl after a fine Horatio. The greatest appeal for performers and audience alike was the simplicity, ingenuity and spontaneity of it all. This inspired discussion about an extended 'Shakespearean' Vaudeville – songs, sketches, novelties, dances – something to celebrate the traditions of theatre clowning.

The choice of the mechanicals from *A Midsummer Night's Dream* at first was a serviceable one – an economically viable cast, effective narrative and great characters. Tony and Keith scripted scenes and developed the scenario which Belvoir grabbed as a hot potential for its pre-Christmas slot in 1987.

A Midsummer Night's Dream is Shakespeare's reverie on the interpenetrating themes of moon, madness, metamorphosis, acting, enchantment, imagination, love, dream and death. Minus the magic of the fairy world .and the glamour of the royal rulers, *The Popular Mechanicals* still aims to pit Shakespeare's amateur thespians against such big themes, and invent, in the genre of a vaudeville show, an Elizabethanish language and story for our contemporary stage. The MEX now stand alone, reliant wholly on their own bonds of camaraderie and their naivety. Behind the routines and the cobbled Bard lies the heart of clowning – their admirable if misguided aspirations to perform beyond their true capabilities.

The fictional world of *The Popular Mechanicals* is a hybrid one – one leg in the twentieth century and the other in the seventeenth, where starched ruffs nestle against polyester skivvies, gold phones stand near cow-pats, poo jokes share scenes with iambic pentameter. In a yellow world of madness, there is gunge and gloss, like the bit of floor between your stove and your fridge.

Of questionable legitimacy, its ancestry however can be traced haphazardly back in its creators' experience to the *Hills Family Show*, *Clowneroonies!*, *Hamlet on Ice*, collective childhood memories of Sorlies and the Tiv, and all the good and bad Shakespeare we've ever done or seen.*

Being academic about clowning is tricky territory. Ctibor Turba, a Czech theatre clown, got it down to a definition of 'rhythm and gags'. There is no thesis really to be made on *The Popular Mechanicals*. Its statement is on the stage in front of you with your participation as its audience. Having performed across Australia, we thank Belvoir for inviting us back into the repertoire. Prithee, enjoy.

Geoffrey Rush

* Tony Taylor co-created the *Hills Family Show* in Melbourne in the 1970s. Rush co-created *Clowneroonies!* in Queensland. *Hamlet on Ice* was a Christmas panto of Sydney's Nimrod Theatre in 1971. 'Sorlies' refers of a variety show that toured, especially rural towns, from the 1920s until 1961. The 'Tiv', short for 'Tivoli', is a large theatre still operating in Melbourne.

The Popular Mechanicals was first performed at the Belvoir St Theatre, Sydney, on 16 June 1992, with the following cast:

Snug	Paul Blackwell
Nick Bottom	Bille Brown
Robin Starveling	Lucia Mastrantone
Peter Quince	Keith Robinson
Francis Flute	Tony Taylor
Tom Snout	Kerry Walker

Director Geoffrey Rush
Associate Director Marion Potts
Designer Stephen Curtis
Lighting Designer Mark Howett

Characters

Nick Bottom, *a weaver.*
Peter Quince, *a carpenter.*
Francis Flute, *a bellows mender.*
Snug, *the joiner.*
Tom Snout, *a tinker.*
Robin Starveling, *a tailor.*

Starveling is played by a woman, as a woman.
Snout is played by a woman, as a man.

Setting

The play is set Now and Then.

Act One

Scene One

A lush romantic fanfare.

Voice-over (*in the dark*) A very long time ago in a faraway, moonlit country a prince and princess were about to be married; and so, six lowly workers – let's call them rude mechanicals – decided to put on a play to celebrate the marriage, and to fulfil their dream to perform at the palace. This is their story.

Lights up. Music. The company nervously make their way out in front of a very home-made curtain. Blankets, tea towels, drapes pinned together.

Quince If we offend (*Cough.*) ... If we offend (*Cough.*) ... If we offend – (*Coughing attack.*) If we offend, it is with our goodwill. That you should think, we come not to offend, but with goodwill. But as for you!

Opening song by the company each accompanying on a percussion instrument.

Quince (*on cymbals*) NOW SOME OF YOU WILL CHAT

Snug (*on slide whistle*) DID YOU DOUBLE LOCK THE FLAT?

All SSH.

Starveling (*on wooden rattle*) CAN I SIT WITH MY FRIEND?

All SSSSSSSSSSSHHHHHH

Bottom (*on triangle*) ONE WILL JOT

Snout (*on drum*) OR HISS THE PLOT
  AND GIVE AWAY THE END.

Flute (*on tambourine*) A JOKER IN THE CROWD

WILL BURP OUT LOUD
AND THEN A FLASHBULB POPS

Quince   AND THERE'S ALWAYS TWO
WHO REACH THEIR PEW
AS THE FIRST-ACT CURTAIN DROPS.

Flute   BUT WE

All   LOVE YA
WE LOVE YA
WHAT A JAPE, WHAT A JOKE, WHAT A LARK!
YOU TWISTIE-CRUNCHING, MINTIE-MUNCHING
MONSTER IN THE DARK.

Pause.

Starveling   THERE'S THE BRAINY DON
WITH THE GLASSES ON

All   HE REALLY GETS OUR GUTS

Flute   COS HIS LITTLE TORCH SHINES
ON OUR CLASSIC LINES

Snug   AND HE YELLS OUT ALL THE CUTS.

All   BUT
WE LOVE YA
WE LOVE YA
WHAT A JAPE, WHAT A JOKE, WHAT A LARK!
YOU TWISTIE-CRUNCHING, MINTIE-MUNCHING

Snout   BRONCHIAL WHEEZING

Bottom   MULTIPLE SNEEZING

All   MONSTER IN THE DARK.

Short percussion break.

Starveling   AND NOW GET THIS
OH JOY! OH, BLISS!
YOU ALL DECIDE TO COUGH

Snout   AND IT'S JUST FINE
ON THE STROKE OF NINE

WHEN YOUR DIGITALS GO OFF

Bottom THERE'S ONE WHO KNITS

Flute AND ANOTHER WHO SITS
WITH A WALKMAN ON HIS HEAD

Starveling AND JUST LAST WEEK
ONE WOMAN HAD THE CHEEK

All TO ACTUALLY DROP DEAD!

BUT
WE LOVE YA
WE LOVE YA
WHAT A JAPE, WHAT A JOKE, WHAT A LARK!
YOU TWISTIE-CRUNCHING, MINTIE-MUNCHING

Snout BRONCHIAL-WHEEZING

Bottom MULTIPLE-SNEEZING

Flute KNUCKLE-CRACKING

Quince DENTURE-CLACKING

All MONSTER IN THE DARK.

Short percussion break with limited choreography.

Snout THERE'S THOSE THAT SHOUT
AND CALL THINGS OUT

Starveling YOU DON'T KNOW HOW IT FEELS

Snug LIKE
THIS IS ART!

Quince HE TAKES A GOOD PART

Bottom AND
WHICH ONE'S COLIN FRIEL'S?

Quince / Starveling NOW HALF OF YOU
WILL SLEEP RIGHT THROUGH

Snug / Snout SO HALF OF IT YOU'VE MISSED

Flute HALF OF YOU WON'T UNDERSTAND

All AND HALF OF YOU ARE PISSED!

BUT
WE LOVE YA
WE LOVE YA
WHAT A JAPE, WHAT A JOKE, WHAT A LARK!
YOU TWISTIE-CRUNCHING, MINTIE-MUNCHING

Snout BRONCHIAL-WHEEZING

Bottom MULTIPLE-SNEEZING

Flute KNUCKLE-CRACKING

Quince DENTURE-CLACKING

Snug MUCUS-CLEARING

Starveling HARD-OF-HEARING

Snout BANGLE-RATTLING

Bottom DOMESTIC-BATTLING

Flute CHEWING-GUMMING

Quince OFF-KEY-HUMMING

Snug GARLIC-PONGING

Starveling SINGALONGING

Snout NEVER-CLAPPING

Bottom CHOCOLATE-WRAPPING

Flute LOUDLY-SNORING

All DEADLY-BORING

Snug (*holding up a rubber chicken*) Is this a dagger which I see before me?

All No!
MONSTER IN THE DARK!!

Tableau.
Here follows a madrigal sung by the company in three-part harmony.

All FEAR, FEAR, FEAR NO MORE, DARLINGS,

FEAR NO MORE,
WE ARE DECEIVERS EVER.
ONE AIM TO PLEASE,
ONE TO DEPLORE,
IN ONE THING CONSTANT NEVER.
THEN SIGH NOT SO,
BUT LET US SHOW
THAT WE BE FAIR AND FUNNY,
AND FUNNY, AND FUNNY, AND FUNNY
AND BE WE FAIR AND FUNNY.
CONVERTING ALL YOUR WORLDLY WOE

Quince / Bottom INTO HEY NO NONNY...

Starveling / Snout INTO HEY NO NANNY...

Snug / Flute INTO HEY NO NUNNY...

Quince Hold it. Hold it. People! Hold it. Who sang nunny?

Starveling I sang nanny.

Quince I said, who sang nunny?

Starveling / Snout We sang nanny.

Starveling *and* **Snout** *link their little fingers.*

Starveling Chaucer.

Snout John Donne.

Bottom I sang nonny. It says nonny, so I sang nonny.

Quince I know you sang nonny. I was with you. I said, who sang nunny?

Starveling Nunny?

Quince Yes.

Snug I did, and he did.

Snout No I didn't.

Flute He didn't. I did. I sang nunny.

Quince   Well, it shouldn't be nunny. It should be nonny.

Bottom   That's right!

Flute   I haven't got nonny.

Starveling / Snout   Nor have we.

Starveling *and* **Snout** *link their little fingers.*

Starveling   Ovid.

Snout   John Donne.

Bottom   I could sing nunny if you want. It's just as easy.

Quince   It isn't nunny. It's nonny.

Starveling   Not nanny neither?

Quince   No! No, no, no!

Snug   Actually, it should be nunny. Actually.

Quince   Why?

Snug   To rhyme with funny.

Quince   What funny?

Snug   The funny we put in when we changed Shakespeare's words.

Quince   We didn't do that!

Bottom   Yes we did, I remember.

Flute   I was there when we did it.

Starveling   Yep – we did that all right.

Quince (*remembering audience*)   Look, can we talk about this later?

Flute   BUT . . .

They move into half-tempo rockettes kick-line.

All   WE LOVE YA
   WE LOVE YA
   WHAT A JAPE, WHAT A JOKE, WHAT A LARK

YOU TWISTIE-CRUNCHING, MINTIE-MUNCHING

Snug (*holding up string of sausages*)   Is this a dagger which I see before me?

All   No!

Bravura Rossini-like finale with much repetition.

MONSTER IN THE

Quince / Bottom / Snug   MONSTER MONSTER MONSTER MONSTER

Flute / Starveling / Snout   IN THE DARK IN THE DARK

All   IN THE DARK THE DARK
THE DARK THE DARK THE DARK
IN THE DARK!

Blackout. Stirring Rossini music.

Scene Two

Quince's *place. Thursday evening, cocktail hour.* **Snout** *is reading the newspaper.*

Flute   This apartment hath a pleasant seat, Peter.

Quince   Thank you. Yes. I fell in love with the willow cabin at the gate, and when I saw that view I had to have it. Living on the edge of the woods one finds tongues in trees, books in the running brooks, sermons in stones and good in everything. I would not change it.

Snug   Here's a pleasant picture, Peter Quince. Is this a Degas which I see before me?

All   No.

Quince   Where is Bottom? (*They all throw a look at the door.*) More mead, anyone?

Snug / Flute (*highly excited*)   Mmmmmmm.

Quince   There are sausage rolls without.

Snug / Flute   Ooooooh!

Snout   Without what?

Quince   There are sausage rolls without, and tomato sauce.

Snug   Can I have mine with?

Quince   With what?

Snug   With tomato sauce.

Quince   Sauce? Of course.

Quince *heads off.*

Flute   Without.

Quince   Yes, they are without.

Quince *heads off.*

Snug   I thought you said there was sauce.

Quince   There is. That too is without.

Quince *heads off.*

Starveling   What? Sauce by itself?

Flute   Errrrrrgh!

Quince   Look! There are sausage rolls and there is tomato sauce withal, and they are both without!

Flute   Withal?

Snug   Without.

Starveling   Whither?

Snout   What?

Quince   In the kitchen.

Pause.

All   Oh.

Snout Hark you each and every one. We get a mention.
'Theseus plans big bash. At a pertinent point in the
reception proceedings, one lucky group . . .'

Flute That's us.

Snug That's right.

Starveling We hope.

Snout '. . . will have the honour . . .'

Flute The honour.

Snug That's right.

Starveling We hope.

Snout '. . . of being selected from a list of entertainments
to perform for Theseus and Hippolyta, the Royal
Newlyweds.'

Flute Hoorah!

Snug Bravo!

Starveling Don't count your capons before they're
hatched.

Quince No . . . No . . . Where's Bottom? Look how the
sun begins to set; How ugly night comes breathing at his
heels.

All (*in mild rapture*) Mmmm.

Flute The dragon wing of night o'er spreads the earth.

All Mmmm.

Starveling The world's comforter with weary gait his hot
task hath ended in the west.

All Mmm.

Snout Light thickens and the crow makes wing to the
rooky wood.

All Mmm.

Snug   The sun's going down!

Quince   And where is Bottom?

Bottom (*off*)   Keep the change! (*He enters.*) Sorry I'm late. The bear-baiting went overtime. And I had to hail an oxcart outside the Frog and Parsnip. Didst thou know they have a merry hour from half past four? Oh, and Cicely Hackett's in the stocks again.

All   No!

Quince   We were called at five. Now is all our company here?

Flute   Ooh! What's burning!

They all sniff.

Flute   Peter Quince! Thy sausage rolls!

Quince   Oh God!

Quince *exits.*

Bottom   Come on, Peter Quince, the clock upbraids us with the waste of time. Light thickens and the crow makes . . .

All   Wing to the rooky wood. Yes.

Snout   I said that before.

Enter **Quince**.

Quince   Well, we'll just have to go without.

The others start to leave.

Sausage rolls!

Long Pause.

All   Oh.

Quince   Right. Now is all our company here?

Bottom   You were best to call them generally, man by man, according to the script.

Quince   Here is the scroll of every man's name which is thought fit through all Athens to play in our interlude before the Duke and the Duchess, on his wedding day at night.

Bottom   Peter Quince, get on, say what the play treats on; then read the names of the actors; and so grow to a point.

Quince   Marry, our play is 'The most lamentable comedy and most cruel death of Pyramus and Thisbe'.

All   Eeergh!

Bottom   A very good piece of work, I assure you, and a merry. Now, good Peter Quince, call forth your actors by the scroll. Masters, spread yourselves.

Quince   Answer as I call you. Nick Bottom, the weaver?

Bottom   Ready! Name what part I am for, and proceed.

Quince   You, Nick Bottom, are set down for Pyramus.

Bottom   What is Pyramus? – a lover, or a tyrant?

Quince   A lover, that kills himself most gallant for love.

Bottom   That will ask some tears in the true performing of it. If I do it, let the audience look to their eyes: I will move storms, I will condole in some measure. To the rest; yet my chief humour is for a tyrant. I could play Ercles rarely, or a part to tear a cat in, to make all split.
   The raging rocks
   And shivering shocks
   Shall break the locks
   Of prison-gates;
   And Phibbus' car
   Shall shine from far
   And make and mar
   The foolish fates.
This was lofty. Now name the rest of the players. This is Ercles' vein, a tyrant's vein: a lover is more condoling.

Quince   Francis Flute, the bellows mender?

Flute Here, Peter Quince.

Quince Flute, you must take Thisbe on you.

Flute What is Thisbe? A wandering knight?

Quince It is the lady that Pyramus must love.

Flute Nay, faith, let not me play a woman: I have a beard coming.

All Whooooo!!

Quince That's all one: you shall play it in a mask; and you may speak as small as you will.

Flute *is distressed.*

Bottom And I may hide my face, let me play Thisbe too. I'll speak in a monstrous little voice: 'Thisne, Thisne', 'Ah, Pyramus my lover dear! Thy Thisbe dear, and Lady dear!'

Flute *is hysterical.*

Quince No, no, you must play Pyramus; and Flute, you Thisbe.

Bottom Well, proceed.

Quince Robin Starveling, the tailor?

Starveling Here, Peter Quince.

Quince Robin Starveling, you must play Thisbe's mother.

Starveling Rightyo.

Quince Tom Snout, the tinker?

Snout Here, Peter Quince.

Quince You, Pyramus's father; myself, Thisbe's father; Snug the joiner, you the Lion's part. And I hope here is a play fitted.

Snug Have you the Lion's part written? Pray you, if it be, give it me; for I am slow of study.

Quince   You may do it extempore, for it is nothing but roaring.

Bottom   Let me play the Lion too. I will roar, that I will do any man's heart good to hear me. I will roar, that I will make the Duke say: 'Let him roar again, let him roar again!'

Quince   And you should do it too terribly, you would fright the Duchess and the Ladies, and they would shriek: and that were enough to hang us all.

All   That would hang us, every mother's son. (*They all link fingers.*) John Donne.

Bottom   I grant you, friends, if you should fright the Ladies out of their wits, they would have no more discretion but to hang us. But I will aggravate my voice so, that I will roar you as gently as any sucking dove; I will roar you an 'twere any nightingale.

Quince   You can play no part but Pyramus.

Bottom   That's it! I'm going back to me loom.

Quince   For – For – For Pyramus is a sweet-fac'd man; a proper man as one shall see in a summer's day; a most lovely, gentleman-like man: therefore you must needs play Pyramus.

Bottom   Well, I will undertake it. What beard were I best to play it in?

Quince   Why, what you will.

Bottom   I will discharge it in either your straw-colour beard, your orange-tawny beard, your purple-in-grain beard, or your French-crown-colour beard, your perfect yellow.

Quince   Some of your French crowns have no hair at all, and then you will play bare-faced. (**Quince** *and* **Bottom** *cack themselves knowingly. One by one the others sort of get it. They laugh and laugh and laugh.*) But, masters, here are your parts; and I am to entreat you, request you, and desire you, to con them by tomorrow night.

All   Tomorrow night?!

Quince   And meet me in the palace wood, a mile without the town, by moonlight.

All   Moonlight?!

Snug   Without the town?

Quince   There will we rehearse, for if we meet in the city, we shall be dogged with company, and our devices known. In the meantime I will draw a bill of properties such as our play wants. I pray you, fail me not.

Bottom   We will meet, and there we may rehearse most obscenely and courageously. Take pains, be perfect. Adieu!

Quince   At the Duke's oak we meet.

They all leave.

Bottom (*off*)   Enough; hold, or cut bowstrings.

Dramatic 'Pagliacci' music. They all burst back into the room, wailing, and strike an heroic tableau, arms outstretched to heaven.

Quince (*over music, shouting*)   Saturday night! Two days be not an ideal rehearsal period one is forced to admit – and we've got our day jobs to think about!

Scene Three

Friday. At work.

Lights up on **Starveling** *who is on the phone.*

Starveling   Starveling's Stichery, Robin prating. Aye, Mistress. Linen bossed with pearl, valance of Venice gold in needlework. But not until after the weekend. Our play for the Royal Wedding, thou knowest. Sorry, Mistress, I'm in great haste.

Montage sequence, set to music. The full company goes about their

day jobs while learning lines etc. **Quince** *sands a lathed table-leg.*
Flute *puts screws into a bellows.* **Bottom** *winds yarn.*
Starveling *sews.* **Snout** *Teflon irons.* **Snug,** *up a ladder, bangs
in nails. All of this, plus wiping of brows, etc., very rhythmical. Light
change. All freeze.*

Starveling   Cicely, get me Snout the Tinker.

Snout's *phone rings.*

Snout   Thank you for calling. You have dialled Snout's
Tinkerage. I'm sorry I am unable to take your call at the
moment . . .

Starveling   Snout, it's Robin here. (*Another of*
Starveling's *phones rings.*) I'll call you back. (*Hangs up on*
Snout. *Picks up ringing phone.*) Aye? Master Lysander. New
breeches and matching hose? Eleven shillings. Doublet?
Twenty-two!

*She hangs up. Music up. The rustics show off their handiwork, learn
lines, practice gestures.* **Snug** *hits his finger with the hammer and
discovers the perfect 'roar'. Light change. All freeze.*

Starveling   Cicely, get me Snout again.

Snout's *phone rings. He answers the iron.*

Snout   Oowww. (*He answers the phone.*) What?

Starveling   Snout, are you busy?

Snout   Yes. I'm busy on the Teflon.

Starveling   So am I. (*Her other phone rings.*) Hang on. (*She
answers the phone.*) Mistress Quickly!!! (*Another phone rings.*)
Yup? Ah, Mistress Paige! Aye, thy costume's concluded.
No, thy drapery is done. (*Returning to* **Quickly**.) Couldst
thou speak more slowly, Quickly? (*Back to* **Paige**.) Look
luvvy, I've finished your frock. (*Back to* **Quickly**.) I'll have
to say goodbye, Quickly. (*Quickly*) G'bye.

Starveling *hangs up. Back to* **Snout**.

Starveling   Snout, have you conned your lines yet?

Snout   Eh?

Starveling   Have you sussed your scenes?

Snout   Prithee?

Starveling   Snout, what have you learned today?

Snout   If the iron rings, don't answer it.

Flash of light. They all wipe their brows in unison. Blackout.

Scene Four

Friday evening. The Duke's Oak. In the blackout, all except **Quince** *and* **Bottom** *are huddled behind a canvas flat.*

Flute   Wait for me.

Snout   I can't see a thing.

Snug   Look out for the spiders.

Flute   Pretty.

They make cat's eyes with two of the torches (They play with their flashlights). They sing a snatch of 'Memory' from Cats. *They flit around the darkened stage in pairs. Some Mendelssohn 'Dream' music. They almost step in a cow-pat.*

All   Ohh poo!!

Quince *bursts in.*

Quince   Sorry.

All   Aaarh! (*They shine their torches on him.*)

Quince (*to Bio-box*) Go cue 28. (*Lights come up slightly.*) 28B (*Light to full.*) Oh, look, the moon's just come out from behind the clouds. Now, where's Bottom?

Snout   Is this the Duke's Oak?

Flute   What a funny name.

Snug   The Duke's Oak?

Flute No. Bottom!

Snout Bot. Tom. (*They giggle.*)

Flute BTM.

Snug (*shaking **Starveling***'s *hand*) Bottom.

Starveling What would he be if he went swimming in the ocean! Bottom of the sea.

Snout And if he were under leaves? Bottom of the heap. (*They love it.*)

Snug And what was he, pray, at school?

All Bottom of the class.

Snug (*dejected*) Yes.

Flute What would they call him if he was a statue? Rock bottom. What dance would he do? Black Bottom. What would he be if he were stretched on a rack?

Snug Rack Bottom!

Flute No. Long Bottom! What would he do if he ran out of smokes? Bot'em!

Quince *finally joins the others in laughter.*

Snug What would he do if he had the chicken pox? Spotty Bottom. What would he do if he fell in a cow-pat? Pooey Bottom. What would he do if *he* did a poo? Smelly Bottom.

More laughter.

Starveling What did his mother say to the neighbours when he was born? Do you want to kiss my little bottom?

They are hysterical. The doorbell rings.

Quince Ooh, ooh, after three, everybody. 'Bottom.' One, two, three.

All Bottom.

Bottom *enters.*

Bottom   Aye.

Flute   Why, Bottom, where hast thou been? We have looked for thee from top to bottom.

Bottom   I just . . .

Snug   Bottom! Bottom of the morning to thee, Bottom.

Bottom   Ah, I see, I am the butt of your feeble wit.

All   Whooo! Dear Bottom.

Bottom   Enough. Enough.

Quince   I'm so glad you've arrived. We were getting behind.

Starveling   Aye, Bottom, 'tis late. We can see Uranus.

Bottom   No it's not, it's Mars.

Flute   Bottom, a word in your rear.

Snug   Bottom, a word in your bottom.

Quince   Sweet Bottom.

Flute   Neat Bottom.

Starveling   Petite Bottom.

Snug   Bully Bottom.

Snout   Woolly Bottom.

Bottom *storms upstage.*

All   Nice Bottom.

Quince   Nay, Bottom. Stay, Bottom.

All (*to him*)   Our Bottom. (*They turn and present their bums. Then, linking fingers.*) William Shakespeare!!

Bottom   Oh, enough of your wisecracks!

The others wet themselves with laughter.

Quince   Come, come, Bottom. We jest. Come drink. Here's to your health.

Bottom   Oh thank you very much.

All   Bottoms up. (*Uproar.*)

Bottom   Are we all met?

Quince   Pat, pat; oh, pat. (*Steps over cow-pat.*) And here's a marvellous convenient place for our rehearsal. This green plot shall be our stage, this hawthorn-brake our tiring-house; and we will do it in action, as we will do it before the Duke.

All   Ooh! (*They take up standing-by positions.*)

Bottom   Peter Quince!

Quince   What sayest thou, Bully Bottom?

Bottom   There are things in this comedy of Pyramus and Thisbe that never please. First, Pyramus must draw a sword to kill himself; which the Ladies cannot abide. How answer you that?

Snout   Byrlakin, a parlous fear.

Starveling   I believe we must leave the killing out, when all is done.

Bottom   Not a whit; I have a device to make all well. Write me a Prologue, and let the Prologue seem to say we will do not harm with our swords, and the Pyramus is not kill'd indeed; and for the more better assurance, tell them that I, Pyramus, am not Pyramus, but Bottom the weaver. This will put them out of fear.

Quince   Well, we will have such a Prologue.

Bottom *and* **Flute** *strike poses. The others stand by again.*

Snout   Will not the Ladies be afear'd of the Lion?

Starveling   I fear it, I promise you.

Bottom   Masters, you ought to consider with yourselves, to bring in (God shield us!) a Lion among Ladies is a most dreadful thing; for there is not a more fearful wild-fowl than your Lion living; and we ought to look to't.

Snout   Therefore another Prologue must tell he is not a Lion.

Bottom   Nay, you must name his name, and half his face must be seen through the Lion's neck; and he himself must speak through, saying thus, or to the same defect: 'Ladies,' or 'Fair Ladies, I would wish you,' or 'I would request you,' or 'I would entreat you, not to fear, not tremble: my life for yours! If you think I come hither as a Lion, it were pity of my life. No, I am no such thing; I am a man, as other men are'; and there, indeed, let him name his name, and tell them plainly he is Snug the joiner.

Quince   Well, it shall be so. (*They set up again*). But there is two hard things: That is, to bring the moonlight into a chamber; for you know, Pyramus and Thisbe meet by moonlight.

Long pause.

Snug   Prologue?

Snout   Doth the moon shine that night we play our play?

Bottom   A calendar, a calendar! Look in the almanac; find out moonshine, find out moonshine!

Quince   Yes, it doth shine that night.

Bottom   Why, then may you leave a casement of the Great Chamber window – where we play – open; and the moon may shine in at the casement.

Quince   Aye; (*moment of genius*) or else one must come in with a bush of thorns and a lantern, and say he comes to disfigure or to present the person of Moonshine. Then there is another thing: we must have a wall in the Great Chamber; for Pyramus and Thisbe, says the story, did talk through the chink of a wall.

Snout   You can never bring in a wall. What say you, Bottom?

Bottom   Some man or other must present Wall; and let him have some plaster, or some loam, or some roughcast about him, to signify Wall; and let him hold his fingers thus, and through that cranny shall Pyramus and Thisbe whisper.

Quince If that may be, then all is well. Come, sit down every mother's son, and rehearse your parts. Pyramus, you begin. When you have spoken your speech, enter into that brake; and so everyone according to his cue. Speak, Pyramus! Thisbe, love, stand forth! (*He demonstrates.*)

Bottom (*as Pyramus*) Thisbe, the flowers of odious savours sweet −

Quince 'Odorous'! 'Odorous'!

Bottom (*as Pyramus*) . . . odorous savours sweet. So hath thy breath, my dearest Thisbe dear. But hark, a voice! Stay thou but here awhile, And by and by I will to thee appear.

Bottom *exits.*

Flute Must I speak now?

Bottom (*off, mimics*) Must I speak now?

Quince Aye, marry, must you. For you must understand he goes but to see a noise that he heard, and is to come again.

Flute (*as Thisbe*) Most radiant Pyramus, most lily-white of
    hue,
  Of colour like the red rose on triumphant briar,
  Most brisky juvenal, and eke most lovely Jew
  As true as truest horse, that yet would never tire.

Bottom *comes on at his cue but goes directly back off when* **Flute** *continues.*

Flute I'll meet thee Pyramus, at Ninny's tomb, and there, we'll love and love and . . .

Quince 'Ninus' tomb', man: 'Ninus' tomb' − why, you must not speak that yet; that you answer to Pyramus: you speak all your part at once, cues and all. Pyramus, enter! Your cue is past; it is 'never tire'.

Quince *cues* **Flute**.

Flute (*cranky and savage*)   As true as truest horse, that yet would never –

Flute *stops as he sees* **Bottom**, *offstage, metamorphosing into an ass. One by one the others join* **Flute** *and watch horrified. Finally* **Quince** *joins them. They are bathed in an eerie light.*

Quince (*softly*)   Oh, fuck! O monstrous! O strange! We are haunted. Pray, masters! Fly, masters!

All (*throwing their scripts in the air*)   H E-E-E-L-P!!

Music. There is bedlam. They run around in a panic, falling over one and other. They madly sweep the sky. Strobe lighting. Screaming, they run for their lives in distracted fear. **Quince** *tumbles in terror.*

Quince   O Bottom, thou art translated!

Blackout.

Scene Five

Quince's *place. Saturday morning. Dawn. Gentle, sad music.* **Quince**, **Snug**, **Snout** *and* **Flute** *are standing wrapped in a rug.* **Quince** *is handing out tea down the line in tiny cups. There is a cold blue light from the window. They look like the* Titanic *survivors on the deck of the Carpathia. Shocked silence.*

Flute   Who saw the sun today?

Quince   Not I, my lord.

Flute   Then he disdains to shine; for by the book
He should have braved the east an hour ago.
A black day it will be to somebody.

All (*tearful*)   Mmm.

Quince   By the clock 'tis day
And yet, dark night strangles the travelling lamp;
Is it night's predominance or the day's shame.
That darkness does the face of earth entomb,

When living light should kiss it?

All   Mmmm . . . mm?

Snout   Arise, fair sun and kill the envious moon.

All   Mmm.

Snug   The grey-eyed morn smiles on the frowning night,
Chequering the eastern clouds with streaks of light.

All   Mmm.

Enter **Starveling**.

Starveling   Look! The morn in russet mantle clad
Walks o'er the dew of yon high eastward hill.

All   Mm.

Quince   Have you sent to Bottom's house? Is he came
home yet?

Starveling   He cannot be heard of.

They pass **Starveling**, *who rugs up with them, a cup of tea.*

Quince   There's plenty more if you want it.

Starveling   Is it a bottomless cup?

They register this clanger and then weep.

Snout   Ah Bottom. Byrlakin. What could have . . . ?

Flute (*tentatively*)   Where do you think he . . . ?

Starveling   Methought he was a . . .

Quince   Didst thou see what . . . ?

Snug   What was it?

Quince   I know not.

Snout   It haddeth the shape of . . .

Starveling   Aye, it looked like a . . .

Flute   Like a . . .

Starveling   Yes.

Snug   Like a what?

Snout   I know not. Like a . . .

Snug   Donkey?

Flute   Yes! They say that wood is full of cozenage.

Starveling   With dark working sorcerers that change the mind.

Snout   And soul-killing witches that transform the body.

Flute   If we obey them not this will ensue –

All   They'll steal our breath and pinch us black and blue!!

They scream, then link fingers.

Starveling   Sylvia Plath.

Quince   Edgar Allen Poe.

Flute   William Blake.

Snout   Leonard Cohen.

Snug   Pam Ayres.

All shriek. They get rid of the rug. **Quince** *sorrowfully collects the tea things.*

Snug   Perhaps some helpful merchant hath invited him from the wood and he's somewhere gone to brekkie.

Starveling   If you were to ask me 'tis but temperament.

Snout   What do you mean?

Starveling   He hath gone off in an huff.

Snout   Why?

Starveling   Well, some of our performances stink.

Flute   (*angry*)   Dost thou speak of me, thou blear-eyed, hag-borne filth?

Starveling   Aye, thou fly-blown footlicker.

Flute   Green sarcenet's flap for a sore eye.

Starveling   Reeking exhalation of a mongrel cur.

Flute   What?

Starveling   Dog's breath.

Flute *hackles up like a cat.*

Snug   He could be lost.

Starveling   We should not have been rehearsing in the woods.

All   No!

Starveling   We should have been rehearsing in the local hall.

Quince   It's all my fault.

Starveling (*nearly hysterical*)   It's got a tea urn and everything.

Snug   He's lost ... his memory.

Starveling   Yes! He hit his head –

Flute   In the dark –

Starveling   And fell.

Snout   Down.

Snug   And he's lying there –

Flute   Still.

Snout   Perhaps he's gone to that undiscovered country.

Snug   What country?

Snout   That country from whose bourn no traveller returns.

Flute   Golden lads and lasses must, as chimney sweepers, come to dust.

Starveling   You shall hear the surly, sullen bell give

warning that he is fled from this vile world.

Snug   Death, death: O, amiable lovely death?
Thou odoriferous stench! sound rottenness!
Arise forth from the couch of lasting night,
Thou hate and terror to prosperity,
And I will kiss thy detestable bones,
And put my eyeballs in thy vaulty brows,
And ring these fingers with thy household worms!!!

Quince (*dazedly*)   It's all my fault.

Others   Murderer!

Quince   Your pardon I beg; for go too far you do.

Others   Bottom-slayer!

Quince   I beseech ye, masters, take that back right now.
Right now, go on; right now, rescind it straight.

Others   No!

Quince   I see; is that the thanks I get?

Others   Yes!

Quince   Yes, well, I see that is the thanks I get:
My fingers I have workèd to the bone, For what?

Others   Bony fingers!

Quince   A motley crew of patches.
Shame on you. O, that I were as great
As is my grief, or lesser than my name,
Or that I could forget what I have been,
Or not remember what I must be now!
What must the director do now? Submit?

Others   Yes!

Quince   The director shall do it: deposèd be?

Others   Yes!

Quince   The director shall be contented then: Must he
lose the name of director?

Others   Suit yourself!

Quince   Swell'st thou proud heart? I'll give thee scope to
  beat
Since foes have scope to beat both thee and me.
We are amaz'd; show us the hand of God
That hath dismiss'd us from our stewardship;
And are we barren and bereft of friends?
Yet know, my masters, God omnipotent,
Is mustering in his clouds on our behalf
Armies of pestilence; and they shall strike
Your children yet unborn and unbegot;
Whilst I, in a mournful house will shut myself,
Raining down the tears of lamentation.

Flute *slaps* **Quince** *out of his hysteria.* **Quince** *slaps* **Flute**
back. A full-on fight about to erupt.

Snout   Hey, lads, jocund day stands tiptoe on the misty
mountain top.

Starveling   The News!

All   Ooooh.

Quince *switches on the radio. They all gather around.*

All   Ssh . . . Sshh . . . Shush!!

Voice-over   And now a Radio Parthenon Royal Wedding
update. It is great morning and the hour prefixed for the
Royal nuptials comes fast upon. Wedding gown designers,
Zandra and Colossus of the House of Rhodes, are
maintaining their silence regarding The Dress. Interest now
centres upon which of the four groups of performers will be
given the chance of a lifetime by being chosen to entertain
at the festivities.

Quince *switches off the radio. Long pause. Heads lowered in*
silence. **Quince** *bursts into deep sobs, then his noble heart cracks.*
They rush to support him.

Snug   Cease to lament for that which thou canst not help.

Quince   Aaagh!

Starveling   He's right i'faith. We've got a show to do.

Quince   Aaaaagh!

Flute   Oh, Quince! Quince! What ails thee?

Quince   You're standing on my foot. (*Gasp.*) I have a young conception in my brain! (*He runs to the phone.*) Cicely – Mmmm – get me the Frog and Parsnip. Yes, I'll hold. (*He bops along to the muzak on the phone.*) Ah, yes, I'll still hold.

He softly sings along to 'Tie a Yellow Ribbon'. The others join in softly. **Quince** *suddenly realises the audience are still there.*

Quince (*to the others*)   Fill in! Fill in!

Starveling   Fill in?

Snug   Who?

Flute (*big ego*)   Me!

Starveling   No!

Snug   Let's do 'That'! (*He makes quotation marks with his fingers.*)

All   Not 'that'! (*They do likewise.*)

Snug   Oh.

Snout   She.

Starveling   Me?

Snout   Thee.

Flute   Thee.

Snug   Thee!

Starveling   Me! (*Spot on* **Starveling**.) Well, I've got a song I like verily much. It was written by our good Queen ... Elizabeth ... the First. And somehow seems ... I don't know ... kind of appropriate. It goeth ... thus.

Starveling *sings 'Upon Mounzeur's Departure'.*

Starveling   I GRIEVE AND DARE NOT SHOW MY

DISCONTENT;
I LOVE, AND YET AM FORCED TO SEEM TO
    HATE;
I DO, YET DARE NOT SAY I EVER MEANT;
I SEEM STARK MUTE, BUT INWARDLY DO I
    PRATE;
I AM, AND AM NOT, I FREEZE, AND YET AM
    BURNED,
SINCE FROM MYSELF, MY OTHER SELF
    TURNED.

The others sing soft harmonies.

SOME GREATER PASSIONS SLIDE INTO MY
MIND,
    FOR I AM SOFT AND MADE OF MELTING
SNOW,
    OR BE MORE CRUEL, LOVE, AND SO BY KIND,
    LET ME OR FLOAT OR SINK, BE HIGH OR
LOW;
    OR LET ME LIVE WITH SOME MORE SWEET
        CONTENT,
    OR DIE, AND SO FORGET WHAT LOVE EVER
        MEANT.

Scene Six

Quince's *place, the same day. Noon.* **Quince** *puts down the phone. Light change.*

Quince   A replacement is arriving imminently to take over from Bottom in the role of Pyramus.

All   A replacement?

Quince   He retired some time ago but he hath served many years once with the King's Players in London.

All (*in awe*)   London!

Quince   Yes. And with the humility of a true professional –

All   Professional!

Quince   He has deigned to step into the breach.

Snug   Who is he, Peter Quince, who is he?

Quince   He is Mowldie.

Snug   Couldn't you get a fresh one?

Flute / Snout / Starveling   Not?

Quince   Yes!

Flute / Snout / Starveling   Oh my God!

Quince   Yes!

Flute / Snout / Starveling   I am agog. We are agog.

Quince   Yes! Yes!

Snug   Who? Who?

All (*ecstatically*)   Ralph Mowldie!

Snug   Who?

Flute   I have heard that dumb men throng to see him, and the blind to hear him speak.

Starveling   My father saw him once. His voice, he said, was of the trumpets, sackbuts, psalteries and fifes; tabors and cymbals, and his shouting made the sun dance!

Snout   He hath crammed many a wooden 'o'.

Quince   All the gallery they say bends as if to Jove's statue, and the pit make a shower and thunder with their caps and shouts.

Snug   He's pretty good.

Mowldie   *is heard from off in a grand voice.*

Mowldie   Howl! Howl! Howl! Howl! Howl!

The company is struck dumb.

Quince   Quickly! Array thyselves!

Mowldie *enters and arranges himself into a grand tragic pose.*

Mowldie   Kill! Kill! Kill! Kill! Kill! (*Awestruck, our fellows fall to their knees.*) Never! Never! Never! Never! Never! Fair be to you, my fair sir, and to all this fair company, fair desires in all fair measures, fairly guide them. (*To* **Flute**.) Especially to you, fair sir. Fair thoughts be your fair pillow.

Flute   Thank you.

Mowldie   Thank *you*!

Quince   My liege ... er ... my lord ... your high ... er ... Master Mowldie. How deeply at once you touch us by graciously coming to our aid in this, our darkest hour.

Mowldie   Your cause doth strike my heart with pity that do make me sick.

Quince   Thank you. Would it please you to receive our company! Peter Quince, director and Thisbe's father. (*He goes blank on each introduction.*) Aah ... Robin Starveling.

Starveling   Thisbe's mother.

Quince   Thisbe's mother. Um ... Tim ... Snom ... aah ... Snot Snout. Tom Snout.

Snout   Pyramus's tinker.

Quince   Pyramus's tinker. And aah ... um. Oh God.

Starveling   Greg.

Quince   Greg. Greg?! Snug the Joiner. Snug the joiner. He's going to be giving us his Loin. Lion! Going to be giving us his Lion. And ... (*To* **Flute**.) ... oh, this is silly ... Thisbe, Thisbe, your leading lady. And you, sir, our Pyramus.

They all applaud **Mowldie**.

All (*but* **Quince**)   Speech! Speech! (**Flute** *goes berserk with enthusiasm.* **Quince** *rams his hand into* **Flute**'s *mouth.*)

Quince   Peace, peace. Master Mowldie may be tired. (*To* **Mowldie**.) I do apologise.

Mowldie   Ohhhhhhhhhhhh!

Flute   Is he all right?

Starveling   Sshhhhhh.

They sit in a semi-circle as his audience.

Quince   Mark how he trembles in his ecstasy. Oh!

Mowldie   ... Grief hath changed me since you saw me
   last;
   and careful hours, with Time's deformèd hand,
   have written strange defeatures in my face –
Oh! See! See! (*He points out and the others look. As they do he
sneaks a drink from his hip flask.*) ... How this grainèd face of
mine be hid in sap-consuming Winter's drizzled snow, yet
hath my night of life some memory.

*He has moved himself and the others to tears. All profoundly
overwhelmed.*

All   Bravo! Bravo! (**Flute** *claps frenetically.* **Quince** *grabs his
hands, and discreetly and swiftly crushes his fingers.*)

Quince   Oh sir, that was indeed an honour, the memory
of which we shall carry to our graves.

Mowldie   I tire.

Quince   Oh sit, my lord, sit. Rest! Rest! A chair, a chair.
(*To the others.*) Witness the exertion of a true artiste. (*To
Mowldie.*) Is there anything we can get you, sir?

Starveling   Spring water?

Flute   Milk?

Snout   A cup of curd?

Mowldie   A divertissement.

Snout   Ah, I think we've only got the curd.

Mowldie   An entertainment. From you. To me. I've
shown thee mine. Now you show me yours.

Quince   Oh, of course. Of course. Ah ...

Snug   Let's do 'That'.

All   Not 'That'.

Quince (*inspiration*)   Ah!

All   The jig!

Quince   Prepare! (*To* **Mowldie**.) Master Mowldie, if you would be so gracious as to sit there, I think you will find that a favourable position from which to view our simple pastorale.

Mowldie   Delighted.

Here follows the jig, 'Beryl the Widow', during which **Mowldie** *drinks at an alarming rate.*

Scene Seven

The jig. The actors parade. The song is to the tune of 'Minnie the Moocher'.

All (*repeat till ready*)   Hi di hi di hi di hi

Snug   HERE BE THE JIG OF BERYL THE WIDOW
WE HOPE YOU NEVER DO WHAT BERYL DID,
   OH!
SHE ATE THIS SOUP AND BLESS HER HEART
SHE DIDN'T HAVE A MATCH TO LIGHT HER ...
   WAY
HI DI HI DI HI DI HI.

Each phrase repeated by **All**, *who encourage the audience to join in.*

HO DI HO DI HO DI HO
FA-LA LA LA LA LA LA LA
OH WHAT HO WHAT HO WHAT HO
HOW NOW NOW NOW NOW NOW NOW NOW
ALACK ALACK ALACK ALACK
FORSOOTH FORSOOTH FORSOOTH
   FORSOOTH
HEY NONNY NONNY NONNY NO.

BERYL, BERYL

All BERYL.

Mowldie Magnificent! I'll drink to that!

The doggerel of the jig is punctuated throughout by percussion and other sound effects made by those not speaking. There are basic costumes, e.g., cape for the witch, skirt for Beryl.

Johnny (Starveling) Sweet Susan, remember the words I have said.

Susan (Flute) That soon in the night you will come to my bed.

Johnny I'll chase thee, embrace thee, my love and delight.

Susan And spend all our time in sweet sports of the night.

Johnny / Susan One play, toupée, three play, foreplay.
(*They mime burlesque intercourse with feather dusters.*)

Mother (Quince) (*entering*) Slut! Slut! Your fool mouth shut.
Out of my house, you whoring nut.

Johnny / Susan But!

Mother Slut and Nut, do not me 'but'
Or else by God I'll have your gut!
I'd rather you would woo a swine.

Susan Have you a mother quite like mine?

Mother *drags* **Susan** *off. Enter* **Witch** *and* **Friend**.

Witch (Snug) Spells! spells! Do I cry!
Will you any of me buy?
Spells to kill? Or hearts to mend!
Or some to drive thee round the bend.

Friend (Snout) Oh hag! Oh hag! Oh hag!
My friend has lost his wag.
He weeps, he moans,

He sighs, he groans.

Witch Come speak to me, you dag!

Johnny Oh woe is me. Was ever man thus crossed?
In my poor plight my love alas I've lost.

Witch What keeps thee from thy treasure, pale young sir?

Johnny My beloved's mother. Oh a pox on her.
She bars me from the sight of my dear heart.
Oh can you help me soften the old tart?

Witch Yea verily! I have a potion old
Which I'll deliver for a piece of gold.
Thou must a bowl of Spanish soup concoct
And into such three drops of this be plopped
And when betimes her nether region blurts.
Entrap the wind from underneath her skirts
And give it her in this same goblet sweet;
From thence your courtship will be most complete.

Exit **Witch** *cackling, and* **Friend**. *Enter* **Susan**.

Johnny Sweet Sue, we must now play our part.
To make your mother, Beryl, fart.

Susan A ghost you'll play to fright her half to death
Then we'll collect a load of rectal breath.

Johnny Till midnight then; a kiss to give thee luck
Then we'll be free to sing and dance and frolic.

Exit **Johnny**, *enter* **Mother**.

Mother Sue! Sue! Sue! My supper set.
A hunger grabs my belly.

Susan Here, Mother, drink this Spanish soup,
It's full of calves' foot jelly.
And now I'll creep beneath her stool.
And wait for it to work.
I hope the witch's spell is true

She goes under **Mother**'s *skirts.*

I feel a proper berk.

Mother   Midnight's struck. (**Snug** *ponderously provides the bongs.* **Quince** *counts them on his fingers, and after five or six speeds them to a conclusion.*)
Oh, help me, Lord
Do not let spirits walk abroad.

Moan off from **Johnny** *as* **Ghost**. **Snug** *provides the farts by blowing raspberries on his arm into a mike.*

Mother (*farts*)   Saints, that soup is goodly strong.

Susan (*emerging*)   Jesus, what a shocking pong.

Moan off from **Ghost**.

Mother (*coughs and farts*)   There's another from a cough.

Susan (*emerging*)   I think the Spanish soup was off.

Mother (*farts*)   Holy Mary, I'm all gas.

Susan   Now, dear John, you stupid ass.

Emerging **Johnny** *appears as* **Ghost**.

Ghost   Wife. Wife.

Mother (*farts*)   What is this I do behold? (*Farts.*)
All my joints do quake with cold. (*Farts.*)
'Tis the spirit of some lewd knave. (*Farts.*)
Newly risen from the grave.

Ghost   Wife. Wife.

Mother (*farts*)   Look how my backside trembles!
(*Farts.*) See how my buttocks quake!
(*Farts.*) Oh, woe is me.

Susan (*emerging*)   Oh, woe is me!

Mother   My arse will surely break.

She farts profusely. Extensive variety of farts which throw her violently about on the stool. Legs banging open in spasms. She eventually collapses. **Snug** *very pleased with himself.*

Susan   Why, Mother, you look almost spent.

Mother   I wonder where my innards went.

Susan   Pray take this medicine up your nose,
Your sickness will be gone. (**Mother** *sniffs the phial.*)

Mother   Why, Sue! I've had a merry thought.
Where is that nice young lad, called John?

Enter **Johnny** *and* **Friend**.

Susan   Oh Mother, may we marry?

Mother   Oh yes, with all my heart . . .

Susan / Johnny   We'll love and woo for all our days.
And never will we far . . . be apart.

Mother   But darlings, that sweet perfume
I long to smell again.

Susan   Next Wednesday you shall have it.

All   When you eat the soup from Spain.

A reprise of the opening part of the jig.

Snug   THAT BE THE JIG OF THE WIDOW'S GAS
AND THE LAD WHO WON HIS BONNY, BONNY
LASS.
AFTER SHE'D DONE HER WINDY DANCE
THEY FOUND HER SPHINCTER IN THE SOUTH
OF FRANCE.

Mother   BERYL.

All   BERYL.

Mother   BERYL.

All   BERYL. BERYL. YOW!

Mowldie *staggers back, enthusiastically applauding their performance
and falls down, dead drunk in front of their final tableau. They look
at him in dismay. Blackout. Music.*

Interval.

Act Two

Scene One

Snug's dream – *an entr'acte*

Snug, *sleepwalking, wakes too find himself in front of the curtain. The following is a stand-up comedy routine for* **Snug** *and* **Snout**.

Snug A funny thing happened to me on the way to the theatre this evening. Anyhow. What did Ethelred the Unready say when he saw the mammoths coming over the hill? I'm not ready! What's the difference between a well-dressed man and a sabre-toothed tiger! A well-dressed man wears a doublet and hose and sabre-toothed tiger just pants. (*Pant pant pant.*) What did William the Conqueror and Alexander the Great have in common? They were both big worriers. Warriors. What did Alfred the Great and Simon the Pieman have in common? The. How do you fit four mastodons on to a pony? Two in the front and two in the back. Speaking of ponies, I was going to buy a carthorse the other day and the man said 'Come in', he said – so I went inside the stable and there was a horse lying on the floor with a lotta blankets and sheets covering him up, he said 'That horse'll cost you some money', I said 'It's dead isn't it', he said 'No', I said 'How much do you want for it' he said 'A pound', I said 'A pound', I said 'Blimey, he hasn't got any shoes on', he said 'Well, he's not up yet.'

So, eventually I got the horse outside and I tried to get on and every time I tried to get on he started to kick and he kicked so hard he got his foot in the stirrups, dropped his foot right in the stirrups, I said 'Well', I said 'if you're going to get on I'm goinng to get off!'

So, I got on the horse and it fell down, so I picked it up 'cos I'm a hefty lad, you see, well I got on again and it fell down again, and I told the man I was down. I said 'This horse is no good to me, every time I get on he falls down, and haven't you got some nice horses there, you've got eight or nine in a string,' I said 'I'll have the one in the middle,' he said 'Don't take the one in the middle, they'll all fall down.'

I've just come back from the May Day revels, always have a wonderful time at the May Day revels, because I haven't got one of those wives who says where've you been, how much have you spent, who've you been with, she doesn't say that. No, she comes with me!

I'd like to do a few impressions if I may. Sir Thomas More. (*Adjusts hat.*) Thou dirty rat. Sir Walter Raleigh. (*Adjusts hat.*) Judith, Judith, Judith. Isabella of Spain. (*Adjusts hat.*) I vant to be alone. So like a man. Robin Hood (*Adjusts hat.*) If I know the Sheriff of Nottingham he'll stick to the ridges. Well, how dost thou know what they sounded like?

Snout *appears at side of stage.*

Snug   Where has thou been?

Snout   The Frog and Parsnip. Fair ladies, gentles, Snug, the joiner! (*Encourage applause.*) Wouldst thou like to hear an impression of Ann Hathaway?

Snug   Be my guest.

Snout   Ding Dong. Ding Dong.

Snug   We give up.

Snout   No! Ding Dong, Ding Dong. It's the Avon Lady.

Snug   Now that's enough of that.

Snout   I hast a joke.

Snug   Well, very well, but mind it's funny.

Snout   Why didst the chicken cross the road?

Snug   To get to the other side.

Snout   Oh! Thoust heard it.

Snug   Of course I've heard it. That be the oldest joke in the world.

Snout   But, it's only 1595.

Snug   At any rate, how dost thou?

Snout   With some chicken feathers on a stick.

Snug   What?

Snout   With some chicken feathers on a stick.

Snug   What do you mean?

Snout   Well, you asked me how I dust. And I told you, with some chicken feathers on a stick.

Snug   Nay, nay, nay, thou getst me not!

Snout   I do not want to getst thee.

Snug   Methinks thou spends too much time at the Frog and Parsnip.

Snout   Aye, and I hast heard the most funny joke there. It had every mother's son, and daughter, befalling about.

Snug   Sounds pathetic; let's hear it.

Snout   Fifteen. One to change the candle and fourteen to make a documentary about it.

Snug   Was that the whole joke?

Snout   Nay, there was a bit before that, but that was the line that had every mother's son befalling about.

Snug   How be Dorothy?

Snout   Dorothy?

Snug   Aye, thy wife Dorothy.

Snout   Oh, she be gone.

Snug   Gone?

Snout   Aye, gone.

Snug   Where in the world could she be gone?

Snout   She probably be in Devon by now.

Snug   In heaven?

Snout   No, in Devon.

Snug   Oh, in Devon.

Snout   Aye. When she left ye olde cottage this morning, she said she was going out to buy some Devon sausage.

Snug   Thou meanst she thinks if you want Devon sausage, you have to go to Devon?

Snout   I once told her I liked Brussels sprouts and I didn't see her for six months.

Snug *and* **Snout** *do a soft-shoe shuffle to 'Greensleeves'.*

Snout   Brothers and sisters have I none. But that man's father is my father's son. Who are *you*?

Snug   This family of yours be fascinating. Thou hast a sister.

Snout   Aye. Bessie.

Snug   How be she?

Snout   Bessie?

Snug   Aye, Bessie.

Snout   Oh, she be fine now. But, oh, the other night she woke up in the middle of the night and she let out this awful scream. 'Whoooa.'

Snug   What happened?

Snout   Well, she looked down and she went 'Whoooa. The plague. The plague. My feet have turned black!'

Snug   How dreadful! What did you do?

Snout   We sent for the apothecary.

Snug   What did the apothecary do?

Snout   He took off her stockings and we all went back to sleep.

Snug *and* **Snout** *soft-shoe shuffle to 'Greensleeves'.*

Snout   My niece went up the hill and saw a whole lot of ships coming from Spain.

Snug   Armada?

Snout   No, she went of her own accord. I like that one.

Snug   I saw a cockfight the other night. Yes. It didn't want to get back into my tights.

Snout   I beg your pardon?

Snug   I saw a cockfight the other night. Yes, it didn't want to get back into my tights.

Snout   Snug. We don't work blue.

Snug   I don't work blue. I aspire to the realms of higher thought, expressed in either poetry or prose –

Snout   Oh.

Snug   Dost thou know the difference between poetry and prose?

Snout   No.

Snug   Poetry rhymes and prose doesn't.

Snout   Oh.

Snug   Mark ye. 'My friend went round the mulberry bush
Upon a morning chilly
I went round the mulberry bush
Sing derry daffy dilly.'

Snout   What's that?

Snug   That's poetry because it rhymes.

Snout   Chilly, dilly. Yes.

Snug   But if I were to say,
'My friend went round the mulberry bush
Upon a morning chilly
I went round the mulberry bush
Sing derry daffy hat.'

Snout   What's that?

Snug   That's prose because it doesn't rhyme.

Snout   Chilly, hat. Well, I could do that.

Snug   You could?

Snout   Yes.
'My friend went round the mulberry bush
Upon a morning chilly
I went round the mulberry bush
And I pulled out my . . .'
Now what do you want, prose or poetry?

Snug   Fair ladies, gentles, Master Tom Snout!

Snout   Snug the joiner!

Snug *and* **Snout** *launch into the following song and dance 'Merrye England', and are gradually joined by the full company.*

Snug   WE LOVE OLD MERRY ENGLAND
OOH! IT GIVES US SUCH A THRILL
THE WARS, THE SORES, THE POXY WHORES
AND WRITING WITH A QUILL,
IF THE BLACK DEATH DOESN'T GET YOU
THEN THE FIRE OF LONDON WILL,
WOULDN'T YOU LOVE TO LIVE IN TUDOR
   ENGLAND?

Snout   WE NEVER BATHE IN WATER
BE WE RICH OR BE WE POOR,
THE FLIES, THE FLEAS, THE SKIN DISEASE
AND WAIT, THERE'S EVEN MORE,
WE HAVEN'T ANY TOILETS
SO WE DO IT ON THE FLOOR
WOULDN'T YOU LOVE TO LIVE IN TUDOR
   ENGLAND?

Flute   MY FATHER IS A WORKMAN
BUT A DISCONTENTED SOUL,
HE BIT HIS THUMB AT FRANCIS DRAKE
WHO WAS RIDING PAST HIS HOLE,

I SAW DAD JUST THIS MORNING
WITH HIS HEAD UPON A POLE,
COULDN'T YOU DIE TO LIVE IN TUDOR
    ENGLAND?

Quince   WHEN POINTING OUT A WITCH
WE MUST BE SURE THERE'S NO MISTAKE.
WE TAKE THE DEAR OLD LADY
AND WE THROW HER IN A LAKE,
IF SHE SINKS SHE'S NOT, BUT IF SHE FLOATS,
WE BURN HER AT THE STAKE,
WE'RE HAVING A LOVELY TIME IN TUDOR
    ENGLAND.

Starveling   WE ALL WENT INTO MOURNING
WHEN QUEEN BESS'S DAY WAS DONE,
THEY PUT HER IN A COFFIN
BUT THEY LEFT IT IN THE SUN,
AND WHEN THE THING EXPLODED
SHE REIGNED OVER EVERYONE,
OH, WHAT A TASTEFUL TIME IN TUDOR
    ENGLAND.

Mowldie   I WOULD TELL YOU OF THE
    TORTURES
THAT ARE MADE TO FIT THE CRIME,
THE PINCERS AND THE NEEDLES
AND THE THINGS THEY DO WITH LIME,
AND OF COURSE THE RED-HOT POKER,
BUT WE'RE RUNNING OUT OF TIME,

All   RUN, RUN, RUN,
WOULDN'T YOU LOVE TO LIVE?
HOW MUCH WOULD YOU GIVE?
WOULD YOU LIKE TO GET AWAY?
COME ON OVER FOR A DAY
YOU MIGHT EVEN WANT TO STAY
THERE'S AN AWFUL LOT TO DO
JUST LIKE NINETEEN NINETY-TWO
IN TUDOR ENGLAND
IN TUDOR ENGLAND
IN TUDOR ENGLAND

The tableau at the end of the song is the same as that at the end of Act One.

Scene Two

They break out of the tableau. **Snout** *exits. The others group around the prone body of* **Mowldie** *trying to shake him awake.*

Quince   Master Mowldie! Master Mowldie!

Flute   What ails him? Didn't he like 'Beryl the Widow'?

Mowldie *snores.*

Starveling   He doth but sleep.

Quince   Aye, 'tis but an after-dinner sleep.

All   Sssh!

Flute   We haven't had any dinner.

Mowldie *snores.*

Snug (*sniffs*)   He's drunk.

Flute   Fie that you should say so!

Starveling   The heavens restore thy wits.

Quince   Professional actors don't drink!

Mowldie *snores. This time the others reel from the alcohol on his breath.*

Starveling   Well, how are we going to rehearse?

They move away, deep in thought.

Flute   Cut Pyramus out and call it 'Thisbe'.

Snug   We could always do 'That'.

Starveling / Flute / Quince   Not 'That'.

Snug   Please?

Starveling / Flute / Quince   No!

Snug   It only needs us.

Starveling / Flute / Quince   No!!

Snug   But it's very cheery and besides, it's better than doing nothing.

Starveling   'Nothing' is better than doing 'That'.

Snug   And I have all ye this for 'That' in my bag.

Mowldie *snores and rolls over.* **Quince** *sees the situation with* **Mowldie** *is hopeless.*

Quince   All right, we'll do 'That'.

Starveling / Flute   Oh, no!

They start to prepare, setting up a screen, etc. **Snout** *enters waving piece of paper.*

Snout   Lads! Lads! Tidings! Byrlakin, what's all this?

Quince   We're doing 'That'.

Snout   Oh, no!

Quince   Don't argue, just do it.

Snout   But there are people here. (*Pause. To the audience.*) I'm very sorry.

The chicken galliard begins. Vigorous music: four rubber chooks, in trunk-hose and ruffs, on sticks perform a striking court dance – as a quartet, sometimes in pairs. Minuet: one couple perform a delicate and stately duet. It ends with one chook lying on its back. Frenzied music: the other chook mounts it while the remaining pair whirl in ecstasy. **Snug** *behind, juggles large eggs. Then, upside down, all wiggle their bottoms and exit. Music. Prokofiev's 'The Montagues and the Capulets'. Eight chook heads appear from behind the screen and ascend in rhythm to the music. They promenade back and forth, form simple but impressive patterns and parade in a large circle to and fro. They dive one by one off the screen à la Busby Berkeley, then form a giant pyramid. After some spectacular leaping they promenade once more while a swirling umbrella laden with many chooks opens and carousels* *wildly behind them. The dance ends with a roast chicken on a platter scaring them away.*

During the dance **Mowldie** *wakes, sees the alarming display, mistakes it for a nasty case of the DTs and collapses once more. Lights up.*

Quince (*to audience*) Well, that is 'That'. (*To* **Snug**.) And I hope you're satisfied. (**Snug** *very pleased with himself.*) (*To* **Snout**.) Now, you were saying?

Snout Was I? Oh, yes. (*He exits and then enters, waving paper as before.*) Lads! Lads! Tidings!

They gather around **Snout**.

Starveling Is Bottom found?

Snout Alas, no.

All Oh.

Snout Thou knowest my wife, Dorothy?

All Aye.

Snug She be in Brussels.

All Ssshh!

Snout Well, thou knowest she works in the palace kitchen?

All Aye.

Snug No, Devon.

All Ssshh!!

Snout Well, she has managed to secure me this.

Snout *holds up the list.*

Quince What is't?

Snout What is't? A list!

Snug Boo-boom.

Snout It is a list of finalists.

Starveling   I've missed the gist.

Flute   What is't the list?

Snout   The final list of finalists.

Starveling   The final list?

Flute   Of finalists?

Snout   The final list of finalists.

All   De-dee de-dee de-dee boo-boom.

Snout   Our rival entertainments. We're up against three top acts.

Snug (*carried away by the rhythm*)   Three top hats?

All (*carried away by the rhythm*)   Acts! Acts!

Quince (*carried away by the rhythm*)   Go on. Go on.

Snout   One. 'The Battle of the Centaurs, to be sung by an Athenian Eunuch to the harp.'

Others (*impressed*)   Ooh.

Quince   I've seen it. The title is the best thing about it. Go on.

Snout   Two. 'The riot of the tipsy Bacchanals, tearing the Thracian singer in their rage.'

Flute   Who's doing that?

Snout   The Ajax players.

Others   Ooh.

Starveling   Oh, they're very good. I saw them do 'The White Horse Inn'. You were with me, Peter Quince. You were raving about them.

Quince (*edgy*)   Yes! Yes! Go on.

Snout   Three. 'The thrice three Muses mourning for the death of learning, late deceased in beggary.'

Flute (*ecstatic*)   Oh, they're brilliant!

Starveling   Superb!

Starveling / Flute / Snug   What about that bit where they . . . My favourite bit was when she came down that . . . (*Laughs.*)

Quince   Shut up!! (*To* **Snout**.) How are *we* billed?

Snout   Fourth. 'A tedious brief scene of young Pyramus and his love, Thisbe; very tragical mirth.'

Quince   'Pyramus and Thisbe' tedious?!! (**Quince** *grabs the list.*) Who wrote this? Tragical mirth?!

Mowldie *rises and takes centre stage. He is very hung-over.*

Mowldie   Oh grim-look'd night! O night with hue so black!

Quince (*recognising the line from 'Pyramus and Thisbe'*)   Places! Places, everybody, places. (*To* **Snug**.) Drunk? Ha!

Mowldie *now quite openly drinks.*

Mowldie   O night, O night, O shit . . . O God . . .

Quince *cues* **Flute**.

Flute   O wall, full oft –

Mowldie   Mirth? I can do mirth. And the trick to playing comedy, particularly Shakespearean comedy, is to laugh at the end of your lines, and everyone thinks it's funny. (*Broad West Country accent.*) 'I would there were no age between sixteen and three and twenty, or that youth would sleep out the rest.' (*Laughs.*) You see?

The phone rings.

My agent!

Snout *answers the phone while* **Mowldie** *continues muttering snatches of obscure wit to himself.*

Snout   Hullo. Oh, yes, Dorothy. Yes. Yes. Really, Dorothy? Thank you, Dorothy. Goodbye, Dorothy. (*Hangs up.*) That was Dorothy Masters, the Duke is married and is coming in from the temple.

Quince Oh dear!

Snug If our sport had gone forward, we had all been made men.

Flute Oh sweet bully Bottom! Thus hath he lost sixpence a day during his life; he could not have 'scaped sixpence a day. And the Duke had not given him sixpence a day for playing Pyramus, I'll be hanged. He would have deserved it: sixpence a day in Pyramus, or nothing.

Quince (*to* **Mowldie**) Excuse me, pal, but I think it is best for all concerned if you return to your lodgings.

Mowldie (*his court jester*) Prithee, nuncle, I had rather be any kind of thing than a fool. (*He laughs.*)

Quince I prithee, sir, take your leave, gramercy.

Mowldie (*his simpleton servant*) I think Crab my dog be the sourest-natured dog that lives. (*He laughs.*)

Quince Hence! Avaunt! Vanish like hailstones, go!

Snout Trudge.

Flute Plod away o'the hoof.

Starveling Seek shelter.

Snug Pack!

During **Mowldie**'s *speech the others try to forcibly remove him.*

Mowldie No, my good lord; banish Peto, banish Bardolph, banish Poins; but for sweet Jack Falstaff, kind Falstaff, true Jack Falstaff, valiant Jack Falstaff, and therefore more valiant, being as he is old Jack Falstaff, banish not him thy Quince's company, banish not him thy Quince's company. Banish plump Jack and banish all the world.

Snug Is this a dag which I see before me?

All (*but* **Mowldie**) Yes!

They heave him through the doorway.

Bottom (*off*)   Where are these lads? Where are these hearts?

Quince   Bottom! O most courageous day! O most happy hour!

Quince *rushes to open the door but is prevented by* **Snug** *who imitates a donkey's bray. They retreat, not sure what will appear. The door opens and* **Bottom** *slowly enters.*

Bottom (*rapturous*)   Masters, I am to discourse wonders. (*The others, overjoyed, clamour around him.*) But ask me not what; for if I tell you, I am not true Athenian. I will tell you everything, right as it fell out.

Quince   Let us hear, sweet Bottom.

Bottom   Not a word of me. All that I will tell you is, that the Duke hath dined. Get your apparel together, good strings to your beards, new ribbons to your pumps; meet presently at the palace; every man look o'er his part: for the short and the long is our play is preferred.

Bottom *exits.*

All (*to audience*)   Our play is preferred. (*This sinks in.*) Aaaarrgh! John Donne!

They go to exit. **Mowldie** *enters.*

Mowldie   You sad little men. Pathetic pismires, dabbling on the edge of oblivion, of abject failure, of nothingness. What has life for thee? Jacks of all trades. Masters of . . . nothing. Amateurs!

They all gasp.

Quince   Yes. Amateurs. From the Latin Ama: Love. Teur: For the of.

Snout   Love for the of?

Quince   For the love of! Yes, amateurs! And you, sir, a professional.

All   Ha!

Mowldie   Yes. Professional. Pro: For. Fesh: . . . fesh. On: State of. Al . . . Cohol. Professional. One who drinks like a fesh!

Mowldie *falls out of the room. The others start to leave.* **Bottom** *enters. They rush back on.* **Starveling** *is eating an onion,* **Flute** *a garlic.*

Bottom   In any case, let Thisbe have clean linen; and let not him that plays the Lion pare his nails, for they shall hang out for the Lion's claws. (*Referring to door.*) Who was that? And most dear actors, eat no onions nor garlic, for we are to utter sweet breath; and I do not doubt but to hear them say, it is a sweet comedy. No more words. Away! Go away!

All, except **Quince**, *exit.*

All (*in triumph*)   Amateurs!

During the following stirring speech **Quince** *strips down to his Y-fronts, completes his toilet — cologne, talcum powder, etc., and changes into his tuxedo.*

Quince   Once more unto the breach, dear friends, once
      more;
   Or close the wall up with our English dead!
   In peace there's nothing so becomes a man,
   As modest stillness and humility;
   But when the blast of war blows in our ears,
   Then imitate the action of the tiger;
   Stiffen the sinews, summon up the blood,
   Disguise fair nature with hard-favour'd rage;
   Then lend the eye a terrible aspect,
   Let it pry through the portage of the head
   Like the brass cannon; let the brow o'erwhelm it,
   As fearfully as doth a galled rock
   O'erhang and jutty his confounded base,
   Swilled with the wild and wasteful ocean.
   Now set the teeth and stretch the nostril wide;
   Hold hard the breath and bend up every spirit

To his full height! – On, on, you noblest English!
Whose blood is fet from fathers of war-proof;
Fathers that, like so many Alexanders,
Have in these parts from morn till even fought,
And sheath'd their swords for lack of argument.
Dishonour not your mothers; now attest
That those whom you call'd fathers did beget you.
Be copy now to men of grosser blood,
And teach them how to war!
I see you stand like greyhounds in the slips,
Straining upon the start. The game's afoot:
Follow your spirit; and upon this charge,
Cry 'God for Harry, England, and Saint George!'

*Mendelssohn's 'Wedding March' and light change during which the others enter, dressed in their tuxedos, **Flute** in black evening dress. We are backstage at the palace. Various warm-ups, physical limbering, last-minute directions from **Quince**, etc.*

Scene Three

Fanfare. Bright lights. The company make their way out in front of the curtain. An echo of their initial entrance. But now it's the Palace! They are in various states of nervous tension. **Quince** *(Prologue),* **Bottom** *(Pyramus),* **Flute** *(Thisbe),* **Snout** *(Wall),* **Starveling** *(Moonshine),* **Snug** *(Lion). What follows is an avant-garde conceptual production of 'Pyramus and Thisbe' gone terribly wrong.*

Quince   Your Majesties. (*All bow and scrape to Royal box.*) If we offend, it is with our good –

Snout   We've done that bit.

Quince   Gentles, perchance you wonder at this show;
But wonder on, till truth make all things plain.
This man is Pyramus, if you would know;

They all step forward and back when introduced or mentioned.

This beauteous lady Thisbe is certain.

This man doth present
Wall, that vile wall, which did these lovers sunder;
And through the Walls, chink, poor souls, they are
    content
To whisper. At the which let no man wonder.

All step forward and back.

This man presenteth Moonshine; for, if you will know,
By moonshine did these lovers think no scorn
To meet at Ninny's tomb . . . to meet at Ninus' tomb,
    there,

He dries badly. The others are mortified.

To meet at Ninus' tomb, there to woo!
This grisly beast, which Lion hight by name,
The trusty Thisbe, coming first by night,
Did scare away, or rather did affright;
And as she fled, her mantle she did fall,
Which Lion vile with bloody mouth did stain.
Anon comes Pyramus, sweet youth and tall,
And finds his trusty Thisbe's mantle slain;
Whereat with blame, with bladey braveful blame
He blamed his broach and . . . boiled his bloody breasts
Whereat with blood, with bloody bladey blood
He broached his boils and blamed the Brady Bunch . . .
Whereat with blade, with bloody blameful blade,
He bravely broach'd his boiling bloody breast!
And Thisbe, tarrying in mulberry shade,
His dagger drew, and died.

Flute, *consumed with nerves, vomits.* **Quince** *moves in front of*
Flute *in an attempt to cover.*

Quince   For all the rest, let Lion, Moonshine, Wall,
And Lovers twain, (**Flute** *vomits again onto* **Quince**'s *back.*)
At large discourse, while here they do remain.

Exit all but **Snout** *and* **Quince**, *who cues and gives*
encouragement and direction from the side. Sound of **Flute** *being*
slapped, and wailing.

Snout In this same interlude it doth befall.
That I, one Snout by name, present a wall;
And such a wall as I would have you think
That had in it a crannied hole, or chink
Through which the lovers, Thyramus and Pisbe,
Did whisper often, very secretly.
This loam, this rough-cast, and this stone (*a foam brick*)
   doth show
That I am that same wall; the truth is so:
And this the cran –

He realises he has forgotten to bring on the cranny. After several moments of panic, he comes up with the bright idea of spreading his legs to represent the cranny.

And this the cranny is, right and sinister,
Through which the fearful lovers are to whisper.

Bottom *enters.*

Snout (*to* **Quince**) Sorry. It was in my pocket. It must be on the table.

Snug *enters and punctuates* **Bottom**'*s speech with 'mood' music on guitar.*

Bottom O grim-look'd night! O night with hue so black!
O night, which ever art when day is not!
O night, O night, alack, alack, alack,
I fear my Thisbe's promise is forgot!
And thou, O wall –

Snout Yes –

Bottom O sweet, O lovely wall –

Snout Yes –

Bottom That stand'st between her father's ground and mine; Thou wall –

Snout Yes –

Bottom O wall, O sweet and lovely wall –

Snout Yes!!

Bottom   Show me thy chink, to blink through with mine eyne.

Snout *spreads his legs apart to represent the cranny.* **Bottom** *is bewildered.* **Snout** *points to the cranny.*

Bottom   . . . Thanks, courteous wall: Jove shield thee well
    for this.
  But what see I? No Thisbe do I see.
  O wicked wall, through whom I see no bliss,
  Curs'd be thy stones for thus deceiving me!

Snug *goes overboard with his accompaniment.* **Bottom** *throws the brick at him.* **Snug** *cowers off. Enter* **Flute**, *in gorgeous mantle.*

Flute   O wall, full often has thou heard my moans,
  For parting my fair Pyramus and me!
  My cherry lips have often kissed thy stones
  Thy stones with lime and hair knit up in thee.

Bottom   I see a voice; Now will I to the chink,
  To spy and I can hear by Thisbe's face.
  Thisbe?

Flute   My love? Thou art my love I think?

Bottom   Think what thou wilt, I am thy lover's grace;
  And like Limander am I trusty still.

Flute   And I like Helen, till the Fates me kill.

Bottom   Not Shafalus to Procrus was so true.

Flute   As Shafalus to Procrus, I to you.

Bottom   O, kiss me through the hole in this vile wall.

Flute *shoves his nose between* **Snout***'s legs.*

Flute   I kiss the wall's hole, not your lips at all.

Bottom   Wilt though at Ninny's tomb meet me straight
  away?

Flute   'Tide life, 'tide death, I come without delay.

Exit **Bottom** *and* **Flute**.

Snout   Thus have I, Wall, my part dischargèd so;
  And, being done, thus Wall away doth go.

Exit **Snout**. *Enter* **Snug**. *He roars, revealing a mouth full of plastic fangs.*

Snug   You ladies, you, whose gentle hearts do fear
  The smallest monstrous mouse that creeps on floor,
  May now, perchance, both quake and tremble here,
  When lion rough in widest rage doth roar.
  Then know that I, one Snug the joiner, am
  A lion fell, nor else no lion's dam;
  For if I should as lion came in strife
  Into this place, 'twere pity on my life.
  So . . .

Snug *roars again and exits. Enter* **Starveling**, *with theatre lamp on a stand, a branch and a toy dog.*

Starveling   This lantern doth the hornèd moon present
  (*At the Royal box in a posh voice.*)
    This lantern doth the hornèd moon present;
    Myself the Man i'th'Moon do seem to be.
  (*To* **Quince**.) They don't understand it.
  (*To audience.*) All that I have to say is, to tell you that the
  lantern is the moon; I the Man i'th'Moon; this thorn bush
  my thorn bush; and this dog my dog.

Enter **Flute**. *Exit* **Quince**.

Flute   This is old Ninny's tomb.

Others (*offstage*)   Tomb. Tomb. Tomb.

Flute   Where is my love?

Snug *enters and roars.* **Flute** *runs off, dropping the mantle.* **Snug** *worries the mantle. His fangs fall out. He starts crying.*

Quince (*through curtain*)   Get off!! Get off!!

Snug *exits.* **Bottom** *enters.*

Snug (*off*)   My teeth fell out.

Bottom   Sweet Moon, I thank thee for thy sunny beams;

I thank thee, Moon, for shining now so bright;
For by thy gracious, golden, glittering gleams,
I trust to take of truest Thisbe's sight.

Starveling *swings the light on to him.* **Bottom** *is blinded and can't find the mantle.*

Starveling (*through clenched teeth*)   ... Oh crikey, what's that on the floor? To the left, to the right ... there!

Bottom   But stay! O spite!
   But mark, poor knight,
What dreadful dole is here?
   Eyes, do you see?
   How can it be?
O dainty duck! O dear!
   Thy mantle good
   What! Stain'd with blood?
Approach, ye Furies fell!

The others enter to represent the Furies. Generous physical chorus movements.

Bottom   O Fates, come, come!
   Cut thread and thrum:
   Quail, crush, conclude, and –

All   Quell!

Bottom   O wherefore, Nature, didst thou lions frame,
Since lion vile hath here deflower'd my dear?
Which is – no, no – which was the fairest dame
That liv'd, that lov'd, that lik'd, that look'd with cheer.
   Come tears, confound!
   Out sword, and wound
The pap of Pyramus;
   Aye, that left pap,
   Where heart doth hop: (*Stabs himself.*)
Thus die I, thus, thus, thus!
   Now am I dead,
   Now am I fled;
My soul is in the sky.
   Tongue, lose thy light;
   Moon, take thy flight!

Starveling *exits*.

Bottom   Now die, die, die . . .

The others exit thinking he has finished.

Die.

The others re-enter.

Die.

Pause. The others exit.
Flute *enters and lasciviously straddles* **Bottom**.

Snout (*through curtains*)   Francis Flute, don't be disgusting.

Flute   Asleep, my love?
    What, dead, my love?
O Pyramus, arise!
    Speak, speak! Quite dumb?
    Dead, dead? A tomb
Must cover thy sweet eyes.
    These lily lips
    This cherry nose
These yellow cowslip cheeks,
    Are gone, are gone!
    Lovers, make moan;
His eyes were green as leeks.
    O Sisters Three,
    Come, come to me.

The others enter to represent the 'Sisters Three'. Realising they are 'four', **Quince** *pushes* **Snout** *off*.

Flute   With hands as pale as milk:
    Lay them in gore,
    Since you have shore
With shears his thread of silk.
    Tongue, not a word:
    Come, trusty sword,
Come, blade, my breast imbrue!
    And farewell, friends;

Thus Thisbe ends: (*Stabs himself.*)
Adieu, adieu, adieu! (*Dies.*)

Quince (*sotto voce*) Lunge!

Tableau. **Quince** *exits.* **Snout** *enters. They line up for the curtain call.* **Quince** *rushes on to join them, leads a group call, then steps forward to take a solo.* **Quince**, *overcome, tries repeatedly to quell imagined applause, even if it is non-existant. Finally . . .*

Quince (*to Royals*) Will it please you to see the epilogue, or to hear a Bergamask dance between two of our company?

It is evident that the Royals' reply is in the negative and the company exits bowing and prostrating themselves before the Royals.

Scene Four

The after-show party. Party music. The company are seen bunched together through the free-standing doorflat at the back of the stage. They are triumphant. Much drinking and mutual congratulation. **Bottom** *breaks away and comes to a spot backstage. The others freeze.*

Bottom   Oh Francis Flute, Peter Quince, Tom Snout, Robin Starveling, oh Joiner Snug! I have had a most rare vision. I have had a dream, past the wit of man to say what dream it was. Man is but an ass if he go about to expound this dream. Methought I was – there is no man can tell what. Methought I was – and methought I had – but man is but a patched fool if he will offer to say what methought I had. The eye of man hath not heard, the ear of man hath not seen, man's hand is not able to taste, his tongue to conceive, nor his heart to report, what my dream was. I will get Peter Quince to write a ballad of this dream: It shall be called 'Bottom's Dream', because it hath no bottom.

Music up. **Bottom** *rejoins the party. Light change. The company dance downstage for their farewell.*

Quince Time is like a fashionable host,
That slightly shakes his parting guest by the hand,
And with his arms outstretched as he would fly,
Grasps in the comer: Welcome ever smiles,
And Farewell goes out sighing.

All Mmm.

Flute Goodnight, goodnight; parting is such sweet
  sorrow,
That I shall say goodnight till it be morrow.

All Mmm.

Bottom Here is my journey's end. Here is my butt.

All Mmm!!

Starveling For ever, and forever, farewell, all!
If we do meet again, why we shall smile!
If not, why then, this parting was well made.

All Mmm.

Snout I was never so bethumped with words
since first I called my father's brother Dad.

All Mmm!

Snug Um . . . See ya.

Snug *steps in the cow-pat. Blackout.*

End.

Glossary